Smart Parenting

A Guide to Child Assessment and Therapeutic Interventions

by

Bill J. Duke, Ph.D.

Assistant Professor of Child Clinical Neuroscience
Assistant Professor of Family Medicine

University of North Dakota School of Medicine

Copyright © 1996 DCC Publishing. All Rights Reserved

Smart Parenting

A Guide to Child Assessment
and
Therapeutic Interventions

By Bill J. Duke, Ph.D.

Published by:
DCC Publishing
Post Office Box 10458
Fargo, ND 58103-0458 U.S.A.

Names have been changed in the use of actual cases and in some cases incidental non-critical details have been altered to further protect the anonymity of those depicted.

All rights reserved. No part of this book may be reproduced or transmitted in any form or by any means, electronic or mechanical, including photocopying, recording or by any information storage or retrieval system without written permission from the author, except for the inclusion of brief quotations in a review and the Appendix materials by the owner of each book.

Copyright ©1996. DCC Publishing.
First Printing 1996

ISBN 0-9648838-3-X

Acknowledgements

I am indebted to many friends and colleagues who have enriched my experiences by sharing of themselves and their knowledge. I am also indebted to all of the children with whom I have worked and from whom I've learned. Since the outset of my work in mental health I have encountered an inspiring array of dedicated and compassionate professionals who have helped in shaping my professional identity and clinical methodology. I have been particularly fortunate to have worked with and learned from some of the most talented and brilliant clinicians and scientists within the United States.

In the fields of Child and Adult Psychiatry, I am especially grateful to Dwight Lysne, M.D. for supporting, sharing and teaching me in my post doctoral fellowship in child clinical neuroscience. Likewise, I am indebted to R. Dennis Staton, Ph.D., M.D. as a brilliant teacher of biological psychiatry. I am appreciative that such a person as Arthur J. Prange, Jr., M.D., a luminary in psychopharmacology and biological psychiatry, has served as my mentor and continues to inspire and teach me. I miss, but remain grateful for the warmth, friendship and intellect of our former chairperson of the Department of Neuroscience, the late Richard Stadter, M.D., MPH. Dr. Stadter invited me to come to the University of North Dakota School of Medicine and was a genuine hero of community health. I am thankful to Mark Chenven, M.D., with whom I shared the treatment of many severely maltreated and emotionally disturbed children. I am also indebted to the Village of Childhelp, U.S.A., the University of North Dakota School of Medicine and the U.C.L.A. Neuropsychiatric Institute, Department of Child Psychiatry.

My exposure and collaboration with committed and insightful leaders and educators within the fields of Pediatric and Family Medicine has resulted in my enduring respect, gratitude and friendship with Martin Baren, M.D., Mary J. Spencer, M.D., John Baird, M.D. and Craig Fabel, M.D.

My colleagues and friends within neuroscience, clinical neuroscience, child clinical psychology and clinical psychology have likewise played a principle contributory role in my development of a meaningful integrated biopsychosocial conceptualization of the human condition. I am grateful for the psychophysiological teachings and intelligence of MaryAnne Hunt, Ph.D. and the neurological stimulation and insights of Elliot Ross, M.D. and Alberto Politoff, M.D. I owe my appreciation of developmental process to Constance Vincent, Ph.D. and my appreciation of sociological influence to Patricia See, Ph.D. The courage to create was demonstrated and shared by William Lyon, Ph.D. The exquisite value and meaning of psychological measurement was proffered by David Lachar, Ph.D. The humor, intensity and forward psychobiological thinking of my doctoral advisor, the late Herman Harvey, Ph.D. nurtured my development of an integrated view of biology and psychology within a social and cultural context. I thank Lillian Stover, Ph.D. for the lessons of the "parent as a therapist" and Steve Shoemaker, Ph.D. for supervision in the war zone of severe child trauma. I am grateful to George O'Neill, Ph.D for reminding me of the importance of sound behavioral techniques and to Karen Knutson, Ph.D., Ron Odden, M.A., L.P. and Kevin Schumacher, Ph.D. for their clinical insights and collegial support.

I also extend my gratitude to others with whom I work, including other faculty and administrative colleagues, Zeljko Jocic, M.D., David Carlson, M.D., Stephen Wonderlich, Ph.D., Stephen Setterberg, M.D., Carol Galde, Carla Lustig, Vonnie Sandland and particularly Sandra Ahonen, who in addition to being a university colleague, proofread the original manuscript.

Finally, my thanks and love to my family, who has sustained me throughout this and previous endeavors. My mother, Ruth Magnuson, my mother-in-law, Ruth Singleton, my children, Kim, Sarah and Chris and most of all, my wife and colleague, Denise M. Duke, Ed.D.

BJD

Table of Contents

Introduction 11

Chapter One
Understanding Children 15
    Using the Resource Chapter and Appendixes ... 16
    Normative Psychological and Social Development 18
    Variations of Normality 18
    Deviations from Adaptivity 22
    An Example of a Child with a Severe Behavioral and Emotional Disorder 25
    Summary of the Example 35
    What Can a Parent Do? 36
    Significant Deviations 36
    Seeking Objectivity and a Frame of Reference .. 37
    Introduction to Child Assessment by Parents 38
    Preparation for a Medical Consultation 39

Chapter Two
Child Assessment 41
    Biological Considerations 42
    Basic Neuroanatomy 43
    Common Parental and Environmental Influences 51
    Making General Observations 53
    The Value of Observations 55
    Data Collection and The Scientific Method 55
    General Parental Observations 56
    The Parent Assessment 57
    Assessing a Child's General Adjustment 57
    The Biopsychosocial History 60
    Systematic Observations 62
    The Systematic Observation Scale (SOS) 64
    Chapter Summary 66

Chapter Three
The Family Environment 69
    Common Family Stressors 71

What about the effects of television? 71
Marital Discord 73
An Example of Marital Discord 74
Death 77
Divorce 81
Custody Issues 83
Example of a Divorce and Custody Issue 86
Serious Child Illness 91
A Case of Serious Childhood Illness and
    Behavioral Problems 92
Accidents 95
Real Family Life 96
Self Responsibility in Family Health 98

Chapter Four
Love and Discipline 101
    A Case of Parental Over-Permissiveness 102
    A Case of Excessive Discipline 105
    Behavioral Learning 108
    Promoting Self Confidence and Self Esteem ... 108
    Preemptive Strike 116
    Preemptive Attention 116
    Preemptive Interventions 117
    Refusing to Argue 118
    Time-outs 119
    Time-out Guidelines 121
    Teaching a Child How To Take a Time-out ... 122
    Length of Time-out 123
    Refusal to take a Time-out 123
    Parent Behavior During Time-outs 124
    Time-out Log 126
    Parental Anger 127
    Child Anger 129

Chapter Five
Adjustment Disorders 133
    Adjustment Disorders 135
    An Example of an Acute Adjustment Disorder . 136
    An Example of an Adjustment Disorder Related
        to Chronic Stressors 139
    Treatment of Adjustment Disorders 144

Chapter Six
Disruptive Behavior Disorders 149
    Attention Deficit Hyperactivity Disorder 149
    Oppositional Defiant Disorder 156
    Conduct Disorders 161
    Example of a Male with Conduct Disorder 162
    Example of a Female with Conduct Disorder .. 165
    Treatment of Conduct Disordered Children ... 168

Chapter Seven
Mood Disorders 171
    Childhood Depression 171
    Disturbances in Neurotransmitter Actions 172
    Circadian rhythms 174
    Seasonal Affective Disorder 175
    Dysthymic Disorder 176
    Major Depressive Disorder 178
    Bipolar Disorders 184

Chapter Eight
Anxiety and Movement Disorders 191
    Types of Anxiety Disorders 192
    Panic Disorder 193
    Agoraphobia 193
    Phobic anxiety 193
    Social phobia 193
    Obsessive Compulsive Disorder 199
    Tourette's and Movement Disorders 205
    Treatment of Tourette's and Tics 206
    Exposure 208
    Response Prevention 209
    Extinction 210
    Modeling 210

Chapter Nine
Autism, Schizophrenia and Developmental Disorders . 211
    Autism 211
    Schizophrenia 213
    Developmental Disorders 214
    Causes of Mental Retardation 217
    Fetal Alcohol Syndrome 218

Normalization and Community Living 221
An Example of a Child with a Developmental
    Disorder 228

Chapter Ten
The Therapeutic Parent 233
    Biological Interventions 234
    A Role Playing Exercise 235
    How to Approach Your Physician 237
    Consultation Preparation Tips 237
    Frequently Prescribed Psychotropic Medications
        for Children 238
    Stimulant Medications 239
    Antihypertensive Medications 242
    Antidepressant Medications 243
    Advantages of Serotonin Specific Reuptake
        Inhibitors 247
    Disadvantages of Serotonin Specific Reuptake
        Inhibitors 247
    Mood Stabilizers and Anticonvulsant
        Medications 248
    Neuroleptic Medications 249
    Antihistaminic Medications 250
    Evaluation of Medication Response 250
    Behavior Modification 254
    Cognitive Behavioral Interventions 257
    Basic Principles of Cognitive Behavioral
        Therapy 258
        Aggression 260
        Depression 261
        Attention Deficit Hyperactivity Disorder 262
        Pain and Learning Disabilities 262
    Play Therapy 263
        The Basic Therapeutic Commitment ... 264
        The Therapeutic Environment 264
        Getting Started 267
        Play Materials 267
        Assuming a Therapeutic Role 268
        Permissiveness and Limit Setting 271
        The Therapeutic Process 272

Chapter Eleven
Resources 275
    Interesting Readings 276
    The Mental Health Association 291
    CH.A.D. 291
    Toll Free Help Numbers 293
    Family Medical Books 294
    Family Medical Software 294
    Parenting Books 294
    Books on Child Development 298
    Play Therapy Books 300
    Samples of Research Articles 300

Appendix A
Biopsychosocial History 338

Appendix B
The Systematic Observation Scale (SOS) 340

Appendix C
Time-out Log 344

Appendix D
Play Session Log 345

Index 346

Introduction

At some point in time most parents question their fundamental intelligence and sanity. The parent, however, who is capable and motivated to become informed about children and children's problems, is indeed a smart parent.

Most parents, at some time, have witnessed an intelligent person who isn't very smart at being a parent. Being a smart parent crosses intellectual boundaries. Being intelligent and successful, or the reverse, does not insure good or bad parenting skills. Basic intelligence, however, is not the essence of this book; being smart is. Smart, as it is used in this book, refers to the efficient, effective and meaningful application of intelligence, knowledge and caring to the most important role of parenting.

Being smart at anything requires a certain amount of basic intelligence, knowledge and motivation. People are not necessarily successful despite their innate intelligence. Being smart begins with an investment of effort. An understanding of children and their problems provides the parent with a more objective frame of reference by which to judge the child's situation. The greater understanding the parent brings to a child, the more helpful the parent will be in forwarding the ultimate objective of producing a happy, healthy individual. The parent choosing to become informed, demonstrates a loving and healthy inclination to be a smart parent.

Can parents enhance and encourage the psychological, biological, social and educational development of their children? Yes! Can a child's development be enhanced? Absolutely! Most of us, as parents, hope to enhance and encourage in our children the development of happy, well adjusted and productive traits and lifestyles. Likewise, however, a child's development can be impaired in numerous ways. Some childhood problems have a tendency to snowball as they add new layers of difficulty on top of a fundamental problem.

To optimize child development, a parent, can provide an adaptive model, participate in the child's educational process and become and/or remain informed. Quality family health care is obviously a necessary part of any plan to optimize child development. A medical or psychological difficulty can distort or impede normal or optimal development.

When is a childhood problem something to be concerned about and when is it just a stage a child is going through? This is a common and important question asked by most parents at one time or another. When should a parent intervene in a problem? How should a parent intervene? These questions will be addressed in this book and methods will be presented that will allow you to consider and face these questions as they apply to your own situation.

The most important roles we undertake initially appear intimidating. Parenting, understanding and dealing with children, is no exception. The dynamic changing nature of children presents us with new opportunities and challenges at every developmental transition. A frame of reference by which to understand and deal with childhood problems assists in meeting these important parental demands in productive ways. The tools of common sense coupled with the scientific method can bring order and increased understanding to the complexities and challenges of parenthood.

This text will provide a general frame of reference regarding childhood difficulties, an introduction to child assessment, observational methods and an introduction of methods to be utilized by parents for behavioral and therapeutic interventions. Many of the methods introduced can also be considered as relationship building and relationship enhancing.

The value and potential of this book is obtained when matched with a smart parent's commitment and motivation to be informed. Assessment and intervention strategies that are offered will be facilitated if the parent begins with some simple organization.

How the parent should start

1. Obtain a notebook binder for notes and results of exercises.
2. Make photocopies of the exercise forms from the appendix and place them in the binder.

A critic could argue that this book is suggesting parents analyze or intellectualize their relationships with their children. While this is true to a degree, it is only to the degree that it brings the parent to a better understanding of a child and a child's motives. The parent who understands a child's motives is in a better position to successfully guide the child and to feel close and effective as a parent.

Chapter One

Understanding Children

In the not so distant past there were few who attempted to understand children. Children were looked upon as labor resources and small adults. In many countries children continue to be viewed in this way. Children in poor and less developed nations frequently face what we in the more developed nations consider the survival concerns of adults. Unfortunately, many children in the world must have immediate survival as their primary objective. Despite all of the challenges of crime, drug abuse, discrimination or other social inequities, children in the relatively more secure boundaries of developed nations are able to develop higher degrees of self actualization.

Psychologists have long noted, that higher levels of psychological development require that fundamental security needs be met first. It seems that Mazlow's concept of self actualization has relevance in this very broad view. Mazlow postulated that for an individual to become "self actualized" he or she must be able to transcend the more basic concerns of security. In the context of children's developmentally dynamic nature, given that basic security needs are adequate, the child continues to acquire mastery, confidence and security in many ways (ie. academic ability, social skills, self esteem), at various levels continuously throughout development. A child who has mastered social relationships at an earlier age may be well prepared to master social relationships at later ages but still must accomplish this development to "actualize" to his or her potential. Given the relative prosperity and good fortune of living in a developed society we have the opportunity to attempt to better understand and guide our children in a way that assists them in becoming happy and effective young people. Today, children's studies span numerous academic and professional disciplines and offer insights in providing the secure foundations that can assist our children in their most important developmental challenges.

Today's professionals and parents have massive amounts of information available regarding child development and childhood issues. Unfortunately, as a result, many parents are overwhelmed with the amount of available information and often times don't know how or where to start. This text aims to serve as both a reference source and guide to provide direction for parents when their child is having difficulty. This book is also designed to elicit and organize specific information a parent can, in turn, provide to a physician or health professional with whom they wish to consult.

There are several helpful child reference books to have in a personal collection. If additional books are not in the budget, local or university libraries may be a resource. If a book such as this allows a parent to more effectively discuss a childhood issue with a teacher, doctor or other professional, the user will hopefully feel the book has been worth its cost. The resource chapter of this text includes lists of family medical, child development and play therapy books that are available.

Using the Resource Chapter and Appendixes

Forms to be photocopied and completed in relationship to the exercises are contained in the appendixes. Lists of books and article titles in the resource chapter (Chapter Eleven) includes a set of general bibliographic references. References have been provided to give readers direction for specific subjects and a general "sense" of available literature. For example, a parent may benefit from simply developing a feeling of the book and article titles available relative to the general childhood topics in the literature. Titles of family medical books, general parenting books, child development books and books on play therapy have been included in the resource chapter to facilitate identifying resources that may be of particular interest.

Professionals may wish to use the resource chapter to find or recommend readings or books to parents with whom they work. A professional may wish to recommend that a parent read or obtain one or more of these resources, or a motivated parent may wish to use these references to gain more specific information within their particular area of interest or concern. Many of the research articles cited are of an advanced nature. The advanced topics may be more intimidating to the general reader and may be of greater interest to professional users. Nevertheless, these titles may lead a parent to become better informed or to be better prepared to consult a professional regarding concerns about a child.

One of this text's primary goals is to assist parents in developing their ability to observe, analyze and intervene in general childhood problems. Among the possible outcomes of the parent observation, analysis and intervention may be the development of an effective parental intervention or obtaining a professional consultation. In the case where a professional consultation is sought the methods presented will assist the parent in organizing data, treatment collaboration and in the collaboration of evaluating a child's response to treatment.

One of the fundamental steps to understanding children is the development of a general frame of reference regarding "normal" child development and deviations from normality or adaptive adjustment.

Normative Psychological and Social Development

Most of us have a sense of what is generally considered normal behavior. Normality, in general, is culturally defined. Normal is frequently considered to be whatever is typical or usual for a given situation. A "normal" individual could be described as having the average amount of problems or psychopathology. Personal dysfunction or pathology must be distinguished from whether or not a behavior is typical, average or normal within the social context of it's expression. In daily living it can be difficult to determine a child's behavior as "abnormal". In addition to the social context of behavior, children are dynamically changing and growing. The question, however, as to whether or not a behavior is abnormal, is not what a parent is usually wanting or needing to define. The author can appreciate a child who marches to a different saxophone; the question really is, is the child's behavior adaptive?

Variations of Normality

Many variations of behavior are within the bounds of generally normative behavior. The behavior of a particular child, for example, may be considered as abnormal by some but not by the child's own group. "Normal" behavior means that a person generally conforms to the practices of his or her social and/or cultural group. A person who conforms excessively may be as abnormal as one who does not conform at all. It is more meaningful to describe behavior as adaptive or maladaptive. A gang member may have successfully adapted within his immediate peer group while at the same time demonstrate maladaptive social behavior. A schoolage child may be acting up along with a similarly minded peer group resulting in maladaptive behavior that is not particularly "abnormal".

We understand children better when we consider the various elements that influence the child's fundamental growth and development. In turn we can learn how to effect those elements that impinge on ourselves and our children. To learn more about the biological, psychological, environmental, and social factors facing children today, we must first accept that these elements are interactive and interdependent.

The probability of a person becoming adaptive or maladaptive in his or her adjustment can be viewed as dependent upon the interactions of strengths, vulnerabilities, risk, and protective factors throughout development. Risk factors at birth may include genetic abnormalities or vulnerabilities, poverty, perinatal complications and parental adjustment. Risk and protective factors continuing throughout childhood and adolescence include parental deprivation, degree of central nervous system maturation, numbers of siblings and closeness in age, birth order, serious or chronic childhood illnesses, parental illness, the child's temperament, adequate parental involvement, handicapped siblings, parental unemployment, frequent moves, frequent changes of schools, foster placement, parental death, divorce, remarriage, availability of support, structure and rules within the home, close friends and access to services.

Parents can influence and modify complex biopsychosocial effects to varying degrees. For example, biological factors include the individual's basic biological constitution as well as such factors as adequate nutrition, sleep and health care.

Few would disagree that many countries, including the United States, are facing critical health care issues with a resultant restructuring of services and treatment methods. As services and treatment methods are restructured, individuals are necessarily becoming more active in making certain their health care needs are met. Some types of health care structures, designed to reduce health care costs, provide basic services while having disincentives or obstacles related to identification of health care needs. The current health care environment is one that is rapidly changing toward mangaged health care as a method to deal with diminishing financial resources. While many of these newer health care structures may not purposely ignore an individual's health care needs, some are poorly designed relative to early identification and treatment. Individuals educated about health issues are in a better position to reduce health care costs and advocate for their legitimate health care needs in a managed care environment.

The methods described in this book propose techniques to monitor quality and treatment response while significantly reducing the costs normally associated with biological and psychological interventions for children. These methods are based on a belief that many parents are capable of providing critical assessment and treatment functions that represent substantial cost. These elements include creating and maintaining organized historical data, relevant observations, analyzing the data and providing a range of therapeutic interventions and support. In more complex circumstances these methods facilitate communication and treatment collaboration between parents and a physician or other professional.

How can parents influence a child's development? Parents' first and most important biological gifts are their genes. One of the first ways a parent can influence their child's biological development is during pregnancy. Having adequate prenatal care, good nutrition, adequate sleep and avoiding alcohol and nicotine increase the odds of producing a child with the best opportunity for uncompromised biological expression. Unfortunately, despite all efforts, unavoidable events such as influenza or measles may complicate a pregnancy. Birth defects, biological impairment or vulnerability are also an inevitable probability for some. While some biological attributes are very obvious, others are subtle and difficult to detect. Some biological attributes, vulnerabilities or tendancies are not expressed or evident until the child is older.

Research is underway seeking to define the genetic transmission of many common mental disorders and diseases. The role of stress as a precipitant or "trigger" to various conditions is one of many important environmental effects related to mental disorders that is being investigated. The hypothesis that stress can trigger an underlying biological vulnerability to illnesses, including depression and other mental illnesses, is increasingly supported by reports within the professional literature. The ultimate manifestation of any mental disorder or difficulty is a complex interaction between biology and other influences.

Psychological factors that influence the child's growth and development include intelligence, temperament, learned behaviors and the current state of these factors as they psychodynamically interact and become experienced and/or expressed. Cultural norms and conditions influence each of us to varying degrees as does other environmental influences. Environmental elements that influence an individual's experience and hence his or her development, include family size, number and nature of stressors, educational, social and living conditions. Social considerations include group membership and access to opportunity.

If we are to describe an adaptive and healthy personality we may be describing attributes that are not necessarily statistically "normal". A person with a healthy personality could be described as able to perceive the world around them accurately and able to relate and interact with others in meaningful and rewarding ways. A person with a healthy personality also benefits from a degree of resiliency while adapting to the general environment. This is not to say that they are problem free, but that they learn from their mistakes and adapt to their given circumstances in a constructive way.

Deviations from Adaptivity

Minor deviations from adaptive behavior, unfortunately, beset all of us at one time or another. Hopefully, we become aware of our maladaptive behavior quickly enough that we don't cause irreversible damage. Most of us have at some time had somebody we love and trust tell us to quit acting like a jerk. Hopefully we listened. As most adults can testify, life's lessons come at significant cost. We all make mistakes and our children will as well. What's most important isn't for our children to be without mistakes but to learn from them. To further the goal of understanding and supporting our children it is helpful to understand common difficulties they experience.

A child's, even an infant's, temperament can be described in several general ways. For example, does a baby mildly fuss when needing a diaper changed or does the baby scream? Observing or recalling traits such as this may suggest whether the child tends to have intense reactions or is mildly reactive to discomfort. Does the child (did the infant) demonstrate stable rhythms relative to sleep and eating patterns? Activity level, ability to adapt to changes, mood, attention span, distractibility and response threshold to stimulation all reflect temperament in the infant and young child. As the child develops, these same traits may continue to reflect temperament or evolve into adaptive or maladaptive styles that are more a reflection of mental state or personality.

Minor deviations from adaptive behaviors will be short lived and will frequently self correct or be responsive to mild intervention. A parent is usually in the best position to provide the child with the most honest feedback. How the child receives the feedback can suggest the child's responsiveness to change. Suggestions on how to provide feedback to a child will be presented in Chapter Four, "Love and Discipline" and in Chapter Ten, "The Therapeutic Parent". Table 1 lists some common childhood difficulties and maladaptive behaviors.

While the problem list is not exhaustive or complete, it does list some common problem behaviors that become expressed by children. How these problems develop or resolve has much to do with how a parent approaches them. Whether the following behaviors are present or not, can, with any given child, mean something entirely different. In one instance a behavior may be a transient expression of unhappiness or anger. In another instance it may reflect a more stable or serious underlying difficulty. We will explore these distinctions as we proceed in the text.

Table 1

Common Childhood Difficulties

social exclusion	bossiness	bed wetting	crying	fighting
poor esteem	impulsivity	homework	bullies	irresponsibility
denial	anxiety	defiance	habits	shyness
sleep	oppositionalism	learning	clown	tantrums
manipulative	whining	isolation	jealous	moody
aggression	withdrawal	hostile	negative	concentration
lying	attention seeking	destructive	meek	immature

These preceding behaviors are frequently transient for children and for a brief period the behavior may be adaptive. The behavior can be considered maladaptive if it results in an eventual personal or socially negative outcome. Frequently maladaptive behaviors result in the individual losing social or familial esteem and/or support. If the child relies heavily on one or more of these styles it suggests a more stable maladaptive behavior which will ultimately have a cost. One way to distinguish between a minor maladaptation versus a moderate or severe maladaptation is to consider the frequency and duration of the maladaptive behavior. A typical maladaptive behavior that has existed less than three months or is occasional (not present at least once every week) can be considered a minor deviation. The child, for example, who is usually compliant may be showing a healthy inclination if he or she questions a parent's decision or confronts a parent with a contradiction.

For our purposes moderately maladaptive behavior will be defined as maladaptive behavior present for over three months or demonstrated more frequently than weekly. A child who goes through a period of opposing his or her mother or father may be looking for clear guidelines or reassurance and respond well to an understanding yet firm parent. On the other hand, unchecked or unchallenged, that child may not be reassured and may escalate the behavior resulting in alienating a friend or a member of the family to the point where he or she is isolated and sometimes, at some level, rejected. Certain types of children have a greater risk and tendency toward these types of difficulties and frequently represent children with moderate or severe behavioral or emotional problems.

An Example of a Child with a Severe Behavioral and Emotional Disorder

Many children push others away as a result of their difficulties. When children have psychological problems it is not unusual for them to have more than one problem. The following case illustrates such an instance. This will be the first of many cases that will serve as examples throughout this book. For the sake of clarity, examples of children are incorporated that best illustrate the issue or topic at hand. Situations, such as will be described, come in all degrees of severity and from every imaginable set of circumstances. As a result, some of these cases will demonstrate extreme or unusually traumatic circumstances. Examples of extreme or severe difficulties sometimes better illustrate the elements that influence such difficulties than if more subtle or mild cases were examined. It will therefore be important for those reading this material to use caution and to not over generalize the causes, motivations or outcomes of severe or extreme examples to other children, similar in some aspect to the example. On the other hand, these examples are offered as a method of developing insight and appreciation into the various and multiple influences that shape and affect our children.

This first example is of a 10 year old boy named John. Included in the example is a summary of his initial evaluation and reports of his initial response to treatment. John represents a particularly complex case in that at the time of referral he had significant behavioral and emotional difficulties for several years, he had never been evaluated or treated for those difficulties in the past, he had significant environmental stressors and was on the verge of being sent to a residential treatment facility. John was large for his age and physically assaultive toward other students. John was stubborn, oppositional and had temper outbursts when confronted by his mother or other adults.

This example illustrates the importance of diagnosis (in order to define an initial treatment strategy), an effective biological intervention and the continuation of evaluation as treatment proceeds. In this case, an effective biological intervention was necessary in order to provide a foundation for psychological treatments to successfully begin and proceed. This example also provides an illustration of how the initial biological interventions were best viewed as medication trials and required close monitoring and adjustments based on treatment response. The specific medication names and doses will be left out of some examples since inclusion of that information could be misleading and not particularly appropriate for another similar child. In Chapter Ten specific medications will be discussed by name and amounts to familiarize readers with medication types and strategies.

John was referred for evaluation due to learning and behavioral difficulties. A physical examination, complete history and psychological evaluation revealed a physically healthy, depressed, 10 year old boy who was aggressive, hyperactive, mildly self abusive and impulsive. At the time of the initial evaluation the single parent was very angry at the child and was extremely frustrated with his behavior. The evaluation included the administration of a variety of neurological and psychological assessments as well as a clinical interview. The following is a presentation of the findings of his evaluation, treatment recommendations and his initial treatment response.

Summary of Findings and Clinical Impressions:

John was referred for evaluation by the school district. John was dropped off for the meeting by his mother, whom John stated had to leave to transport a sibling. The biopsychosocial history was provided by John and later confirmed by his mother. In response to the question as to why he was being seen for treatment John stated, "Because I make bad choices in school. The teacher tells me to do a lot of math problems in three minutes and I get mad. I don't yell but I feel like it, so I just don't do it and let my anger build up". John was in the 5th grade. John appeared appropriately groomed and displayed a mildly depressed and guarded appearance. His mood appeared mildly depressed and congruent with the tone of the self report. John appeared oriented to time, place and person and he reported and displayed no unusual perceptions. John reported difficulties that included learning, allergies (sinus), bossiness, irritability, headaches, impulsive behaviors, trouble concentrating, behavioral problems at home and at school, hyperactivity, picky eater, defiance, particularly irritable upon awakening, social interaction problems, sleep disturbances (mid awakening, sleep onset difficulty, hypersomnia), destructiveness, aggression, frequent crying, anger dyscontrol and poor social skills. Trauma was self reported as out of home placement (at the time of the evaluation he had been living with maternal grandparents for approximately 5 months). Despite many years of serious behavioral and emotional difficulties, John had not previously had any type of mental health evaluation or treatment. John's family history was positive for depression, alcoholism and possible bipolar (manic-depressive) illness. John's biological father was absent and John had never met him. John was right handed; his vision normal and his expressive and receptive language appeared age normative. John demonstrated an impressive ability to discuss his difficulties and expressed a fear of being "sent away to a boarding school".

John's content of thought centered around losing his temper. John's recent and remote memory appeared intact as did his retention and immediate recall, however, significant inattention was reported. John was able to accomplish basic calculations and demonstrated a somewhat below average fund of general knowledge. John demonstrated a fair degree of awareness of many of his current difficulties. John's most recent behaviors related to school and family relationships suggested impulsivity and poor judgement. In general John appeared to be a reliable informant and his mother later confirmed the information he provided.

John's overall evaluation suggested that his general emotional and behavioral state was moderately to severely maladaptive. John's projective drawings demonstrated qualities that suggested immaturity, poor visual motor integration, impulsiveness, hostility, depression and concerns over family or environmental issues. John's sentence completion responses further suggested prominent concerns and issues regarding acceptance, rejection, control of hostile impulses, authority, school, teachers, performance, peers, parents and to some degree, morbid ideation.

John's personality inventory profile reflected clinically significant elevations on numerous scales. The configuration and degree of elevations present suggested the presence of a major depression, a coexisting behavioral/personality disturbance and hyperactivity. The presence of sleep and appetite symptoms, academic impairment, current acting out, and poor social skills were also indicated.

Diagnosis:
296.21 Major Depression, single episode, mild without psychotic features-Rule out Bipolar Disorder

314.01 Attention Deficit Hyperactivity Disorder, Combined

313.81 Oppositional Defiant Disorder

Recommendations:

It appeared John would benefit from both biological and psychotherapeutic interventions in addition to continued academic support, remediation, encouragement, counseling and possibly special services. John had no previous psychotropic medication trials. He indicated his placement with his grandparents might be in jeopardy if his behavior did not improve. Based on John's history and assessment it appeared John would most likely benefit from an initial stimulant trial and the probability of adding an antidepressant in the future. The medication plan was discussed with his primary care physician. Family issues addressed included the stability and consistency of parental direction and discipline and issues related to both an absent father and mother. Personality characteristics focused on in individual psychotherapy included oppositionalism, avoidance, low self esteem, fear of failure, poor frustration tolerance and impulse control.

The following reflect progress notes of John's initial response to treatment:

1st session:

John began his stimulant medication after the evaluation and prior to the first therapy session. John's grandparents, his mother, John and the school all reported a positive initial response that lasted approximately two days. Subsequent to the initial response all (including John) felt that everything was pretty much back to the state prior to medication. As previously planned, John's medication was increased. Coordination of services with the school, family and the physician continued.

Assessment:
Anticipated response to initial low dose stimulant trial without adverse or untoward effects.

Plan:
1. Increased stimulant medication.
2. Weekly psychotherapy and treatment monitoring until stable then reduce frequency.
3. Coordinated services with physician adjusting the stimulant until adequate and adding additional pharmacological strategies as appropriate dependent on treatment response.
4. Coordination of treatment monitoring between school, home and physician.

Session #2:
John was seen for individual psychotherapy and treatment monitoring. The clinician had spoken with John's teacher and she indicated that John had produced more work over the previous two days but also had been quite aggressive, depressed, oppositional and angry. The stimulant trial was continued with a plan to add an antidepressant beginning the next week. John had also been seen the previous week by his physician for a brief physical. Coordination with the school, family and physician continued.

Assessment:
Continued early trial of stimulant. John still appeared significantly depressed.

Plan:
1. Continued stimulant at current dose.

2. Considered plan to add antidepressant.

3. Continued psychotherapy until stable.

4. Coordinated treatment monitoring between school, home and physician.

3rd Session:
John was again seen for individual psychotherapy and treatment monitoring. John reported he was doing very well and this was confirmed by his mother and grandmother. The school reported the previous week they only saw him one day due to an absence and a reduced school schedule. John's mental status was as follows: His appearance was somewhat subdued and restricted, however, less than at previous visits. His mood was mildly depressed but he smiled spontaneously several times during the session which was an improvement over the mood reported and observed at baseline. He complained of no side effects. He did report having a headache during that session.

Assessment:
Continued early trial of stimulant. John still significantly depressed.

Plan:

1. Continued stimulant at current dose.

2. Started antidepressant at 1/2 target dose with instructions to increase to target dose after three days.

3. Continued psychotherapy until stable.

4. Coordination of treatment monitoring between school, home and physician.

4th Session:

John was seen for individual psychotherapy and treatment monitoring. John and his mother reported that he had been doing very well. John reported that he was now in the regular classroom all day. John's mental status was as follows: Affect was somewhat broad, his mood was euthymic (neutral) and he smiled spontaneously several times during the session. He was oriented to person place and time and complained of some gastro-intestinal distress, however, had not used the antacid as had been recommended. No other side effects were reported.

Assessment:
Continued early trial of stimulant and anti-depressant. John still appeared significantly depressed.

Plan:
1. Continued stimulant at current dose.

2. Continued antidepressant at target dose.

3. Psychotherapy until stable.

4. Coordination of treatment monitoring between school, home and physician.

Session 5:

John was seen for individual psychotherapy and treatment monitoring. John was seen briefly together with his grandmother in order to obtain her observations of his treatment response.

John's grandmother mentioned that John had been much better but still wanted to sleep a lot and had been difficult to get up in the mornings. She indicated that he had been sent home once in the past week for talking in class and that he had lost his temper with her when she insisted that he do homework and not go out with friends. He went outside, threw snowballs at her window and walked down the middle of the street. John discussed these incidents productively with his grandmother and the clinician.

All agreed that the impulsiveness and anger dyscontrol that John had demonstrated was much less than prior to treatment; the behaviors, nevertheless were dangerous and self defeating. His grandmother stated that he clearly remained significantly improved over his pre-medication state and was very pleased with his response. John's mental status was as follows: Affect was broad, his mood was euthymic and he smiled spontaneously and frequently during the session. He was oriented to person, place and time and complained of less GI distress since using antacids. No other side effects were reported or observed.

Assessment:
John's school reported significant improvement with aggression, social interactions and to some degree, academics. He appeared to have had a positive response to the stimulant and antidepressant medications. In regard to his current antidepressant treatment he appeared to have had a significant but partial response.

Plan:
1. Continued stimulant at current dose.

2. Continued antidepressant at target dose for one more week and then increase.

3. Psychotherapy until stable.

4. Coordination of treatment monitoring between school, home and physician.

Summary of the Example

This child had clearly worn out his welcome at home and school and was threatened with expulsion from school and removal from his home. The child's evaluation demonstrated the presence of an attention deficit hyperactivity disorder, a major depression, the possibility of an underlying bipolar disorder and the potential to develop a conduct disorder (which is another term used to indicate a stable, maladaptive personality adjustment). John was treated with a combination of medications, a stimulant and an anti-depressant and psychotherapy. John's positive initial treatment response occurred over a period of approximately two months.

In a case such as this, it is important to recognize that long standing untreated emotional and behavioral problems pose a complex treatment challenge. Additionally, when medications are used as part of an intervention, their close monitoring and effective adjustments are a critical part of the initial and ongoing treatment strategy. The proper biological interventions in place allows the child or youth to gain the greatest potential benefit from psychotherapeutic interventions. From the point of referral to the fifth session required two months of evaluation and treatment for John. It was at this point that higher order concerns were able to be addressed.

The acquired biological stability allowed John's family to begin to enjoy his presence rather than avoid it. John began to make friends and improved significantly in school. This particular child's severe and previously untreated hyperactivity caused those previously exposed to him to reject him. This rejection later contributed to the onset of a major depression which, in turn, caused him to become much more seriously disturbed.

What Can a Parent Do?

Methods by which a parent can better understand, assess and collaborate efficiently in the treatment of their child will be presented. These methods have been designed for parents to make an assessment, specific observations and determine intervention strategies. These goals are furthered by first defining types of maladaptive emotional and behavioral states.

Significant Deviations

Clinically significant deviations from adaptive behaviors are probably more common than most people think. Although major deviations are challenging in regard to treatment, early identification and intervention are always a help. Minor deviations frequently correct themselves or benefit from forthright parental intervention. Moderate and severe maladaptation frequently requires the help of a physician or mental health professional in league with the "therapeutic parent". In any case, whether minor, moderate or severe, maladaptive behaviors are best approached in an intelligent, objective and methodical way. A reasoned approach will increase the odds that maladaptive behaviors will be understood and effectively treated. Major difficulties include severe depressive and anxiety disorders, psychotic disorders, antisocial behaviors, conduct disorders, assaultive behaviors, self abusive behaviors, child maltreatment and trauma.

Seeking Objectivity and a Frame of Reference

Making general observations is the starting point of obtaining a more objective understanding of any child. By defining behaviors beforehand and determining areas of interest or concern, a parent can build in a certain degree of potential objectivity. That potential is diminished every time a parent's biases affect the observations. Since most who will read this book will be observing their own child there will be a contaminating bias that influences the observations. Nevertheless, if a parent conducts observations in the spirit set forth in this text, they will approach a greater degree of objectivity and will certainly have a clearer picture of their child than had they not made the described types of observations.

Most parents are amazed at the power of the observations. Observing parents are much less intimidated by certain childhood behaviors. Frequently, parents become anxious because they don't understand why a child is acting in a certain way. If the behavior is frequent or increasing in frequency it may invoke a fear that the behavior will escalate into a major problem. By making systematic observations parents obtain a more objective picture of a child's behavior. By systematizing and documenting observations, patterns associated with specific behaviors become more apparent. The observations suggested can help parents better understand a child as well as suggest how or whether to help the child in a particular regard.

The value of the observations extend to a parent's contribution to a child's problem. The parent, for example, may see a relationship between the child's behavior and their own. Collecting data or observations allows us to get a measurement which in turn can be correlated to behavioral consequences, rewards or interventions. Child assessment and observational methods are further described in Chapter Two. The assessment will consist of examining the child's educational, developmental, familial, psychological and social adaptation. Observational methods will then be described that will contribute to the initial an on-going assessments.

Introduction to Child Assessment by Parents

For parents who are not needing a formal psychological evaluation but want a better understanding of how to enhance a child's development and deal with common childhood problems, the recommended parent assessment methods should suffice. It is not suggested that a parental assessment can substitute for a formal professional psychiatric, psychological or educational evaluation. Parents, however, who determine they need a professional evaluation will get a superior evaluation if they provide the evaluator with the observations and information suggested by this book.

There are several ways to generally assess your child's psychological and emotional adjustment. In fact, parents assess their children's psychological and emotional states constantly. Day care, school and friendship adjustments are typically the way we assess our children. If our children are developing as expected, learning as expected in school, have good family and friend relationships then they certainly can be considered well adjusted. Well adjusted children are a delight and require generous doses of love, understanding, firmness, resolve and consideration.

Frequently, the well adjusted child is not expected to have periods of difficulty. The process of learning and adjustment, however, requires that children have periods of difficulty. It is important for us as parents to provide both understanding and guidance for our children during such times.

A secure and loving environment is one in which children learn both self tolerance and self discipline. In assessing your child it is important to keep in mind the context of your child's circumstances. What is your child's daily routine? How stressful is your child's routine? How supportive or stressful is your family life? The following chapters are designed to help you assess and qualify your ability and motivation to attempt objectivity in assessing your child. Some parents may find their evaluation helpful in simply better understanding their child or in designing a strategy for developing a better relationship with their child.

Preparation for a Medical Consultation

Frequently, by the time parents consult their physician regarding a concern they have about a child, the problem they are seeking help with, is significant. The physician's ability to advise the parent is limited by how well the physician knows the child and family as well as the availability of documented historical facts that assist the physician in making a diagnosis. Even when a child or family is well known by the physician, the fundamental biopsychosocial history is usually not known or documented unless a previous psychological or mental health evaluation has occurred. Consequently, the first visit for this purpose is usually spent providing historical and symptomatic information.

It will not be unusual for a primary physician such as a pediatrician or family physician to ask you to observe your child for a period of time and return to discuss this issue again. Another option that may be suggested is for the family to seek a professional evaluation which in turn can be made available to the physician so a collaborative effort may take place. Both of these approaches are reasonable options, but involve time and significant cost.

Preparation for a medical consultation can provide the physician with the documentation and information from which a much more specific strategy may be deemed appropriate or provide the physician with information which will make the ultimate referral much more valuable. If the assessment outlines recommended in Chapter Two, the Biopsychosocial History in Appendix A and the Systematic Observation Scale in Appendix B are completed prior to a medical consultation, it will facilitate a productive discussion and expedite a plan. These techniques will facilitate a parent's important involvement in the therapeutic process and offer the potential to minimize cost and maximize quality while enhancing the parent-child relationship.

Chapter Two

Child Assessment

In order to provide a frame of reference for understanding a particular child, as distinguished from understanding children, the focus will turn to a discussion of biological considerations, common parental influences and environmental factors. The aim of this chapter is to build a contextual framework that allows for recognition and appreciation of the multiple elements that shape and determine what we ultimately see expressed by children. These elements, for a given child, are better understood when isolated, defined by systematic observations and reassembled in the service of understanding.

One of the disadvantages of writing to a relatively broad audience is that there is a constant danger of writing too "technically" for some while dealing with issues too "basically" for others. Nevertheless, it is recognized that even among professional readers a review of fundamental components can be helpful. On the other hand, the parent or lay reader should not feel intimidated by unknown terms or statements suggesting complex biological, psychological or environmental interactions. This overview of biopsychosocial influences will create a foundation which will allow for a more meaningful discussion of specific mental disorders and difficulties as they are presented in later chapters. In order to approximate objectivity in understanding a child, it is important to first take stock of broad biological, parental and other environmental influences. It is then possible to further identify specific attributes of the various influences being reflected in the emotional and behavioral state of the child.

Biological Considerations

The saying "You can't tell a book by it's cover" is apropos when discussing the multidimensional nature of mammalian biology. In addition to interactions with extra-biological influences, complex interactions also result from intra-biological interactions. An overview of general biological issues related to genetics, structural brain abnormalities, neuroendocrine and neurotransmitter relationships will be woven into the text in order to provide a cornerstone from which to consider specific biopsychosocial interactions and treatment strategies.

Advances made over the past twenty years have added clarification related to the underlying genetic and molecular mechanisms implicated in several medical disorders. Evidence for genetic involvement for some of these disorders, has come from twin and family studies. In other disorders, evidence of a genetic component was found as a result of the tremendous advances in biological techniques. Progress in molecular biology coupled with recombinant DNA procedures has resulted in separating and characterizing genes with mutations accountable for some of these disorders such as Huntington's Disease and cystic fibrosis.

Genetic factors have been implicated in a number of mental, behavioral and developmental disorders of childhood onset as well. Evidence that genetic factors are significant in the ultimate development of many childhood psychiatric disorders is abundantly clear in much of the current scientific literature. Advances in DNA recombinant technology will illuminate genetic components of many human illnesses at an accelerating rate.

How then, might genetic aberrations influence or cause childhood mental illness or developmental disorders? It cannot be emphasized too strongly that genetics, however important, are just a component of the many interactions that result in a final outcome. Many circuitous arguments revolve around whether a particular mental disorder is caused by "nature or nurture" or *"environment or biology"*. This is a meaningless exercise since mental difficulties have multi-dimensional elements that are individually unique and defy exact quantitation. Nevertheless, understanding broad concepts regarding genetic influences can assist in weighing the components of a particular child's situation and ultimately assist in defining treatment strategies should they become necessary.

One way to consider genetic influences as they relate to most of us is to think of them as predispositions. Another way to consider genetic influences is to consider them as constitutional strengths or vulnerabilities. Some of us may be extremely vulnerable or impervious to various other biological or environmental "triggers".

Advances in neuro-imaging are also increasing our knowledge regarding functional aspects of the brain. Current methods in neuro-imaging include the study of brain structure and the study of the brain while it performs specific tasks. These studies have uncovered critical data on an assortment of mental illnesses such as abnormalities in brain blood flow and metabolism. As a result of these advances, neuroscientists are currently developing innovative methods of treatment based on brain chemistry.

Basic Neuroanatomy

The brain is a collection of cells which weighs approximately three pounds. The brain has a marvelous ability to change in response to both external and internal influences. Brains actually change with both structural and chemical changes which can be measured in response to external and internal conditions. For example, nerve cell branches are added in response to learning. The brain is divided into two cerebral hemispheres, left and right, that are divided by a deep groove called the longitudinal fissure. Other grooves further separate the hemispheres into lobes. The grooves are called fissures or sulci.

The part of the brain (see figure 1) in front of the central sulcus is the *frontal lobe* which represents approximately a third of the hemispheric surface. A large part of the frontal lobe is involved in executive functions; that is, planning, predicting and deciding issues important to the individual's needs. A thin portion of the frontal lobe just forward of the central sulcus is referred to as the motor area and controls distinct bodily movements. The lower aspect of the frontal lobe, predominantly on the left hemisphere, is a speech area important for the articulation of speech. The *temporal lobe* is beneath the lateral fissure. The upper aspect of the temporal lobe is particularly involved with hearing. The medial (inner) surface of the temporal lobe is involved with memory processing, while the remainder of the temporal lobe integrates auditory, visual and tactile (touch) sensory data. The *parietal lobe* is behind the central sulcus and includes a primary sensory area. The primary sensory area is involved with nerve impulses resulting in sensations of pain, pressure, touch and temperature. Some reading disabilities have been associated with structural abnormalities in the lower portion of the parietal lobe. The *occipital lobe* is situated behind both the parietal and temporal lobes. The occipital lobe processes visual information.

Although the left hemisphere is slightly larger in most people than the right, they are otherwise structurally similar and are inter-connected and intra-connected by billions of sub-cortical (beneath the surface of the cortex or outer layer of the brain) myelinated (insulated) fibers called *commissures* and *association tracts*. Commissures are fibers that connect one hemisphere with another while association tracts have both short and long fibers which connect cortical areas of the same hemisphere. The subcortical centers are connected to the cortex by *projection fibers*. Figure 2 offers additional views of the brain noting functional capacities of the lobes that have so far been identified.

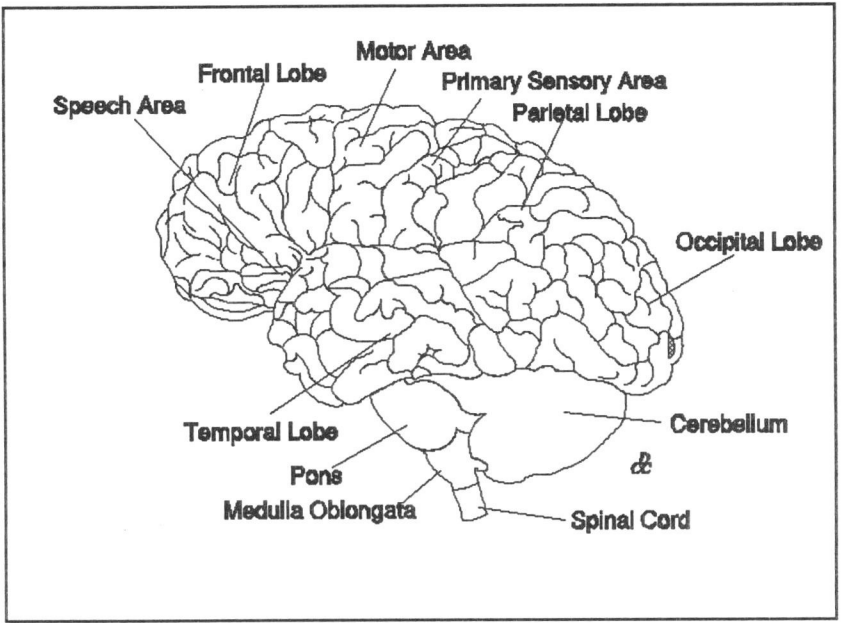

Figure 1

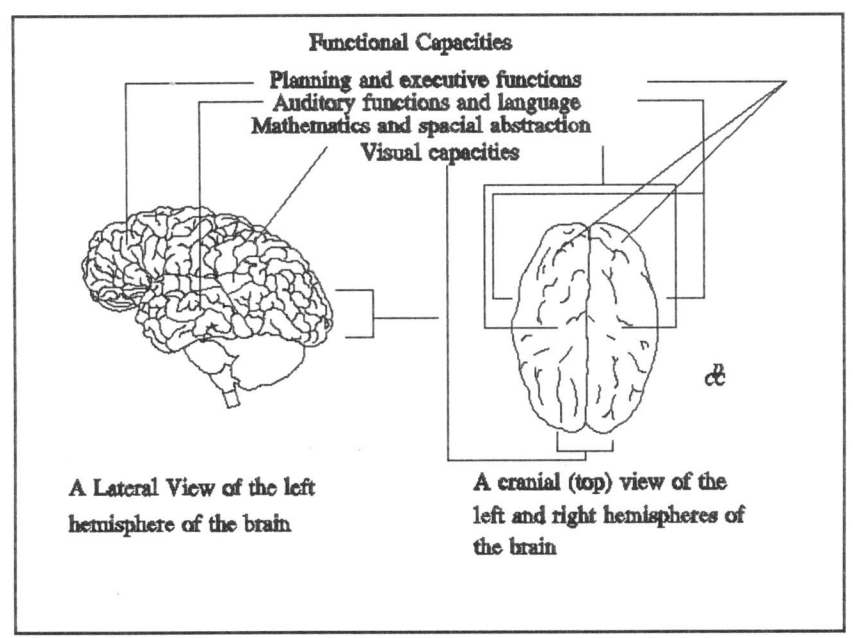

Figure 2

Neuron

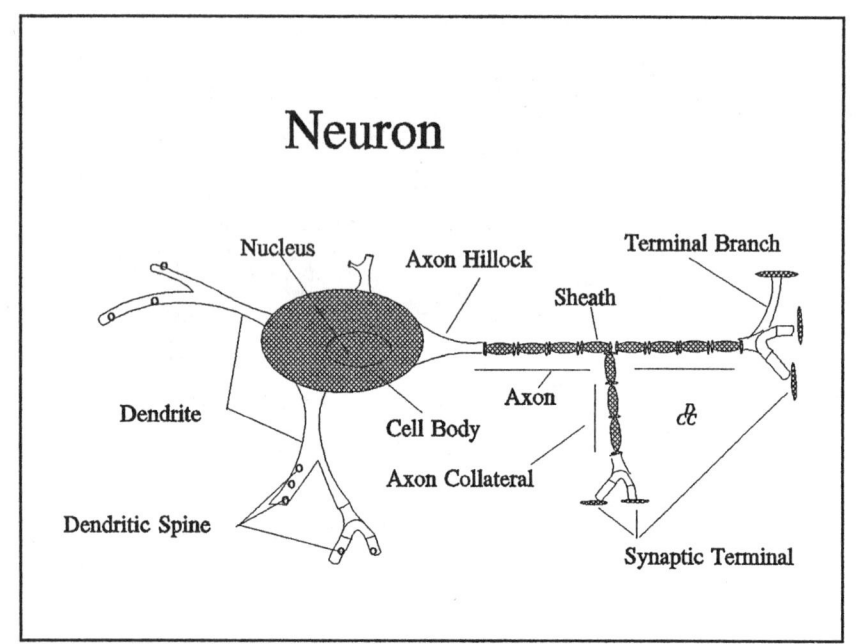

Figure 3

Figure 3 illustrates the appearance and basic components of a neuron. The *neuron*, which is simply a brain cell, is the basic information processing component of the nervous system. Hundreds of billions of these nerve cells are interconnected and integrated throughout the human central and peripheral nervous systems. The neuron is made up of a cell body, a nucleus and extensions which project from the cell body. The extensions which project from the cell body include *dendrites* which branch out from the neuron cell body like a tree. Dendrites allow for various other neuronal information to be communicated to the neuron. A single process called an *axon* also extends from the cell body and serves to conduct impulses away from the cell body. The direction the axon takes is dependent upon its source neuron and its aim. Most axons are about 100 micrometers in length although some exceed one meter in length. Axons are covered with a sheath, some with a lipoprotein insulator called myelin and some without. Axons, like dendrites, may branch out and thereby communicate information to several areas of the nervous system at once.

Structures within the neuron manufacture and package proteins such as *neurotransmitters* for transport or discharge. The role of neurotransmitters and proposals regarding how they are involved in specific disorders will be addressed in the chapters dealing with aggression, mood, anxiety and psychosis.

In recent years the general public has become more aware of a genetic role in schizophrenia. This has been in part due to increased dissemination of the genetic findings through television and news reports. In some cases, however, the contribution of genetic factors to the development of schizophrenia may be overestimated. The term "schizophrenia" is a group of psychiatric ailments typified by disturbances in thought mechanisms, mood and behavior. Abnormalities that occur during brain development may contribute to the cause of schizophrenia. Different events may occur during pregnancy that interfere with the normal development of brain structure and function. Maternal influenza during pregnancy and complications during delivery have both been found to be common among histories of schizophrenic patients. Post mortem examinations and neuro-imaging studies have also found various abnormalities in the brains of schizophrenic patients. Relative to the genetic predisposition or influences, the incidence of schizophrenia is higher in some families than in others.

Cultural influences interact with biology and environment as well. Clinical research has indicated that different ethnic groups respond differently to drugs used to treat major mental disorders. Keh-Ming Lin, a psychiatrist from Taiwan, has been named to head the Research Center on the Psychobiology of Ethnicity at the Harbor-University of Los Angeles Medical Center in Torrance, California. The Center is one of several centers studying cultural aspects of mental health care. The Center also investigates ethnic factors that determine drug responses. Several drugs that are commonly used to treat mental disorders appear to be therapeutically effective at considerably lower blood levels in Asians than in Caucasians.

These differences may in part be the result of environment and/or biology.

Drug response differences could result from ethnic variability in metabolism, in peripheral protein binding (in the blood), or in receptors located on brain cells to which these drugs bind. Studies have also shown that the environment plays a role in drug responses. An interesting study drew comparisons among Sudanese living in the Sudan and in Britain, and Caucasians living in Britain. The investigators demonstrated that the metabolic rates for a drug that uses the same enzymes that are activated by psychopharmacological agents were similar for the two groups living in Britain, regardless of the cultural group. Diet or other environmental types of exposure may be responsible for this particular finding. The goal of the Research Center on the Psychobiology of Ethnicity has been described as not focusing on the biology of racial variation, but on the ways various ethnic groups react to biological interventions for mental disorders.

It may be helpful to keep in mind that environmental influences are not exclusively psychological or social in nature. Differences expressed as a result of diet are one of the many cases of environmental influences that have direct physiological consequences. Other such influences include pesticides, chemical exposure, alcohol or other drugs, radiation and under some circumstances possibly sustained exposure to high voltage electrical current. The physiological consequences of any type of influence has much to do with the state of prenatal or post natal development that is being considered.

A particularly interesting area of current investigation has to do with the role of hormones and neurotransmitters related to development and the development of disease (pathogenesis). These areas of research remain complex and poorly understood. It is a daunting, if not impossible, task to determine if an undesirable hormonal or neurotransmitter effect is a reflection of a structural or production abnormality, an abnormality of metabolism or a result of abnormal receptors interacting with these substances. Abnormal neurotransmitter states or effects can also be the result of various combinations of conditions and interactions of environment and biology. To complicate matters even further there are differences of opinion in terms of what is considered a neurotransmitter. Some consider thyroid hormone to be a neurotransmitter. The anatomy and physiology of neuroreceptors is another area of rapidly growing knowledge intertwined with many confounding variables.

A more concrete example may be illustrative of the potential effects of an abnormal hormone state in the developing fetus and infant. Most infants have a transient surge of thyroid stimulating hormone (TSH) shortly after delivery. This stimulates the release of thyroid hormone and potentiates certain developmental processes. Both prematurity and fetal alcohol exposure have separately been shown to result in an absence of the otherwise normally expected transient surge of thyroid stimulating hormone shortly after birth. Thyroid hormone plays a critical role in stimulating brain and other development. The fetal hypothalamic-pituitary-thyroid (HPT) unit is active in the developing fetus *in utero*. There is a defined sequence of HPT function as the fetus matures. The major circulating fetal thyroid hormone is T4 (some of which becomes metabolized to T3, the active hormone in the brain), while T3 values are low. Postnatally, in more mature pre-term neonates (gestational age >30 weeks), the dynamic function of the hypothalamic pituitary unit is quantitatively similar to that of the term infant, but quantitatively less in that the TSH, T4 and T3 secretory surges are less dramatic. In gestationally immature (<30 weeks) pre-term infants, thyroid hormone secretion is depressed postnatally, increasing slowly after two weeks of age. The absence of the normal thyroid stimulating hormone surge or the relatively lessened quantitative presence of thyroid hormone may be a marker of neurodevelopmental immaturity within the Hypothalamic-Pituitary-Axis or the Hypothalamic-Pituitary-Thyroid Axis.

The developmental impact of thyroid dysregulation can result in mental retardation, cerebral palsy, attention deficit hyperactivity disorder and learning disabilities. Developmental deviations of thyroid functioning have been identified as a risk factor contributing to the development of cerebral palsy. Premature delivery, which is the single most important antecedent of cerebral palsy, is also associated with immature Hypothalamic-Pituitary-Thyroid Axis development.

One of the most frequent causes of cerebral palsy in many parts of the world is prenatal iodine deficiency. Neurologic cretinism, is a form of spastic diplegia (cerebral palsy) associated with deafness and mental retardation found in areas with soils severely deficient in iodine. A paradoxical finding in such children is that unlike the child with classical endemic cretinism, hypothyroidism is absent as are the other stigmata of congenital hypothyroidism. It has been suggested that neurologic cretinism arises when iodine deficiency is exclusively prenatal; that is, when nutritional conditions are such that although prenatally deprived, the infant has sufficient iodine in the diet to prevent post-natal hypothyroidism.

An example of the complexity with which these variables interact returns us to the role of genetics. The influence of genetics and genetic mutations may result in many variations of vulnerability and expression as well. Recent findings by Peter Hauser and associates addressing the relationship between a genetically transmitted generalized resistance to thyroid hormone (GRTH) and attention deficit hyperactivity disorder further illustrate the depth of potential complexities of these disorders. This resistance to thyroid hormone is expressed in different degrees (by various mutations). To literally make a long story short, an individual with GRTH may have adequate supplies of thyroid hormone in their system but be unable to utilize it efficiently.

Some children have difficulties that have little or no genetic, structural or biochemical brain influences of primary significance. Similarly, some children have difficulties that have little or no primary psychological or environmental influences of significance. Developing a sense of the weights of the various influences is helpful for those designing strategies to intervene in a particular childhood difficulty. These distinctions will be considered relative to specific childhood problems and mental disorders throughout the text.

The primary influence involved in a childhood difficulty may take on secondary importance over time. For example, an environmental stressor, may over time, precipitate or trigger a biological state that becomes more significant as a concern than the original precipitant. The other side of the coin would be a biological state, such as a major depression, that results in increasingly significant environmental or psychological components. The negative secondary effects of a major depression may include social alienation due to an individual's moodiness, irritabilty or withdrawal. Clearly, the duration and quality of any influence will have a bearing on an individual's response.

Common Parental and Environmental Influences

Common parental and environmental influences on children and children's problems include parental attitudes toward discipline and permissiveness. Additional influences include the effect of marital and other personal adult difficulties on children. School and neighborhood environments have important influences as well. While many parents are aware of these considerations, it is easy to be blind or otherwise insensitive to a child's view and perceptions. Identifying significant negative influences and attempting to determine their effect on children can be useful.

Children, like adults, are not immune to the effects of moving, death, divorce, illness, unemployment, victimization or any other environmental curve ball. Events such as these can precipitate major consequences for children as well as for adults. Death of a parent is a tragic event for the surviving spouse (if there is one) and children. Divorce, as many can attest, is multifaceted in it's effects on children. Despite the difficult challenges faced by all parties in a divorce, continuing marital discord is no picnic either. Marital discord often has a much greater influence on children than parents care to admit. The fact is that every day most children are influenced by a multitude of events and circumstances beyond their control. Our awareness can be magnified by considering many of the common situations that prove difficult for children and frequently precipitate or contribute to childhood difficulties.

Parental upset, whatever it's cause or form, rarely goes unnoticed by children. Children may or may not acknowledge the parent's situation even if the parent has been quite open with the child. Anxiety, for example, is contagious. When children see or sense their parents as anxious they also tend to become anxious. If the parent on whom they rely is worried, then there must be something to worry about. It is not suggested that a parent be deceptive, but a parent does not have to be completely and totally honest when to do so increases the child's anxiety with no benefit. For example, a father who learns that his job may or may not be ending depending on the winning of a new contract, may have concerns he will be laid off. This father may be extremely anxious in terms of the consequences for himself and his family. To share the information with his children in an anxious way will most likely increase the children's anxiety. On the other hand if the children sense something is wrong with the father or if the parents argue and are tense, it may relieve some of the children's anxiety to know what the general circumstances of concern are.

School environments include the child's relationship with his or her teachers, peers and schoolwork. It is easy for us as adults to forget the complexity of the school environment. A child may be very sensitive to a teacher's criticism or a teacher might be particularly anxious, stern or moody. Other children may be targeting a particular child for teasing because that child has a strong reaction or gets easily upset. Children experiencing parental separation or divorce manifest their reactions in a variety of ways. One generalized effect of those children on others is that it makes other children more acutely aware that marriage is not always permanent. Many bright children become anxious when they find schoolwork to be difficult or not immediately mastered. Children are affected by the degree of control and comfort within the classroom. Children are quite aware when others get away with breaking a class rule. The child's school environment is the equivalent to the adult's work environment with all of the rewards of accomplishment and the pressures of performance.

Neighborhoods vary tremendously and have the potential of being extremely supportive, stressful or neutral. It is important when attempting to understand a child to gauge his or her place within different environments and the environmental influences. Are there other children in the neighborhood? How does this child fit in with the other children? Are the parents in the neighborhood supportive and consistent among themselves with regard to the children in the neighborhood? Does the child have others to play with? Are there bullies in the neighborhood? Even when circumstances are difficult or cannot be changed, it is helpful to be aware of daily influences facing children.

Making General Observations

Up to this point this chapter has addressed general factors that affect children. Family life, school adjustment and peer relationships are obvious examples of environmental factors. In subsequent chapters specific case examples will be provided that illustrate the potential outcomes of these and various other influences. Understanding the factors and forces shaping children is heightened by examining the fabric of troubled children's experiences. Our relationships with children will profit when we remind ourselves of the environmental and developmental currents from which children grow and evolve. Even so, we are usually motivated to understand children better when a specific situation with a child has been challenging or difficult to understand.

The observational methods suggested are offered as a way to understand a specific child within the context of the many factors that shape or effect individuals. It is helpful for the professional as well as the parent to keep these various general environmental factors in mind when attempting to better understand a child. When an adult feels a child has not responded to their guidance or discipline, it can be helpful to attempt an objective assessment of the circumstances associated with the given situation. One way to facilitate understanding is to plan and conduct directed observations of the child. Most people have had the experience of looking more closely at some common object and discovering many new elements they had not previously observed. The same experience will be true for those who make thoughtful observations of a child. Observations become more rewarding when they are pre-determined and pre-defined events.

It should be made clear that it is not being recommended to "spy" on a child. What is being suggested is that the observer make a determined effort to study some area of the child's environment and behavior. A note of caution should be added at this point. The motive and goal of what is being suggested truly needs to be a greater understanding of a child. Observed difficulties can be addressed and this book will suggest methods toward that purpose, however, the first order of business is to obtain data; not just a single or a few observations.

It is very easy for a newly observant or more observant adult to become overly critical of a child, especially if the parent observes a difficulty of concern. Obviously, if a child feels watched or observed it will diminish the validity of the observation. For the sake of illustration and gaining observational experience the following parent exercise is offered.

Exercise 1

Pick a behavior such as how your child goes to bed at night. Decide to observe and briefly note your child's bedtime behavior for five nights in a row while attempting to maintain your normal reciprocal behaviors. Observe who initiates the bedtime routine. Does the child start to bed on his or her own accord? Does the child wait for you to tell him or her it is time for bed? Is the bedtime routine a comfortable, pleasant process or is it a difficult and frustrating one? Do you like how you feel or interact with your child? What is usually happening in your home at this time of evening? Have you had a chance to talk to your child about his or her day? Is there something about your child's bedtime routine that you would like to change? After five observations, do you see a trend? Are there big differences on different nights? If so, can you relate them to other differences in routine? Save your notes for future exercises.

The Value of Observations

By making a concerted effort to be more observant you will notice more about yourself and your child's behaviors. Ultimately you will be rewarded with a greater understanding of your child and possibly, of yourself.

Data Collection and The Scientific Method

The type of data collection that is used will depend on the nature and severity of a given child's problems. For a typical child having transitional difficulties that are primarily at home, general observations made by the parents may suffice in order for them to consider ways to help the child or prevent the development of maladaptive styles. For a child who has more significant difficulties that extend into school or other settings, more specific observations that focus on specific difficulties of concern may be obtained by the parent and others having contact with the child.

General Parental Observations

Parent observations by nature of their built-in bias cannot be rigorously scientific. They can, nevertheless, be very helpful and certainly increase the level of objectivity a parent brings to interactions with their children. Although many parents feel they know their children well, most are still amazed at how much better they understand a behavior once they have made a specific observation of their child. Invariably, parents have a greater understanding of a child's behavior once they have made a concerted effort to watch what is happening; including their own and other adult responses to the behaviors being observed.

As in scientific data collection, objectivity and quantity of data combined with consistency of the methods used, increases the reliability of the observations. With this in mind, methods will continue to be discussed throughout this book on how to approach data collection. It should be stated at this juncture that there is an important role and value of singular observations as well. It is not uncommon in science for a single event to lead to more specific observations related to that event. With a child, a certain type of behavior may lead you to study more closely the elements that support or reward that behavior.

In making these types of observations a temporary sort of minor detachment from the behavior is being suggested. Most parents can relate to being angry and frustrated with a child. The moment the parent is reacting to some behavior is not the time to analyze it. Later, at a time when the child is not present, is a time when a parent can reflect on what caused the difficulty or frustration. A parent may state for example, "I've had it! I told him to go to bed ten times and he is still up! Now I am trying to watch the news and I am having to deal with this!". After the news is over and the child is asleep the parent may more successfully analyze what occurred. Why did I get so angry? I don't like ending the day on a bad note and that makes me angry. I told him ten times and that makes me angry because it continued to demand my attention well after his bedtime. With this type of reflection a parent can decide how to handle this issue the next night.

The Parent Assessment

This manual proposes that a parent can make an assessment of their child's general adjustment. This assessment, of course, is no substitute for a professional or clinical assessment. In fact, if a parent utilizes the proposed method it may suggest whether or not a professional assessment is in order. If a professional assessment does seem indicated, the parent can present their findings, observations and notes to the professional for inclusion in the professional's assessment.

Assessing a Child's General Adjustment

In order for a parent to gain a general frame of reference about a child, the following method is suggested. Photocopy the assessment outline found in the appendix and complete it as you read along with the text following the general outline as shown in Exercise 2.

Exercise 2

Following along this general outline, make notes about what fits for your child and what doesn't fit. These items are intended to stimulate your thoughts, so feel free to add to any areas. Once you have read over the complete outline and your notes you will have a general summary result.

I. Educational
- A. Academic interest
    1. Interested in learning
        a. Specific interests
    2. Not interested, bored or resistent
        a. Specific non-interests
- B. Academic attitude
    1. Likes school
        a. Specific likes
    2. Doesn't like school
        a. Specific dislikes
- C. Academic achievement
    1. Areas of strong achievement
    2. Areas of poor achievement
    3. Areas of average achievement
    4. Responsibly completes homework
    5. Completes homework with encouragement
    6. Has difficulty completing homework
- D. Parent relationship with teacher
    1. Positive
    2. Negative
    3. Neutral
- E. Child relationship with teacher
    1. Positive
    2. Negative
    3. Neutral
- F. Parent educational involvement
    1. Parent looks at schoolwork daily
    2. Parent looks at schoolwork weekly
    3. Parent watches scientific or educational programs with the child
    4. Family has educational outings-museums etc.
    5. Child reads to parent(s) on a regular basis
    6. If a two parent home-both parents participate in educational stimulation and motivation.
    7. Child has a positive feeling about parent educational involvement
    8. Child has a negative feeling about parent educational involvement

II. Developmental
- A. Medical
    1. Child is healthy
    2. Child is ill
    3. Child is frequently ill

4. Child has had a physical within past year
   5. Child's physical development is age normative
B. Psychological
   1. Child's intellectual development is advanced
   2. Child's intellectual development seems average
   3. Child's intellectual development seems delayed
   4. Child's emotional development seems advanced
   5. Child's emotional development seems average
   6. Child's emotional development seems delayed
C. Family relations
   1. Is well liked within the family
   2. On-going difficulties with one or more family members
   3. Is particularly close to a family member
   4. Enjoys family outings
   5. Dislikes family events
D. Social Skills
   1. Has many friends
   2. Is well liked
   3. Has few or no friends
   4. Actively participates with peers at school
   5. Actively participates with peers in neighborhood
   6. Avoids other children
E. General Environmental Considerations
   1. Has had recent trauma
   2. Family or marital discord
   3. A parent, relative or friend has died
   4. A pet has died
   5. Divorce
   6. Other stressors
F. Outline Assessment Summary
   1. Areas in which the child excels or is advanced.
   2. Areas which are neutral, average or unremarkable.
   3. Areas of delays or demonstrated difficulties.

By considering a child's adjustment related to these various domains a parent will gain both a global sense of his or her general adjustment and identify areas of both strengths and weaknesses. Children, like those of all age groups, have strengths and weaknesses that defy uniformity and often progress at different rates. If a child is experiencing difficulties that have been persistent or having difficulties in many of the outlined areas, closer observation and possibly a professional assessment may be helpful.

The Biopsychosocial History

The completion of a biopsychosocial history provides a method of creating and maintaining a historical context in which to view an assessment of a child's adjustment. A biopsychosocial history format is provided that will assist a parent seeking to clarify a child's difficulties within the changing context of the child's development. The biopsychosocial history will be described here and a form suitable for photocopying can be found in Appendix A.

Exercise 3

Read the following section describing the biopsychosocial history, photocopy and complete the form "Child Biopsychosocial History" from Appendix A, and place in your binder.

The elements that make a biopsychosocial history valuable and useful to a parent include it's ability to convey and organize important information for documenting a period in time. Additionally a history such as this can be copied and provided to a collaborating clinician, should professional services be indicated.

It is not unusual for a parent obtaining professional services to repeat a summary of a child's difficulties or particular concerns several times in an effort to provide critical background information. Depending on time constraints, the clinician's style or particular questions, the parent may end up feeling as though a complete picture was not well presented. An organized historical summary can be completed once, used for later review or copied, and provided to others involved in a treatment process as deemed appropriate by the parent.

Child Assessment 61

The first section of the history is basic identification information. This is particularly important if this form is to be copied for a collaborating clinician. It allows clerical staff to place it in the proper file and provides a documentation for the clinician that further indicates critical information regarding the child such as the name of the informant (person completing the form), relationship to the child (parent, foster parent, social worker etc.), the date the history was completed, the name of the child, the child's age, home phone number and date of birth. Next, information regarding others who may play an important role in coordinating current efforts to help a child; namely, the school and the child's physician, is provided. Last in this section is a space for a brief indication of the primary concern about the child and referral source, if applicable.

The next section allows for an indication of the parents with whom the child resides, their relationship to the child, parents who do not reside with the child, circumstances of absent parents and visitation information, and names and ages of siblings residing both in and out of the home of the child. Developmental and educational history is provided by indicating circumstances of the pregnancy, pregnancy or birth complications, description of the child as an infant and toddler, attitude to preschool, kindergarten and descriptive comments regarding each educational year. Any significant features of physical growth, motor (walking etc), speech and language, developmental milestones exceeded or delayed can be included in this section. Current difficulties are next indicated by circling the applicable indication of the presence or absence of the specific symptoms. Space is then provided for indications of previous psychiatric or psychological evaluations, previously prescribed medications, presence or absence of seizure history, medication allergies or trauma.

The final section of the history provides for a family medical history, the developmental course of the current difficulties and for final parental remarks.

Systematic Observations

The Systematic Observation Scale (Duke, 1988) was developed in response to a perceived need for more objective treatment response data. While the author was working within a residential psychiatric treatment facility for severely maltreated children, the need for objective data was apparent. It is not uncommon for children to conduct themselves differently from one setting to another. They may also be perceived quite differently during the same time period by different observers. It was with this in mind that the Systematic Observation Scale (SOS) was developed. An example based on that particular setting is illustrative.

Sam was a 10 year old boy who had failed a foster home placement and was referred to residential treatment. Sam had been the victim of physical abuse by his mother's boyfriend. He had a history of a head injury that resulted from a fall while running, tripping and hitting his head on concrete. During the time Sam lived with his mother and her boyfriend, he was frequently punished by being hit on the head and face. While still in the home Sam was a frequent problem at school and had been diagnosed as having attention deficit hyperactivity disorder. The school referred him to a physician which resulted in his receiving a stimulant medication. The school documents reported that he initially had some benefit from the medication, however, he was later expelled from school after some rather bizarre episodes in which he defecated in various school rooms.

Sam was removed from his home by child protective services after being beaten by his mother's boyfriend. His mother's boyfriend was charged with child abuse. Rather than face a certain jail term, the boyfriend and Sam's mother fled the state taking Sam's brother. After several months of absence it became apparent that Sam's mother had abandoned him. Despite Sam's many difficulties, he was a likable child. He was depressed, hyperactive and at times physically aggressive and explosive.

A typical incident for Sam was to have a period of exceptionally good behavior and emotional control followed by an explosive outburst in which he would become indiscriminately assaultive and violent. After such an outburst he would be genuinely remorseful about his actions. While the therapy and school staff saw Sam as improving considerably after a course of treatment which included medication, the cottage staff which dealt with him in his living environment felt that he had not benefitted at all from the treatment. The issue became significant when the consulting child psychiatrist was attempting to determine the response to the medication trial and the staff members disagreed widely over the benefit of the medication.

An analysis of the "cottage staff's" views revealed that they were concerned about this child's potential to do serious harm to staff and other children. Sam was a large strong child and on one of his many violent episodes, had narrowly missed a staff member's head when he hurtled a heavy trophy across a room at major league speed. Sam had also had numerous previous episodes in which he unpredictably exploded and assaulted those in his proximity requiring the staff to protect others and restrain him. Given the difficult management issues confronting the staff, it was no wonder that they were angry with this child and the challenges he presented. A thorough team review of Sam's behaviors and critical incidents provided an interesting finding. While Sam had continued to have serious incidents, the frequency of the incidents had been reduced by over fifty percent while on the medication. It became apparent that while the cottage staff correctly identified Sam as a continuing danger, they had not objectively reported his response to treatment. The cottage staff's concerns were of course legitimate but were misleading to the treatment staff. A partial response is different than no response and may provide important information regarding adjustments, changes or other strategies relative to biological and psychotherapeutic interventions.

The Systematic Observation Scale (SOS)
©1988. Duke Children's Clinic

General Description and Instructions for using the Systematic Observation Scale

The SOS offers a method of observation and documentation that facilitates the physician-parent partnership in the treatment and on-going evaluation of a child. It is particularly valuable in observing, recording, tracking and evaluating children's responses to psychopharmacological and/or psychotherapeutic interventions. Observations by parents and teachers in the form of the Systematic Observation Scale (SOS) record, provides a direct communication link between the educational or child care setting, parents and the clinician. The SOS was developed to provide a method to make specific multiple observations over time, quantify the observations and graphically represent these observations over individually determined time intervals. The SOS is comprised of five specific observational scales and an observation summary graph. The PH scale observes physiological symptoms. The AD scale tracks symptoms that are associated with attention deficit and hyperactivity. The AG scale tracks physical, verbal and self aggression. The AF scale tracks affective or emotional states. The fifth scale is the specific problem tracking scale. The SPT scale tracks any specified problem the parent and clinician wish to observe. The uses of the SOS include it's utility in documenting and graphically demonstrating relative changes over a treatment course. Parental and educational settings observations aid in assessing treatment results and variations of treatment. The SOS is easy to use and step by step instructions and tips are provided for observers and evaluators.

An example of the flexibility of the SOS is its ability to observe on a daily, weekly or monthly schedule. Observations will most commonly be characterizations of the day, week or month, but can also be made more rigorous by planning direct observations at randomly assigned times. Systematic observations usually begin with one or more observations representing pre-treatment conditions. In order to avoid the effects of inter-rater differences in a series of observations, the individual observing should ideally remain consistent. Multiple observers, should have his or her individual SOS records of dated observations to be made available as needed. If an observer must be changed during an observational series, it can be indicated and taken into consideration when evaluating the observations. The SOS establishes a data base from which treatment responses can be evaluated, monitored and documented.

The SOS consists of these descriptive and instructional remarks, item definitions, an observation sheet and an observational summary graph. Instructions are provided for accommodating single or multiple observers. Each observation summary graph allows for thirty observations on each of the five dimensions. The instructional remarks, item definitions, an observation sheet and an observational summary graph can be found in the appendix. The purchaser of this book is permitted to make unlimited photocopies of the SOS and other forms in the appendix for personal and non-commercial use.

The figure that follows is a representation of what an SOS observation summary graph might appear like if there had been a pre-treatment observation and two subsequent treatment conditions. The sample graph has utilized different patterns in filling the bars to indicate different treatment conditions. In addition to the bar pattern or color, the space above the vertical line of a given observation allows for a treatment condition code. A key can be written at the bottom of the graph page indicating the treatment condition number or code and what treatment that represents. Many parents have found it helpful to sub-total a particular scale, mark an X in the scale observation square equal to the score and then highlighting the bar from the zero point up to the X. A visual representation of treatment response can be made more apparent by using a text highlighter, markers or colored pencils to fill in the bars. When a treatment condition changes, a color change can be keyed to the change as a further assistance to viewing treatment response over numerous observations and/or treatment conditions.

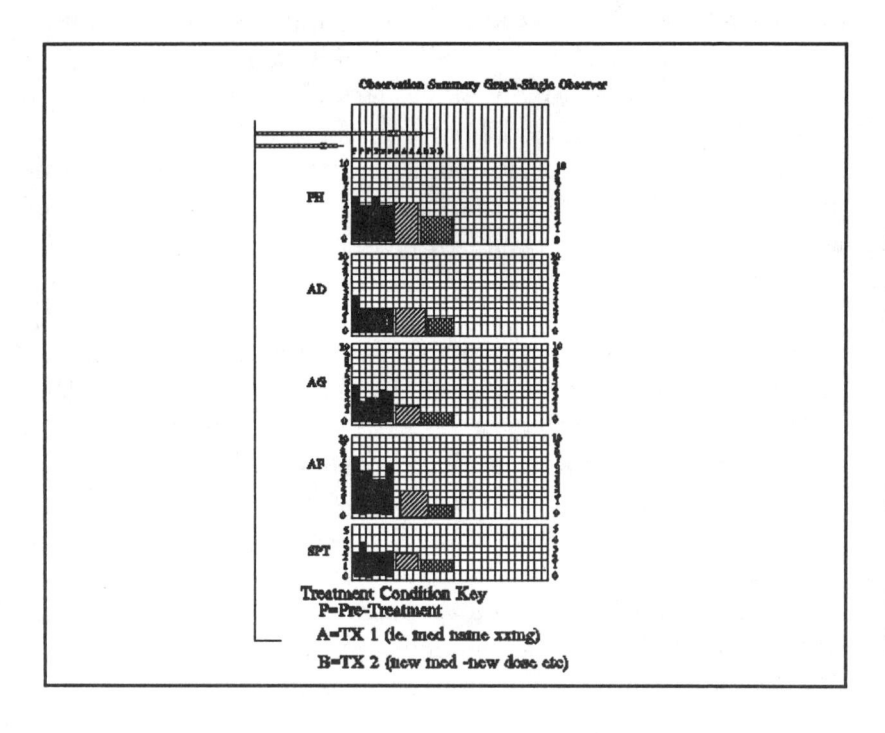

[Figure: Observation Summary Graph-Single Observer, showing bar graphs for PH, AD, AG, AF, SPT across treatment conditions. Treatment Condition Key: P=Pre-Treatment; A=TX 1 (ie. med name xxmg); B=TX 2 (new med -new dose etc)]

Exercise 4

Photocopy the SOS instructions, item definitions, an observation sheet and the observational summary graph. Follow the instructions and complete your first observation, noting the date and the presence of any treatment condition that is occurring as the observation is made. Place the completed observation in your binder, determine an observation schedule and continue to use the same summary graph for subsequent observations. Many parents find that frequent (hourly; various periods of the day or daily) observations are helpful when there are frequent and wide ranging variations of behavior and emotional states whereas less frequent (1-2 times a week) observations are adequate when behaviors and emotions are relatively stable. It is common for parents to have more frequent observations occurring at the beginning of treatment with frequency reductions as the child becomes more stable.

Chapter Summary

In this chapter methods have been suggested for gaining a general frame of reference from which to better understand your child. Methods for making observations and making a general assessment of your child's adjustment have been provided. In becoming more aware of your child and his or her world you will also become more aware of your own. It is important to consider your own stressors as well as those in your child's life. Some stressors such as routines and the way a family chooses to recreate and interact are controllable. Some stressors such as death, divorce, illness, personal crimes against yourself or your child and so on are uncontrollable. It is a tragedy when a child has been severely traumatized by crimes or other events; while those incidents cannot be undone, their effects on children can be lessened by understanding the child.

I'm going to treat my headache just as instructed on the bottle of aspirin. I'm going to take two and keep away from children.

Chapter Three

The Family Environment

The family environment is generally the most critical environmental factor in a child's life. That is even true when a child is not in a typical home environment. There are many children living "out of home" in foster homes and residential treatment centers. It is helpful to provide a brief general discussion of these children because much can be learned from their hurt and trauma that can benefit more traditional homes and families. There is definitely the analogy to learning new medical techniques or methods from the horror of war casualties. Discussing some of the issues confronting out-of-home children can illuminate some of the effects and issues present in traditional homes. In some small way this may help maltreated children by making others more aware of their situation and needs.

Most informed people in our society are to some degree aware of child abuse and child maltreatment. However, many are not aware of much more than the occasional news reports of incidence or alarm at the frequency of these occurrences. The fact is that thousands of children are placed out of their homes as a protective measure or as a measure of necessity. Maltreated children, orphans and children of incarcerated parents are frequently placed out of home in foster homes or residential treatment facilities.

Above and beyond the stress and hurt that results from their initial home removal, these children continue in stressful circumstances by nature of their out-of-home placements. For children who fail in foster placements the ultimate placement is usually a residential or hospital treatment placement. In these placements it is easy to observe the result of trauma and ongoing stress. Despite many fine and loving foster parents and some outstanding treatment facilities, these circumstances remain unnatural and stressful for the children involved.

Fortunately, most children are not in these dire circumstances. Previous research with this population of children (Duke, 1987) has demonstrated that maltreated children are at heightened risk for depression as a result of the confluence of biological vulnerability, genetics, cognition, learning, environment, psychodynamic and personality considerations coupled with maltreatment. From a child's point of view, maltreatment can be viewed as an uncontrollable stressor. Numerous animal studies have demonstrated the biological results of depression that have been precipitated by the animal being placed in a situation of uncontrollable stressors.

The effects of emotional and behavioral disorders among maltreated children have substantial consequences. Many maltreated children fail in foster placements due to undiagnosed and untreated emotional and behavioral disorders. The lesson for society is two fold; not only do we have a moral responsibility to these children but we also have a self interest in these children being effectively cared for. Maltreated children require and deserve complete psychological assessments, support and treatment starting when they are initially removed from their homes. Most foster children don't receive services until they have demonstrated a serious problem. Social service agencies are very frequently overwhelmed by the demands for child protective services, foster care and related services. Most of these agencies are understaffed and wanting of foster parents and financial resources. It is not unusual for the typical foster child to have multiple foster placements over a short period of time. This, of course, increases the stress the child endures. The lesson for other families is that stress is best identified, recognized and minimized when possible. Emotional and behavioral problems can, of course, occur in the absence of identifiable stress; the presence of continued stress, however, can result in serious difficulties for anyone.

When stress is identified it can provide the parent with important information regarding how a child can best be supported. Even in situations where the stressor cannot be changed, the aware parent can counteract some of the negative effects by being aware of the stressor and offering supportive measures. Later in this text parent play therapy methods will be presented which is one such measure of support. The following text will discuss common stressors experienced by children and adults.

A Comedian's Tradition

A young comedian has described her family holidays as an event where the family all gets together and criticizes one another until one of them has a seizure. Then they have pie.

Common Family Stressors

All people are faced with stress. How people react to and deal with stress, however, varies tremendously. Pain and stress are experienced in some ways as relative to what one is accustomed to. Additionally, some people seem to have a higher threshold for pain or stress. Some have very low thresholds for stress and/or pain. Nevertheless, if the pain or stress is overwhelming it probably doesn't matter what you've been used to or for that matter, what your threshold is. This section will consider common family stressors and discuss methods by which their effects can be countered.

What about the effects of television?

Certainly television offers a significant richness to our children and ourselves. Educational and informational materials are plentiful and have evolved into very entertaining formats.

72   Smart Parenting

The Public Broadcasting System, The Discovery Channel and the Learning Channel as well as other channels have many examples of fine programming. The comic relief and dramatic programming provided by television also serve a real purpose for most children and adults. Nevertheless, television plays a large role in shaping children and their views. Some interesting statistics regarding television were reported previously by The Cable Guide (Volume 11, Issue 130, September, 1992). For example, according to this survey, what is the top rated activity of the 6-17 year old age group after school? What do you expect is the percentage of kids who would prefer to watch television than read? What do you suppose are the recommended and estimated numbers of hours per day that American children are viewing television? How many total hours has a typical first grader spent watching television? The top rated after school activity for those 6-17 years old is watching television. 41% of children responded that they would prefer to watch television than read. According to The Cable Guide "experts" recommend two hours of television viewing per day, while it is estimated that American children view television approximately four hours a day. How many commercial minutes within one hour, in weekday children's programming do you think are legally permitted? Twelve minutes of commercial programming is allowed per hour during the weekdays and 10.5 minutes per hour on weekends. The average number of commercial minutes per hour in the United States is 13.5 as compared to .83 in France.

What about television violence? The Cable Guide report goes on to state that there are 5 to 6 violent acts per hour on prime time television. The number of violent acts per hour during daytime children's shows was reported as between 20 and 25, and during Saturday morning cartoons, 26 per hour. By age five the report estimates that a child will have seen 200 hours of violent images. By age 14 the typical child will have seen 13,000 killings on television. Twenty percent of those five to seven years old (and 89 percent of those 11 years old) have seen Nightmare on Elm Street. During a typical week children will be likely to see 30 policemen, 7 lawyers and 1 scientist during their television viewing.

While 58% of parents reported feeling uncomfortable with the content of what they see on television with their children, only 25% of parents make any restrictions on what their children watch. The report also shares a somewhat surprising finding. Although Japanese children spend more time doing homework, they also spend more time watching television. The report's findings were that 73% of 13 year old Americans watch three or more hours of television a day compared to 88% of 13 year old Japanese children. The percentage of 13 year old Americans who spend more than two hours a day doing homework is 27% compared to 62% of Japanese who are 13 years old. The Japanese children must be watching television while they are doing their homework.

Marital Discord

Marital difficulties are probably one of the most common family stressors. There are, of course, minor, moderate and severe types of marital difficulties. It should be noted, however, that even minor marital difficulties can be misinterpreted by children and result in stress. It can be helpful for parents to point out to their children that even people who love each other sometimes fuss and fight. It can also be helpful for children to witness their parents doing what their parents usually instruct them to do in disagreements: apologize, compromise and otherwise work things out by open communication.

It is not being suggested that parents air their private grievances in front of their children purposely, but if the children find themselves party to such an argument or discussion there are ways to make it instructive rather than destructive. It can be helpful for them to hear their parents say things (if they are said genuinely) like, "Let me see if I understand what you are saying....", "This is what I heard you say but I disagree, I think....", "I love you, but, sometimes I feel angry at you", "I don't want to argue any further about this, let's both think about this and discuss it tomorrow". When children are watching their parents arguing it can represent an opportunity to demonstrate constructive problem solving and communication. Children learn much of their communication and problem solving skills from watching their parents interact. It can also afford the opportunity for very destructive modeling.

We all sometimes displace our angry feelings on those we trust the most. What is more important is that anger displacement does not become a habit or a routine. Many children are sensitized to fears regarding divorce due to friends and peers who are going through such transitions. Some children are unnecessarily stressed by fearing their parents will separate or divorce because they overhear their parents making such threats. Habitual arguing or spousal mistreatment suggests moderate or severe marital discord and can have a very negative effect on children and their development. Not only does constant bickering result in anxious children but it also has a devastating effect on many children's own social skills. If moderate or severe marital discord is occurring, the children and parents will most likely benefit from a marital intervention such as marriage encounter, a good self help book or marriage counseling.

An Example of Marital Discord

Ron was a 10 year old boy whose teacher recommended that he be seen for evaluation and treatment. The teacher pointed out that Ron would become very easily frustrated both in the classroom and on the playground and would begin crying if he made mistakes or didn't get his way. The teacher became increasingly concerned when this behavior continued and became more frequent. As a result of these behaviors other children had begun teasing Ron which made him even more upset.

Ron's mother provided the history. Ron's father was a physician and was not able to attend the first meeting. Ron's mother was college educated, described a relatively affluent lifestyle with frequent family trips and activities. Ron's mother had chosen to discontinue working after the birth of Ron and devoted her time to PTA, church activities, her children's activities and other volunteer commitments. Ron's mother seemed very easy going, intelligent and pleasant. She reported a family history of severe depression on her husband's side of the family. She indicated that her husband's sister had suffered from severe depression and had been hospitalized on numerous occasions. She then went on to describe her husband as extremely demanding, irritable and at times, explosive. When asked if she believed he was depressed she indicated that he wouldn't admit it, but she felt he was.

Ron was an above average student and was described by his mother as irritable, moody, immature and anxious. He had few friends, cried a lot at home and was whiny. When inquiring about the younger brother, he was described as very similar. The mother decided that she wanted an evaluation of him as well.

Psychological assessment of each of the boys confirmed the historical and clinical impression of depression. Anxiety and family relations were also indicated as being significant components of the children's difficulties.

Both parents were present at the subsequent session in which the results of the assessment and recommendations were made. The father acknowledged that he and his wife had frequent difficulties, however, essentially blamed those difficulties on his wife. One of the boys had made a family drawing as part of the assessment process in which he and his brother were on a surf board surrounded by sharks. These boys clearly felt they were in a hostile environment. Treatment recommendations were made related to the children to which the parents agreed. Conjoint (couple) therapy was also recommended for the parents, Tom and June.

The treatment for the children coincided with the parents' conjoint sessions. It was critical to the treatment of the children's depression to reduce familial stress to the degree that it was possible. It quickly became apparent that Tom was a tyrant with an explosive temper. He would threaten June with divorce and berate her unmercifully over very minor issues. She was slow to show her anger but continued to do the minor things that Tom would later blow up over. The following dialogue was typical of their couples sessions. June would smile and say something like "I forgot to pick up those fixtures for Tom at the hardware store because I was taking the kids to their lessons and had to stop by the church to leave some food...etc." Tom would respond by yelling something like "Can you be that stupid! All I asked you to do was to pick up one thing for me! You say you love me but none of my needs are important to you!"

There came a point where individual therapy was recommended alternating with the couples therapy. Tom resisted the idea that he was in fact depressed and ultimately admitted that he feared being mentally ill like his sister. Tom admitted in individual psychotherapy what he would not admit to his wife, that he was committed to the relationship and did not want to end it. Tom eventually agreed to begin an anti-depressant medication which significantly reduced his tirades. Nevertheless, he continued to be a likable but mildly arrogant and difficult character. June was also committed to the relationship and had to learn how to be direct, fight her timidity and not allow herself to be intimidated.

The family began having significantly reduced conflict. Tom and June took some trips by themselves and had several fun family trips. Family trips had previously been continuous arguments which were very destructive and stressful. The planning of family trips became a family activity with all sharing the responsibility of planning in a way to minimize conflicts. Tom continued to be a somewhat difficult patient in that he had a partial positive response to the anti-depressant medication but refused to increase it to the recommended dose.

In a way he may have been attempting to deny the severity of his depression by needing only a "low dose" antidepressant. Ron, the ten year old child, had a sustained positive response to the combination of anti-depressant medication and psychotherapy. Ron's medication was later discontinued and Ron remained without symptoms. The younger brother benefitted from brief psychotherapy and all of the family benefitted from a reduction in the degree and intensity of conflict.

Death

Children experience and react to death in a variety of ways depending on their age and level of development, their relationship with the individual who passed away and their perception of how they view the rest of the family dealing with the event. The circumstances surrounding a death are also important. A murder has a different impact than an accident but both are unexpected. Death preceded by a long illness can have complex feelings attached for the survivors. It is important for parents to understand that children may not experience their grief in the same way or at the same time as the parent. Death is a difficult concept for young children. As with most traumatic events, children will take many of their cues from the adults around them as to how they should feel and act. Children may get anxious and laugh and act giddy. To adults such behaviors can be misunderstood. In the same way that parental anxiety can be contagious, so can morbid ideation and rumination.

It is wise to understand both how resilient children can be and how deeply they can hurt. Generally speaking, in traumatic circumstances, taking into consideration the child's level of understanding, honesty is the best policy. Children want to know, as best they can, what has happened, to make whatever sense they can of it, and to be honestly reassured when possible.

A few words about honesty. There are some parents who feel the need to subject their children to too much information. While they may feel that they are simply being honest there is no benefit for a child to hear about details they either poorly understand or are helpless to respond to. While most will agree that it is important to be honest with children, there are times when it is appropriate to withhold information that they do not need or desire to know. For example, an adult trauma victim may need to recount the details of an attack, crime or accident scene in order to overcome continuing anxiety. Sharing that information with their child, could traumatize the child. It is best if the traumatized adult works through these issues with a therapist. In a less dramatic but more common example, a parent may make a child anxious by telling them about all of their bills, problems and concerns. This kind of information can only make a child anxious by contagion since they have no way to change those problems for the adult on whom they rely.

Cases of Parental Death

Parental death is certainly one of the most difficult events that a child may face. The age of the child, the nature of the child's relationship with the deceased parent and the relationship with any surviving parent and/or other relatives, is a very important factor in regard to the child's ultimate adjustment. Even siblings with very similar environments may have very dissimilar effects from such a tragedy. Several unfortunate cases are illustrative.

One Thanksgiving day many years ago, a child therapist was paged and asked to see two boys, ages 6 and 8, whose father had been murdered. The police investigating the murder had assisted the boys' mother in reaching the therapist and asked if the children could be seen that day. The meeting was arranged and the therapist learned from the mother that she had not yet told the children of what had happened. She asked the therapist's advice on how to give them this news.

Before advising the mother on how to proceed historical information about the boys, the family and each child's relationship with the father (who will be referred to as Hank) was obtained. Additional information about the circumstances of the murder was also gathered. The father had been shot in the head and dumped on a little used road. At the time of the therapist's first meeting with the boys the murderers had not been apprehended. As with most human situations, they are rarely clear cut or without their own unique complications. In this case there were several aspects that were significant in regard to approaching the children. The first was that the family had a very unstable history with frequent parental arguments. Hank had been physically and verbally abusive, particularly so with the older of the two boys. It was not uncommon for the father to be gone from the home for days at a time. Hank had been dishonorably discharged from the military and was involved in using and selling drugs at the time of his death.

Although the mother was approaching the children's current needs appropriately enough, her general judgement was in question. The boys were described by her as being hyperactive and having behavioral problems at school and at home. The mother was currently being considered as an important informant and witness that investigators felt would lead them to the party or parties involved in murdering her husband. As a result, she and her children were potentially in danger.

The issues presented were considered, and it was suggested to the mother that the best course appeared being honest and direct with the children. It was suggested that the boys be told as best as possible what had happened and then be available to answer questions and to provide support. The mother agreed. The boys entered the setting and at the mother's request the therapist informed them that their father had died. Their first question was to ask how it happened. They were told that he was shot by someone and that the police were currently trying to find the person or persons who had done it.

It was clear that it was difficult for them to completely understand, and they were surprised but not initially very upset. The therapist then took time with each of the boys individually and talked with them about their relationship with their father.

The older boy expressed ambivalence, pointing out that he was sorry that his father had been killed but that he was "mean" and would "throw me down the hall and punch me when he got mad". He expressed a mixture of sorrow and relief. The younger boy had been a less direct target of the father's anger and had a somewhat more idealized vision of his father even though the father actually did little with him.

It was arranged for the therapist to see these boys individually for a complete evaluation and ongoing psychotherapy. Both boys had an attention deficit hyperactivity disorder (ADHD), demonstrated the effects of parental neglect and had developed styles of poor self control and low self esteem. Coordination with their physician and school provided a way to assist the mother in becoming more constructively involved in observing their response to treatment. The mother was referred to a female therapist and parenting classes. Both boys did well on relatively low dose stimulant medication for the ADHD and responded well to the therapeutic relationship.

The boys' mother was instrumental in the investigation that ultimately led to the arrest of several individuals across several counties who were manufacturing, smuggling and distributing drugs. As it turned out, the boys' father had an extramarital affair with an 18 year old young woman whom he had encouraged into the use of drugs. In later court proceedings, the young woman indicated that she had a precipitous involvement in drug use. The credibility of her drug use history was supported by her previously conventional lifestyle and accomplishments. In the height of her drug use, the boys' father somehow fatally angered his co-conspirators by either stealing from them or otherwise double crossing them (it never became clear). According to the young woman friend of the boy's father, one of the more menacing members of the drug ring told her that Hank had broken a rule and had to be killed. He threatened Hank's girlfriend and told her she would have to shoot Hank while he slept or "they" would kill her. She also made the case at her trial that she was continually on drugs supplied by this group. She was given a gun and told when and how to kill Hank. After the murder the conspirators came in and disposed of Hank's body.

This case illustrates several victims in addition to the children. Over time the boys were able to understand their father in a more realistic way and understand better the events that led to his death. A major factor in addition to effective treatment for ADHD was that their mother became more appropriately part of the boys' lives at school and home. The boys improved in school and in their behavior. The mother later met and married a man who was stable, hard working and liked and accepted the boys. When treatment was discontinued the boys were doing well and being maintained on stimulant medication for ADHD by their pediatrician.

Divorce

Regardless of peoples' intentions or wishes divorces do occur. While divorce can be extremely disruptive for children, so can their exposure to a chronically destructive relationship. It is similar to the old question about whether a child is better off with a mother who works or one who does not. Most of the research has demonstrated that the important variable is whether or not the mother is happy working. Children tend to feel secure and happy if their parents do. Some children are clearly better off after their parents have divorced. Some are not. Many children have been hurt and damaged by drawn out post divorce fighting and custody struggles. On the other hand, many who divorce, are able, after a transition, to have workable relationships that serve the child's interest.

In divorce situations, children usually don't care about the events that ultimately led to the end of the marital relationship. Most children love both parents and miss the mother when they are with the father and miss the father when they are with the mother. It can be helpful for a child when the parent they are with is not offended at or refrains from taking issue with the child's longing for the absent parent. There is no winner in that type of competition.

A common complaint of parents with whom the child primarily resides is that the other parent, on visitations, spoils the child. It can be frustrating for the parent of the child's primary residence to be stuck with all of the drudgery of daily routines, chores, homework and housework only to see the child go on a weekend of Disneyland and restaurants. On the other hand, the absent parent may be in a new living situation that is not convenient or comfortable for the child or where other children are not available and outings may offer the best situation for positive parental interaction. Overcompensation by both parents, however, is common during transitional periods subsequent to divorce and should be guarded against. It is, of course, possible for either parent to spoil the child as a way to compete with the other parent or as an attempt to compensate for the divorce circumstance. Parents also spoil their children for many other reasons as well. As the term implies, "spoiling" a child is destructive and will be discussed in more detail in Chapter Four, "Love and Discipline".

What is the ultimate effect of divorce on children? The question is complex and dependent on many variables specific to the families involved. Professionals examine the effects with mixed results. Judith Wallerstein, who is now 73 has been concerned about the effects of divorce since 1970 when she began a study of 131 children whose parents were divorcing. Dr. Wallerstein began her study at the University of California, Berkeley, within the School of Social Welfare. After the first 18 months, Dr. Wallerstein went against the conventional wisdom and academic beliefs that ending a negative marriage led to the long-term advantage of all involved. She reported that one and a half years after the divorce study she and her colleagues determined there wasn't a single child who was well adjusted. Many of her colleagues were unconvinced. Her continuing reports now exceed 25 years in duration. This largest and longest-running examination of divorced children continues to document a picture of anger and mourning. The study describes children with social difficulties and later as young adults with relationship difficulties, attributed to their parents' divorce. Dr. Wallerstein's conclusions are that family life has radically changed and as a result is changing the social fabric of society at large.

> An analysis of step-parenting approaches and their influence on adolescent adjustment demonstrated that teenagers who obtain support from their stepparents are more apt to be well adjusted. These findings are irrespective of the level of control exercised by their stepparents. The Supportive style with high support and low control was the best style for ultimate adjustment. The disengaged style with little support and control was the worst. The study was based on a sample of 80 Caucasian step families.
>
> Margaret Crosbie-Burnett. Adolescent adjustment and stepparenting styles. Family Relations Oct 1994, v43, n4, p394(6).

Others challenge Dr. Wallerstein's methods and conclusions. Some challenge her results directly. Professor Frank Furstenburg Jr., University of Pennsylvania, has countered that the overall effect of divorce is modest to moderate. Methodological criticisms include the fact that Dr. Wallerstein did not have a control group and therefore has no way of knowing if her study participants are anymore poorly adjusted than other similar age persons from troubled but enduring marriages. Also countering the idea that marital preservation is better than divorce, is a more recent but lengthy University of Virginia analysis that established that children of divorce were better off than children in families with highly dysfunctional marriages.

Custody Issues

There is no question that there are legitimate and necessary custody proceedings to determine the best interests of a child's legal status relative to the child's biological parents. The most obvious case is for the child who has been placed in protective care. Difficult issues must be addressed regarding removing a child from his or her home, short or long term foster care, the appropriateness of parental visitation and, in some cases, termination of parental rights. Despite overwhelming evidence of repeated non-accidental injuries and child maltreatment many abusive parents will contest protective actions at every legal juncture. Frequently children will be ambivalent about their placement. Regardless of the circumstances, a child who is the focus of a custody determination will be insecure, anxious and uncertain until a determination is made. It cannot be overstated that stress such as this is frequently a precipitant of adjustment, mood, anxiety and behavioral disorders in children and adolescents.

A bitter custody dispute is clearly one of the most destructive conflicts that can develop as the result of a divorce. Over the past two decades the pendulum has once again swung and courts have come to take fathers' rights more seriously. The period of fathers having essentially ownership of their children evolved to a system where mothers, almost exclusively, were granted sole custody. Unfortunately, in some cases, greater equality of parental rights results in protracted legal skirmishes and dirty tricks aimed at making the opponent look bad. There are numerous examples that are conspicuous because of the celebrities involved. There are countless examples of cases where tens and even hundreds of thousands of dollars and several years have been expended only to eventually settle for terms that had been proposed in the beginning. States address these issues in various ways. In Connecticut and in New Jersey a judge can order parents to share joint legal custody even if one parent is opposed to it. In New York, however, a landmark Court of Appeals ruling, Braiman v. Braiman, ruled that joint custody is not awarded if the parents are embattled and seriously antagonistic toward each other. As a result it is difficult to get joint custody in New York State unless the parents work out the agreement themselves. Dr. Wallerstein's work found that joint custody works well under circumstances where parents communicate effectively and have a genuine commitment to make the agreement work and that it clearly does not work when parents are still fighting.

It is sad to acknowledge, but there are numerous examples of needless, bitter custody disputes. Many cases become resolved as the combatants meet with their attorneys. They may begin to heal from the wounds of a new divorce and begin to grasp the reality of cost, the lengthy proceedings involved and the likelihood of their obtaining some custodial advantage. From the opponents' point of view the goal in a child-custody trial is to make the other parent look as awful as possible. Attorneys frequently tell their clients that they should expect to be followed or investigated by a detective and they should be prepared to have their conversations taped. In some cases there may even be video surveillance. Parents can also plan to have a new lover or spouse pulled into the battle. The lengthy nature of these types of proceedings gives rise to many fraudulent allegations. The most damaging allegations are of sexual abuse. Even in the tragic circumstances where a young child has physical signs of sexual abuse the issue of how to best protect the child is not always clear. In one such case a three year old girl was examined by a hospital physician, expert in conducting physical examinations for children who have been sexually abused or who have alleged sexual abuse. The mother brought the child to the hospital after the child reported pain. The child was unable to identify the perpetrator and the child's mother immediately accused her ex- husband, the child's father. The child's father, in turn, offered to take a polygraph, be psychologically examined and expressed his belief that his daughter was sexually molested by his ex wife's boyfriend.

While both fathers' and mothers' rights groups frequently feel that their opponents are treated preferentially, it is generally not at all clear. The biggest losers in most of these proceedings are the children. Children frequently seize the natural opportunity to take advantage by playing one parent against the other. There is ongoing debate about whether a child should be allowed to choose a parent with whom they wish to reside. While it is critical to listen to what children want, most psychologists and psychiatrists have reservations about giving children the ultimate decision. Many children enduring a battle between their parents demonstrate the effects of the stress with stomach aches, poor concentration, lack of sleep and other somatic manifestations.

Example of a Divorce and Custody Issue

The following letter from a child psychotherapist to a superior court represents an example of some of the issues involved in custody disputes. Names have been changed to protect those involved.

To All Interested Parties:

Since the letters I have received indicated that both attorneys agreed upon myself as therapist and since it was also indicated that the court requested that I "begin working with these parties and incorporate the step-parents into therapy as you deem fit" I began by meeting with both natural parents separately and arranged to evaluate David.

I have since had an opportunity to meet with Mrs. Smith, Mr. Doe and David Doe. I obtained partial histories from Tyrone Doe and Zada Smith separately, David's father and mother, and administered the Personality Inventory for Children to both parents. I have also observed David in a structured play therapy setting, administered projective drawings, completed the Children's Sentence Completion Test and have conducted clinical interviews with him. A history was provided by Zada Smith, David Doe's mother. David is a 9 year and 8 month old male who resides with his natural mother and step-father, Zada and Peter Smith. David's natural father, Tyrone Doe, remarried and his wife, David's stepmother is Melinda Doe. David visits his father in accordance with current court agreements. David was Zada and Tyrone's only child. Zada and Peter Smith have been married approximately 1 year. Zada is a homemaker and Peter works in the aerospace industry; Tyrone is a contractor. David was born without complications. David walked at 13 months. Zada described David as fairly easy as a toddler. David attended a preschool where Zada describes him as initially having language problems; David's first language is Hungarian. During kindergarten David's language difficulties improved and were not apparent at the time of his evaluation. David's grade by grade educational adjustments were characterized as: 1st grade, Catholic school-did well, 2nd grade, public school, 3rd grade, was improving in school, 4th grade, average. David is currently in the 4th grade. David's current problems include: trouble concentrating in school and lying at home. David is very well liked by his peers. David is currently receiving no medication. Zada and Peter Smith have not obtained a previous psychological consult on David. The family history includes no known psychological problems. Zada's major concern is that David has been lying quite a bit at home lately. Tyrone also noted David's school and behavioral problems.

In approaching the task set forth by the court I informed both parents separately of my findings related to David's evaluation and suggested a starting approach to this inter-family dilemma. Mr. Doe was receptive to all of the points and suggestions I made and indicated he would cooperate with my recommendations. Mrs. Smith, on the other hand, took exception with one of the details of my proposal and left the session prematurely and without hearing the whole of my proposal. My assessment of the current issues related to these parties has resulted in the following proposal. First of all I believe that all parties must understand that David is manifesting psychological difficulties that are exacerbated as a result of continued conflict among the parental parties. David is ambivalent and conflicted in his own role within the family and may unconsciously and/or consciously complicate the already tense relationship as a way of acting out his own conflict if allowed ie. complain to Mrs. Smith about Mrs. Doe, complain to Mr. Doe about Mr. Smith etc. It will be harmful to David to encourage or support this behavior, or to put David in a position of deciding who or how he wants to visit or which parent to live with. David loves both parents and despite the difficulties is becoming increasingly adjusted to the step-parents. David's evaluation demonstrates him to be a highly intelligent child who is mildly anxious and depressed. There were multiple signs in David's testing of potential for greater acting out and more serious depression and anxiety should the stress he is experiencing continue. Even under optimal conditions I see David as a child who has difficulties that need to be addressed. My proposal is for a three month initial plan which includes David attending a peer psychotherapy group each Wednesday at 4:00pm, a monthly meeting with Mr. and Mrs. Smith and one of the clinic staff, a monthly meeting with Mr. and Mrs. Doe, and a three month meeting between myself and Mr. and Mrs. Smith and Mr. and Mrs. Doe in order to review David's progress and reduction of tensions between families. I also recommend that we all form an agreement to bring forth any claims of mistreatment made by David to the clinic rather than to each other (ex-spouses). I also believe that it will be important to have a set visitation schedule that does not allow for continued difficulties related to visitation details.

In summary, I believe that David's interest must guide the process and that continued inter-parent conflict is endangering his psychological well being. I suggested to Mrs. Smith that she might bring David to the group and he might have the evenings on Wednesdays with his father for dinner. It was at that point that Mrs. Smith began picking up her belongings and stating that Tyrone just wants to prevent her from moving and that her husband works in LA and that this is ruining her family and that she will not agree to seeing me any further. I can appreciate the difficulties for all in this process, however, I have not ruled out recommending an entirely new arrangement after the proposed three month attempt to reduce these tensions. It may not be unreasonable, in the future, for David to live in LA with his mother and visit his father every other week and for extended vacations. It also may not be unreasonable for David to reside with his father and have a visitation arrangement with his mother if that is in his best interest.

It is not my belief that Tyrone Doe is trying to limit Zada's mobility, but it is my impression that he is trying to appropriately assure and protect his parental rights. It also seems appropriate to mention that the point here isn't who is winning but who is losing, and currently David is losing. David loves both parents. It is damaging for him to feel that his parents are hurting each other or lacking in respect for each other. He is a part of both. I am somewhat concerned with Mrs. Smith's focus on whether or not she can move rather than the effects of the divorce on David. While I have been specific in my recommendations for dealing with these issues I also realize that Mrs. Smith has indicated that she does not want to work with me. If she continues to feel this, I believe another therapist or facility should be found that can also provide treatment services for David and continue in an advisory capacity to the courts. Sincerely,

Should B. Fishing, Ph.D.

Subsequent to this report Mrs. Smith reconsidered her position and chose to continue the process recommended by Dr. Fishing. The following is a three month progress report to the court. This particular case had a generally positive outcome. Frequently such situations drag on unresolved until the child is so disturbed that neither parent wants custody.

January 5, 199X

RE: Marriage of Doe
San Diego Superior Court Case #DNXXXXX

To All Interested Parties:

At this time psychotherapy has been provided for David Doe in a peer group for a period of three months and Mr. and Mrs. Doe and Mr. and Mrs. Smith have each been seen. Mr. and Mrs. Doe and Mr. and Mrs. Smith were seen both as couples separately and in the most recent meeting, all together. David appears to have benefitted from the group experience and family intervention. It also appears that tensions between the Doe's and Smith's have been significantly reduced. Recommendations to these parents (which have been expressed the joint meetings) and the court is as follows:

1. The Smith's retain primary physical custody of David Doe and be allowed to reside in the Los Angeles area.

2. Mr. Doe have every other weekend visitation in addition to once a week, weekday visits which are presently on Wednesdays.

3. Mr. Doe has requested that his weekday visits begin at the close of the school day. This is appropriate since it also will afford Mr. Doe the opportunity to be

more involved with David's educational process and interact with David's teachers.

4. In the course of the evaluation of David, a school observation was also made. The school indicated that David may have a learning difficulty, and they plan an educational evaluation. It has been recommended to all parties that this evaluation should take place in the school in order to better determine David's ongoing educational needs.

5. It is recommended that the parents (all four) meet at least quarterly in order to consider David's interests and to share information. The parents have asked this therapist to mediate the next such session.

In summary, all of these parties love David and have reduced their inter-familial tensions in his interest. Please feel free to contact me if there are any further questions or if I can be of any further assistance.

Sincerely,

Should B. Fishing, Ph.D.

Serious Child Illness

Having a child who is seriously ill is tragic for the entire family. Everyone is stressed and it is important for families enduring these types of hardships to seek support groups and friends. Parents in these circumstances are very frequently overwhelmed with the demands placed upon them. Siblings are also affected. The play therapy methods recommended in this book may be appropriate for both the ill child and the well sibling(s). The well child is frequently compelled, as is the rest of the family, by their concern for the ill child. The child may have natural feelings of jealousy and sadness at parental or family loss that may be difficult to express. Certainly, a well child, no matter how much they love an ill sibling, will wish their life to be "back to normal". Like children in other stressful circumstances, if their behavior does not demand intervention, their feelings, anxieties and concerns may go unnoticed.

In circumstances where there is a severely ill child it can be helpful for the parents to enlist the help of the child's well friends. Friends are helpful in keeping the ill child from becoming socially isolated and also help keep the ill child active in their more typical activities. It is also important for the parents to support each other in maintaining as many normal and refreshing activities as reasonable under the circumstances. Whether a severely ill child is chronically or terminally ill or is expected to make a quick recovery may suggest how a family can best counter the heartache and stress of these difficult events.

A Case of Serious Childhood Illness and Behavioral Problems

Amber was seven and a half years old when she was referred by her pediatric oncologist for evaluation and treatment recommendations. Amber had previously been diagnosed and treated for acute lymphocytic leukemia. Although the leukemia appeared in remission at the time of the referral, Amber's emotional and behavioral states were worsening considerably. Amber's parents stated that Amber had increasingly unmanageable and difficult behavior that included destructiveness, aggression and self injurious behaviors. The self injurious behaviors resulted in her frequent removal from class. Amber attended a private school at the time of the evaluation and was in the first grade. Amber appeared appropriately groomed and displayed a restricted emotional demeanor and facial expressions with restricted range of expression. The observed mood appeared depressed and congruent with the tone of the parents' report. Amber appeared generally oriented to place and person, as would be expected due to her young age and her apparent cognitive deficits. She engaged in "rocking behavior" while historical data was obtained from the parents. The parents reported her difficulties to include the following: she picked at her skin, she had recently pulled out a tooth, she had significant learning difficulties, severe irritability, behavioral problems at home and at school, she was defiant, enuresis (bedwetting), social interaction problems, sleep disturbances, destructiveness, occasional withdrawal, immaturity, aggression, she cried easily and had very poor social skills. Her parents noted that she frequently rocked, hyper-extended her fingers and rolled her eyes. Significant history included the birth of a sibling one month prior to the evaluation.

Amber's birth was described as a difficult delivery (C-section) with Amber presenting with respiratory distress. An unusual developmental event was that Amber had been walking and then suddenly stopped walking at age 12 months. She began walking again at 15 months of age. Amber had a medical history of chronic ear infections from infancy to three years of age. Significant history of illness also included her diagnosis of acute lymphocytic leukemia which was in remission at the time of the evaluation. She was treated with methotrexate, which is known to have possible negative cognitive effects in children and may have contributed to some degree along with the other unfortunate events to further reduce her cognitive functioning. The family history was positive for alcoholism in the biological father.

Amber was right handed. Her expressive and receptive language appeared significantly impaired and she demonstrated a difficulty of expression. Unusual speech mannerisms, reaction times and vocabulary were noted. Amber appeared to demonstrate significant receptive and expressive dysphasia.

Neurological assessment suggested that Amber's equilibratory functions of motor coordination were compromised as reflected by her poor fine motor control and poor visual motor integration. Amber's visual fields were not examined and the need for a full visual examination was indicated. Amber appeared motorically age normative with a relaxed posture. Amber's recent and remote memory appeared intact and her retention and immediate recall appeared intact as long as she had attended to the stimulus. Amber demonstrated a below average fund of general knowledge, a poverty of content, a poverty of thought and concrete thinking. Amber demonstrated impaired and limited insight in that she recognized only a few of her problems. Amber's behaviors related to school and family relationships suggested significantly impaired functioning and poor judgement. In general, Amber was cooperative and well behaved throughout the testing process.

Amber's psychological assessment was consistent with the history provided and suggested that her current general emotional and behavioral state was severely maladaptive. Amber's projective drawings demonstrated qualities suggestive of possible psychosis, immaturity, poor visual motor integration, impulsiveness, feelings of inferiority, depression and withdrawal. Amber's sentence completion responses suggested prominent issues regarding acceptance, rejection, control of impulses, performance, peers, parents, morbid ideation and perseveration.

Amber's PIC profile demonstrated clinically significant elevations on numerous scales. The configuration and degree of elevations present suggested the presence several co-morbid conditions. Cognitive and intellectual impairment, depression, a coexisting severe behavioral disturbance, moderate anxiety, mild hyperactivity, disorganized thinking, significant withdrawal, the presence of vegetative symptoms (primarily sleep and appetite disturbances), academic impairment, acting out and poor social skills were all in evidence.

Summary and Recommendations:

The next step recommended was to obtain a child psychiatric consultation and opinion. The pediatric oncologist had recently begun Amber on an anticonvulsant medication and the parents reported a good week at home but noted that the school continued to struggle with Amber. It appeared that the parents, particularly Amber's mother, may have had difficulty in recognizing improvement. The first impression of Amber's mother was that of an overwhelmed parent who had become increasingly demoralized and alienated by Amber's serious illnesses and problematic behaviors. The new baby had also, most likely, brought some feelings forth for both mother and daughter.

Once the consultation and child psychiatric opinion was completed it was suggested that a complete review of Amber's educational placement occur. Amber's mother had indicated that she initially felt that a private school would be able to be more accommodating of Amber's difficulties. Unfortunately, it appeared that they were less able to be accommodating. The private school had a frequent need to call the mother to retrieve the child whereas public school programs had in-school options for disruptive behaviors. The worry and concern of having to get Amber from school was experienced as a significant stressor to the mother who was both caring for a new baby and attempting to complete her own college education.

Amber was responsive to play techniques and it was expected that if the pressing maternal demands of Amber's illnesses and difficulties were reduced, her mother might be able to reduce some of the ambivalence that she appeared to harbor toward Amber. Short term psychotherapy (in the form of play therapy) was provided to Amber for both therapeutic and treatment monitoring purposes. As Amber became increasingly manageable, her mother was introduced to a parent led play therapy technique (described in Chapter 10). The play therapy approach provided a therapeutic outlet for Amber while enhancing her relationship with her mother. Ultimately Amber's mother took over providing the majority of play therapy sessions with occasional professional consultation.

Accidents

Accidents can be extremely traumatic. Two young sisters who were in a family vehicle accident on a freeway illustrate one type of response. The family had left for a daytime outing and was rear-ended on the freeway by a drunk driver. The two young girls were 3 and 5 years old. The family car was hit from behind at a high speed and was knocked into a guard rail. Fortunately the girls were buckled in their seat belt and car seat and suffered no physical damage. The parents and grandmother who were in the car suffered non-life threatening injuries. Nevertheless, these girls watched both of their parents and grandmother taken away in ambulances. They were unaware of their parent's and grandmother's condition until later in the day.

The parents sought treatment for their daughters due to the development of intense separation anxiety and persistent severe emotionality. These children refused to sleep in their own beds, had sleep problems, were tearful, whiny and generally had regressed from their previous level of functioning.

Children, like the rest of us, are reassured by the illusion that we, or in children's cases, parents, are in control of what is going to happen. Accidents, crimes, illness and disaster remove that comfort and confront us with our vulnerability. While we can control much of what occurs in our lives or control much of what we will be exposed to, we cannot control what happens. Children experiencing the reality of trauma can respond anxiously and regress emotionally. The children mentioned, had a successful treatment course and were back to their previous levels of functioning within two to three months. It should be pointed out, however, that one of the treatment complications for those girls was the parents co-existing anxiety and trauma response. The treatment process included parent consultation, play therapy with the children and teaching the parents a play therapy method.

Real Family Life

Families come in all shapes and sizes. Single parent, one, two, three, four or more children; two parents, one or more children; grandparent parents; foster parents; house parents and many other variations. Whatever the family composition, however, there are some universal features. One such feature is that the responsible parental adult or adults will have their own emotional ups and downs and will frequently delay their own needs in order to care for their child or children. While reality dictates that parents often must forgo their own interests, there can be a very real danger in parental self neglect. In cases where parents chronically neglect their own needs, they may as a result resent and damage their relationship with their children. They may, in fact, have less to give as a result of their own self neglect. It is important for parents, while being conscientious, to be self forgiving and to recognize their own needs.

Family environments represent oceans of currents representing all of the various stresses felt by all of the family members. The parent may be concerned financially or frustrated in work, an adolescent may feel left out of a social group or disliked by an admired peer, a child may feel anxious or resistent toward schoolwork or jealous toward a sibling. The point is, that even in the most optimal environments there are converging effects of stress on family members. It is easy to lose perspective regarding ultimate family goals when feeling angry and misunderstood. In two parent homes, for example, an expression of anger and frustration toward a spouse might result in undermining your or your spouse's parental power. It is very important to resist this type of behavior and to choose a more constructive approach and a different battle ground. It is helpful and reassuring to children to see their parents united and mutually supportive regarding children's rules and issues even if they fundamentally disagree regarding some points. When parents disagree they can continue the discussion and agree to consult books, articles or professionals if necessary.

Along somewhat similar lines, it is important that a parent not undermine their own authority. A parent who "puts him or her self down" or otherwise speaks derisively toward himself invites similar behavior from their children and their spouse. Another variation on that theme is the parent who always apologizes to their children about what they don't have or can't have. There are a fair number of over privileged children with parents like this who genuinely come to believe that they are not getting all that they should. Telling your children you should do more or that others are better parents or providers is destructive and self demeaning.

When a parent feels guilty about losing their temper or some other event, it is easy to let kids "off the hook", to not hold them responsible for their normally expected behaviors. It is important, while allowing for some flexibility, to not confuse children about what is or is not acceptable. Letting a child off the hook for a known misbehavior can confuse the child about your seriousness regarding the rule or your resolve to hold him or her accountable. Very often if the parent is compensating for guilt feelings it will not be in the child's ultimate interest. Nobody is perfect. It is better to admit your mistake, apologize and address any appropriate remedies while keeping your child responsible for his or her expected behaviors. Admitting and correcting mistakes can provide important positive modeling experiences for children.

It is possible to shape your child without oppressing him or her. A family that supports, models and encourages mutual respect and concern while providing parental guidance and understanding can successfully counter many of the negative environmental effects that can occur in life. Avoiding over-punishment, over-permissiveness and over-indulgence, while at the same time, recognizing, understanding and dealing with parental, family or child anger can be powerful components to designing a supportive and nurturing home.

Self Responsibility in Family Health

There is little choice but for people to become increasingly self responsible for their health. Health care costs are ever increasing. While there will always be a need for professional health care interventions there are many procedures and interventions that are best performed by parents and individuals. Prevention, pre-natal care, well child checkups and early interventions can reduce ultimate health care expenditures as well. In the case of childhood problems, there are certainly situations that suggest a professional assessment or intervention. There are also many cases where the properly trained parent can provide an effective therapeutic intervention, particularly if they have access to the support and supervision of a professional therapist.

In many cases, a parent can be the most effective and most motivated therapist. It is the author's contention that this will become an increasingly popular alternative to many child psychotherapeutic interventions. This is not to say that the process or techniques that will be described are particularly easy or effortless. The process requires commitment, skill and effort. Nevertheless, it is frequently difficult and many times impossible for a parent to pay or otherwise arrange for weekly individual child therapy. One alternative is for the parent to see a professional (trained in play therapy techniques) for monthly or intermittent supervision and guidance. In some cases, of course, where a child is not having severe, chronic or serious difficulties to begin with, a parent and child can benefit from the play therapy procedure without on-going professional guidance. While some children will clearly require regular professional interventions many children can benefit from supplemental parent play therapy or ultimately transition from professional therapy to a parent process with professional support.

The delicate balance of love and discipline is the subject of the next Chapter.

Chapter Four

Love and Discipline

Love and discipline go hand in hand. Failure to discipline a child is a very common form of child neglect. Providing proper discipline can be a very challenging and sometimes difficult task. How discipline is or is not handled can result in far reaching consequences. For those who provide child protective services there are unfortunately many common scenarios. One such scenario is the neglectful parent who has allowed misbehavior to continue until they can no longer effectively ignore it. It is not uncommon for the child to then be physically abused for the same behaviors that had been previously ignored. A generally less serious and more common example is the parent who allows a child's behavior to escalate to the point where the parent loses his or her temper. This, of course, happens with all parents; however, when it occurs frequently, it suggests a need for a discipline strategy.

Most children are assured by a loving and firm parent. Being firm does not require inflexibility but it does require parental resolve. The resolve to prevail in the child's interest by not allowing the child to successfully manipulate the avoidance of responsibility. A parent must decide what is ultimately in a child's interest, what is important and where to draw the line. The child who is given no limits feels uncared for. Some parents might argue "I try to make my child mind, but nothing works". When and how behavioral training and guidance occur with a child can make a critical difference. It is clearly more difficult to rein in a child who has been out of control or poorly behaved for an extended period of time. It also should be noted that children with certain disorders and difficulties may pose a particular challenge and complexity and as a result require a well thought out behavioral and treatment strategy.

A person who ultimately does not develop a sense of self motivation and self discipline has little probability of success in this competitive and dynamic society. The ultimate goal of providing parental guidance and discipline for a child is for the child to incorporate those values and benefit as a result. While it is common for the term discipline to be considered synonymous with punishment, the term discipline as used in this text refers to guidance, direction and consequences intended to teach a child values, adaptive behavior and self discipline. Providing reasoned discipline from a young age will assist a child in developing and maintaining adaptive behaviors. Consideration of how people learn behaviors can be helpful when designing discipline strategies.

A Case of Parental Over-Permissiveness

The following example is of Katy, who was three years and one month old at the time of the evaluation. Katy's mother had complained to her family physician that she felt Katy was hyperactive. The physician referred Katy for evaluation and treatment recommendations.

This type of evaluation requires beginning with a complete biopsychosocial history and a specific description of current difficulties and circumstances that may have a bearing on the child's problems. Katy's mother reported that Katy had severe behavior problems which included aggression, hyperactivity and pulling out her hair in clumps. Katy's mother admitted to having difficulty setting limits with Katy and frequently giving in to her demands. Katy appeared appropriately groomed and displayed a bright age appropriate demeanor. Katy's observed mood appeared somewhat labile (variable) which is not particularly inappropriate given her age. Katy also appeared oriented appropriate to her immature developmental status and displayed no unusual perceptions.

Katy's mother reported no current or recent physical illness or physiological complaints. Katy appeared to be right handed and her expressive and receptive language appeared age normative. Katy demonstrated no hesitancy to speak and had a general age appropriate spontaneity and degree of impulsivity. Katy's speech was noted as generally relevant and of a level consistent with her age. Unusual speech mannerisms, reaction times and vocabulary were not noted.

A neurological assessment suggested that Katy was essentially age normative. Katy demonstrated no apparent gait disturbances and demonstrated general normative gross coordination of the extremities. Her visual fields appeared intact as evidenced by her ability to track computer monitor images in all fields. Katy appeared motorically age normative. Observations of the parent child interactions illustrated several examples of how Katy's demands resulted in her mother rewarding the behavior. At one point Katy demanded a piece of candy from her mother and her mother said no. Katy began to increase her demanding behavior and essentially threatened to throw a tantrum wherein the mother produced the candy with the admonition "You had better behave yourself or you will not get another piece".

Katy was able to separate from her mother for the remainder of the evaluation without difficulty. Katy's content of thought centered around toys and computer games that were available. Katy did demonstrate demanding and willful behavior with the evaluator but responded to firm limits. Katy was able to sing the "ABC's" while accompanying a computer program that does the same and demonstrated an apparent age appropriate average to above average fund of general knowledge.

Katy's behaviors as reported by the mother focused on home behaviors and suggested poor and impulsive judgement. Katy's psychological assessment suggested that her general emotional state was age normative while her behavioral state was mildly maladaptive. The administration and interpretation of the Personality Inventory for Children (PIC) supported the observations and initial hypotheses suggested by the history and clinical observations. The Personality Inventory for Children provides scales that reflect a child's placement on several personality dimensions as compared to peers (based on a national standardized sample of boys and girls). In Katy's profile the configuration and degree of elevations present suggested mild general adjustment difficulties. More specifically, measures reflecting depression, anxiety, hyperactivity and withdrawal were within the expected normative values. Measures reflecting defiance, misbehavior and inconsistent family relationships were elevated to a degree beyond the normative range. The degree of elevation reflected was suggestive of an unusual degree of difficulty that was mildly maladaptive. Potentially, if unchecked, mildly maladaptive adjustment can result in the development stable behavioral patterns. Given the results of the psychological assessment and history it was unlikely that Katy's behavioral disturbance and emotional lability was suggestive of an underlying depression and/or hyperactivity. The degree of parental inconsistency and lack of behavioral limits better explained the type and degree of maladjustment.

Despite the appearance that Katy's behaviors had been learned, early onset behavioral and emotional difficulties may begin with the types of difficulties presented by Katy. At the time of the evaluation, however, Katy did not meet the diagnostic criteria for either a diagnosis of depression or attention deficit hyperactivity disorder. The inconsistent parenting and lack of clear limits were significant factors that warranted brief intervention directed primarily at the parent.

Diagnostic Impression:
309.40 Adjustment Disorder with Disturbance of Conduct

Recommendations:

Katy's mother was advised to attend parenting classes, to begin making systematic observations, to focus on firmness and behavioral methods and to have Katy participate with her in a structured weekly play session in order to further clarify significant diagnostic concerns. Katy was mildly maladjusted with a family history of difficulty in providing clear limits and consequences for misbehavior. Family issues included instability and inconsistency of parental direction and discipline, problematic sibling relationships, issues related to an absent father and the relationship between mother and daughter. Katy's mother was advised to make continued observations in order to rule out the possibility of a developing depression, early onset bipolar disorder and/or attention deficit hyperactivity disorder.

Plan:
Parenting classes for mother
Continued observations at preschool and home
Weekly mother-child play therapy
Continued diagnostic clarification.

A Case of Excessive Discipline

Allison was a six and a half year old girl referred for evaluation and treatment by a county social worker. When asked why Allison was being seen for evaluation, Allison's mother, Anne, stated that she sought an evaluation of her daughter due to her concerns over the daughter's withdrawal and general adjustment. Allison's mother reported having previously been physically abusive to her three children and was under the supervision of county social services at the time of the evaluation. Anne reported that she had also recently sought out treatment for herself and her son. Anne was extremely flighty and disorganized. She reported that the biological father of her children resided in another state and had severe bipolar disorder. It appeared that this mother may have also suffered from bipolar disorder (impulsive, flighty, pressure of speech, significant instability etc.). The mother was vague about her own treatment, stating that she had been seeing staff at a community mental health center as well as working with her social worker and other support persons.

Allison was appropriately groomed and displayed a quiet, timid and constricted appearance. She was cooperative and seemed to enjoy the attention provided within the evaluation setting. Allison had low self esteem and negative self attitudes ("I hate ...what I do".) Her clinical presentation was consistent with that of a child who had a punitive environment. Allison denied any current abusive treatment. Allison appeared oriented to time, place and person appropriate to age expectations. Difficulties at the time of the evaluation, included irritability, difficulty sitting still at school, some social interaction problems, withdrawal, occasional aggression and some morbid ideation. Allison's history of environmental stressors included past physical abuse, environmental instability and an absent parent. Allison had no previous mental health evaluations or treatment. The family history was positive for both alcoholism and bipolar illness. Allison's expressive and receptive language appeared age normative. Allison's speech was generally relevant and demonstrated no unusual speech mannerisms, reaction times or vocabulary.

A neurological assessment suggested that Allison was developmentally age normative. Allison's content of thought centered around her perception of her misbehavior, her absent father and feeling sad. Depressive trends were evident. Recent and remote memory and retention and immediate recall appeared unimpaired.

Allison demonstrated an average fund of general knowledge. An more extensive intellectual assessment did not appear necessary. Allison's psychological assessment suggested that her emotional and behavioral state was mildly to moderately maladaptive. Allison's projective drawings suggested immaturity, poor visual motor integration, feelings of inferiority, depression, withdrawal, anxiety and concerns over family or environmental issues. Allison's sentence completion responses further suggested prominent concerns and issues regarding acceptance, rejection, peers, parents and morbid ideation (thoughts about death and dying).

Allison's profile on the Personality Inventory for Children (PIC-R) demonstrated clinically significant elevations on several scales. The PIC resulted in a reliable response set with significant clinical findings. The configuration and degree of elevations suggested depression, severe familial stressors, anxiety and mild hyperactivity within a context of relatively good social skills.

Diagnostic Impression:

Axis I
311.00 Depressive Disorder
Rule out
296.70 Bipolar Disorder NOS
314.01 Attention Deficit Hyperactivity Disorder

Recommendations:

It was recommended that Allison would benefit from both biological and psychotherapeutic interventions. Based on Allison's history and assessment Allison was at biological risk for mood disorder in addition to living in a highly stressful environment. Although Allison's mother reported attempting to modify her own past behaviors she was very disorganized and had established inconsistent relationships with multiple mental health care providers. Based on the evaluation, psychotherapy and a psychiatric consultation for Allison was recommended in coordination with the mother's therapist and social worker. Family issues included lack of stability, inconsistency of parental direction and possible continuing abuse or neglect. Additional issues included problematic sibling relationships, issues related to Allison's absent father and a parent alternating between being overprotective and overly punitive. Personality characteristics that became a focus of individual psychotherapy for Allison included withdrawal, avoidance, shyness, low self esteem and poor frustration tolerance.

Behavioral Learning

In the field of psychology, learning theory and behavioral research have demonstrated the power of positive and negative reinforcement as well as the power of modeling and learning by imitation. People learn quickly which of their behaviors become rewarded and which do not. If we consider our interpersonal relations carefully, we can frequently find ourselves rewarding undesirable behaviors and thus encouraging them. This is a particularly common occurrence in parent-child interactions.

> Behavior modification is defined as any procedure that reduces or suppresses an undesirable behavior or increases the likelihood or frequency of a desired behavior. There are both positive and negative forms of behavior modification. Corporal punishment, such as a toddler's slapped hand for biting, is a form of positive punishment. Negative punishment is when something desired is taken away (freedom, privileges etc.). Both positive and negative punishment are methods of suppressing an unwanted response. Reinforcement is the alternative where the goal is to increase the probability of a desired behavior. There are also positive and negative forms of reinforcement. Praise for a job well done is an example of positive reinforcement. A classic and common example of a child using behavior modification on a parent is by the child using negative reinforcement. This is when the child has nagged so much in the store that the parent gives in as a way to quiet the child.

Teaching by example, or modeling, is one of the most powerful ongoing methods by which a parent teaches their children. How much of a parent's modeling is conscious depends on how much the parent stops to consider his or her lessons by example. A parent who is unhappy or angry with a child may unintentionally express their displeasure by frequent criticism, unrealistic demands or even tease them over some sore point. When a child feels unaccepted or criticized, the child may resign him or herself to a generally oppositional or uncooperative attitude. Expecting a shy or reticent child to be immediately comfortable in a social situation, for example, will likely increase the child's anxiety and self criticism. Self examination of the source of parental disappointment is a powerful tool in further understanding an emotional reaction to a child's behavior or interests. In some cases a parent is overly concerned about the "appearance" of a behavior. At other times a parent may be disappointed because a child did not live up to realistic and appropriate expectations. Under either circumstance, the child who feels loved and accepted despite his or her shortcomings will ultimately be more likely to develop self acceptance. A parent who can model tolerance, understanding, self examination, perseverance and resolve will teach their child fundamental skills with which they can manage and move beyond life's obstacles.

Children model other children and other adults. The influence of others on a child is important to consider. Individuals can learn and benefit from negative as well as positive experiences, however, some experiences can be damaging. Examples include, a relatively non-athletic child who is intensely criticized by an overzealous coach; a teacher who is expecting too much of a child or a classroom dominated by misbehaving bullies. These experiences can have enduring negative effects. Children most certainly develop at different rates and have their own unique strengths and weaknesses. Participation in activities where a child's strengths are promoted and the child is encouraged can also have an enduring, positive effect.

Promoting Self Confidence and Self Esteem

Developing self confidence and assurance is an on-going developmental process. As much as parents may want to give their children self esteem and self confidence, parents can't convey self worth to their offspring simply because they value them. Parents may, however, increase a child's or youth's opportunities to build confidence and esteem. Individuals must ultimately develop and recognize their own strengths and weaknesses. A pre-adolescent or adolescent may make statements like "I'm fat", "I'm ugly" or "everybody hates me" and so on. The first parental realization may be to recognize that all young people naturally have periods of self consciousness and insecurity. It is also helpful to determine whether these statements are exaggerations or if the child is truly having difficulties related to physical differences, socialization or other problems.

A large part of our initial view of ourselves is what we feel from those who have cared for us and raised us. Nevertheless, as young people get older, what their peers think of them becomes increasingly meaningful. Parents can help by not demeaning their children's natural inclination toward peer affiliation and their desire to dress and talk like their peers. A young person's transient feelings that they are disliked, unattractive or otherwise undesirable are normative stages of development. These feelings, however, should not be persistent, even though they are usually unresponsive to parental reassurances. There are things that a young person can do that may increase self confidence and self esteem. A focus on personal hygiene and exercise are two ways in which many young people increase their sense of value and appearance.

It is helpful for a parent to examine the expectations they may have for a child. Are the parental expectations realistic? As a parent, are you being overly critical? Are you concerned about the outside appearance of a behavior? It can also help for a parent to make time to talk with their child in a meaningful way about some of the trials and tribulations of growing up. It is always interesting to see how genuinely interested children are in the feelings, difficulties and achievements of adults when they were their age. Making a point of letting the child know you really want to listen to what he or she is experiencing is supportive and helpful, even when

> **A Gifted Teacher's Insights** - Characteristics of Gifted Children. Susan Winebrenner provided "Strategies every teacher can use: meeting the needs of your high-ability students". She points out that teachers' definitions of what they consider gifted is transforming as we weigh a larger scope of "gifts," ranging from visual intelligence to affective abilities.
>
> She illustrates a partial inventory of indicators that may be present in whole or part to assist in recognizing high-ability students. A sampling of the indicators she identifies include advanced vocabulary, an outstanding memory, broad curiosity, many interests and hobbies, intensity, absorbed in activities and thoughts, higher levels of thinking than his or her same age peers, perceptive of subtle cause-and-effect relationships, catches on quickly then resists work, sensitivity, possesses an advanced sense of justice and displays original ideas.
>
> She describes four strategies and examples to stimulate the learning interest and addresses the needs of gifted students. These include finding hidden talents, appointing resident experts on a given subject, allowing students to showcase their abilities and facilitating group activities which redirect leadership qualities. She has found these four strategies successful in building the self-esteem, confidence and intellectual ability of the students involved.
>
> Winebrenner, Susan. Strategies every teacher can use: meeting the needs of your high-ability students. (includes related article) by Susan Winebrenner. Instructor (1990) Sept 1994, v104, n2, p60(4)

that's all the parent can do. One thing a parent can do is to break the regular routine and suggest that parent and youth go out for a malt or soft drink and have some time together. The parent can indicate a desire to understand and help, if possible.

Most children will welcome guidance as long as they don't see it as a parental soapbox from which to lay out changes the parent thinks should be made.

> Whether your child is a toddler or an adolescent, it is natural to want to help when he or she is in a difficult spot. But often we're so intent on keeping our children happy that we hover over them ready to rush in at the first sign of trouble. When we're too quick to offer assistance, we may inadvertently send the message to our children that they can't manage on their own, that they need us to play with them and solve their problems. Moreover, we deprive them of the satisfaction they get when they successfully figure out a solution on their own.

These remarks are suggested in responding to "normal" developmental low points and insecurities. When a self deprecating attitude is persistent it will be important to determine whether or not the attitude is suggesting a degree of difficulty that impairs social, family or school endeavors and if it appears transient. If a degree of "impairment" is noted a parent may wish to consider the issues raised throughout this book and/or consult with a professional to determine the next step. Young adolescents can usually benefit from a parent helping them evaluate what they like about themselves and don't like, what they can change and not change and how much parental assistance they want and don't want. Parental guidance, that is not disciplinary, is most effective when provided in a supportive non-critical and understanding manner. It may be helpful to share similar issues from the parents' earlier years. A regular family meeting is a good opportunity for all members of the family to express concerns as well as plan positive events.

Magazines can help young people feel a needed affiliation as well as help in formation of an identity. Some can

> In a study of parent child attachment, self esteem and adolescence, Cynthia B. McCormick and Janice H. Kennedy reported that fathers were viewed as more independence-encouraging than were mothers at both younger ages and during adolescence. There was continuity in measurement of the parent-child affinity over time as well as a perception of parents modifying their behaviors as their children matured. Parents generally became more independence-encouraging. While no significant gender differences were noted in assessment of parent-child relationships, fathers were perceived as more independence-encouraging, while mothers were perceived as more accepting.
>
> The study subjects who were judged to be securely attached reported their parents to be more accepting and more independence-encouraging than did those judged to be insecurely attached.
>
> Self-esteem was positively related to independence, encouragement, acceptance, and secure attachment to both parents for both initial and current assessments.
>
> Cynthia B. McCormick and Janice H. Kennedy. Parent-child attachment working models and self-esteem in adolescence. IN: Journal of Youth and Adolescence Feb 1994, v23, n1, p1(18)

also assist young people understand that others have similar insecurities and concerns. "Teen Magazine" is an example of a magazine that is read cover to cover by many young teenage girls. Advice about boys, appearance, homework, etc. is well received when available in the attractive, interesting and non-threatening format as provided in this publication. "Hip" is a magazine for hearing-impaired children between the ages of eight to fourteen. "Hip" is published every two months and is available only by subscription. There are no advertisements. The magazine attempts to help hearing impaired children increase their language and vocabulary skills and to better relate to their non-hearing-impaired peers. There are approximately 400,000 children with varying degrees of hearing impairment in the United States. "Hip" is produced in full color and aims to help hearing impaired children expand their reading, vocabulary and language skills; it is also a medium for them to build a sense of community with their peers. Stories are written on the eight to fourteen year old level about successful real-life, hearing-impaired people. Self-esteem, coping techniques and communication are principal topics along with commentary about careers, computers and fashion. Puzzles and contests are also provided. With each issue "Hip" includes articles and art by deaf children and provides a teaching guide for parents and professionals. "Hip" is available by subscription only ($14.95 per year). Address: 1563 Solano Ave., #137, Berkeley, CA 94707. Telephone: 510-527-8993.

When discussing avenues of developing self esteem and self confidence it is interesting to consider various approaches used to encourage self esteem and self confidence. For example, is the Stewart Smalley (Saturday Night Live Character) school of positive self attribution really effective? At one particular elementary school in the United States, 500 students recite in unison "I am a good person. I am an important person." A student teacher, defending the omission of requiring new reading words to her second grade class explained that the most consequential detail is for the students to feel good about themselves as readers. That student teacher has not yet learned what seasoned and skilled teachers most certainly know. A student who does not develop competence will most certainly not develop confidence.

The development of an unrealistic view of one's abilities will ultimately, in the face of reality, result in a loss of self esteem. Harold Stevenson, professor of psychology, in a University of Michigan study, measured math achievement in both Asian and U.S. fifth-graders. The Asian children scored dramatically higher than their American counterparts in actual performance, while the American students rated highest in their confidence in their math skills. In recent reports, Professor Stevenson, has confirmed that the trend for overrating performances is continuing. Professor Stevenson points out that thousands of high school students studied consider themselves above average in looks, athletic ability, and academic ability. One clear disadvantage is when the student is unable to realize the goals which were based on a false sense of ability.

It is possible to compliment a child for working diligently while also providing constructive criticism relative to an educational assignment or project. Involvement in a child's educational activities can be fun if done in a non-judgmental manner. Many children become more interested in an assignment or project when they recognize that the parent has an interest as well. It is important to learn how to praise behavior and accomplishments. Keep praise informative and related to a specific activity. When a young child shows a parent a painting, an effective response might be, "This is good or this is interesting. Tell me about it. Is it the way you wanted it to look? Some experts point out the pitfalls of statements of praise such as "I'm so happy when you clean your room." The child's room being kept clean and assigned household responsibilities should be expected responsibilities of the child. When a toddler creates a project, a parent can remark about it's colors, height or any other feature; however, an overstated compliment or misleading emphatic comment may ultimately be to the child's disadvantage. Parents mislead their children when they try to make them feel good without regard to the level of accomplishment. When everything is special then nothing is special.

It is helpful to keep in mind that under normal circumstances, a child's self-esteem and self confidence, fluctuates with age and situations. When children appear completely confident in situations that are beyond the child's ability or where the child is inexperienced, it is likely they are missing important feedback. Similarly, when they express insecurity or feel incompetent it can be supportive to help the child accept his or her limitations. Children, like adults, benefit

> An analysis of the effect of divorced and non-divorced mothers' employment on children demonstrated some distinct related advantages. The outcomes demonstrated that among children residing in divorced middle class homes, recreational activities within the family and the self-esteem of the children increased with mothers' employment. Advantages related to mothers' employment in two parent non-divorced families demonstrated increases of self-efficacy in children.
>
> Family configuration and maternal employment: effects on family environment and children's outcomes. by Linda Kurtz and Jeffrey L. Derevensky IN: Journal of Divorce & Remarriage March-April 1994, v22, n1-2, p137(18)

in learning how to deal with their frustrations and setbacks while pressing on. The figure of speech "You can do anything you want in life" isn't literally true. It may be true that children may be able to attempt most anything they choose, but all will ultimately encounter limits.

Preemptive Strike

Preemptive strike refers to proactive rather than reactive parental involvement.

Preemptive Attention

Preemptive attention is simply providing a child attention before they demand it. It is very common for parents to come home from work and immediately begin their routine of preparing dinner and attending to chores. A child may be clambering for attention while the parent is busy. It can be very helpful to plan five or ten minutes with your child prior to starting the routines. A parent can tell their child that they want to visit or play with them for five or ten minutes and then start dinner. Often times, this small amount of attention will make a significant difference to a child and will allow the parent to proceed with fewer interruptions during early evening chores.

Preemptive Interventions

The "problem bedtime" example from the previous chapter may benefit from some closure. If the parent in the previous example resolves to make bedtime not their problem they may try the following approach.

The preemptive strike. Deal with the child before you get angry. Select a time that is not close to bedtime and when not angry at the child. The parent can tell the child in a friendly but matter of fact way that they want to speak with them about the bedtime behavior of the night before. The parent can then reaffirm the child's bedtime and assure the child if they do not respond at the first direction that they will receive an immediate time-out (see time-out) and go to bed a half hour earlier the next night. The parent may want to offer to read a short story together before the appointed bedtime. It can also be helpful for the parent to let the child know how they honestly feel (not a guilt trip) when the evening ends on a negative note. At the approach of bedtime, with a loving tone, give one firm statement reminding the child of your earlier talk.

The preemptive communication suggested does not need to suggest the child feel guilty about a previous behavior. The parent who is resolved to have the child ultimately comply will have consequences that will effectively result, if they don't. For the parent who says "I tried that and it didn't work", don't despair. Frequently initial methods or approaches to child behaviors and difficulties don't work. The secret to success is continuing to analyze as objectively as possible why it didn't work and to modify your approach. This most common error parents make related to behavioral methods is to abandon them before they have worked. More information about behavioral interventions and play interventions will be presented in later chapters.

Refusing to Argue

One very effective method of dealing with an oppositional child is to refuse to argue. It is easy for a parent or a professional to become seduced into an argument that is pointless, other than to inflict misery on the intended adult. Being prepared for such an encounter is a helpful defense. A common professional and parental weakness is perceiving a child's behavioral compliance or non compliance as a reflection of professional or parental competence. If behavioral non compliance threatens an adult's self confidence then it has potentially destructive power. If we expect an oppositional reaction and respond to it in a matter of fact manner, we can eliminate much of the potential maladaptive reinforcement. These behaviors, however, are not always in the form of non compliance. Personal verbal assaults are another common child weapon. For example, the child who tells his or her parent "You don't love me" or "You don't care about me, if you cared about me you'd let me spend the night with my friend!" Many oppositional and defiant children learn that adults will simply give in to them in order to avoid a tirade or emotional meltdown. In some cases these types of behaviors begin as a result of a mood disorder with it's inherent irritability and sometimes explosive emotional qualities. If allowed to continue the result can be the incorporation of maladaptive secondary features as adults inadvertently reward the intimidation and emotional extortion by giving in to the demands.

Children who are physically aggressive, hurt parents and run away are typical of youngsters who are out of control. It is easier to keep an authoritative relationship with a child than it is to establish or re-establish it. To become effectively authoritative a parent needs to be genuinely involved with a child, spending time to cultivate and develop the relationship. A parent who is thwarted in efforts to cultivate such a relationship will gain insight into the barriers and hopefully devise some strategies by utilizing the assessment and other procedures outlined in this book. Parents ultimately need to view themselves as leaders, not friends. It is possible to maintain equality of worth between parent and child while maintaining the parental role of authority. Parents are, at times, paralyzed by their desire for their children to like them. If this becomes frequent the child quickly learns how to manipulate the parent. The role of the parent is most effectively achieved by providing guidance for a child and helping that child add age appropriate responsibilities as able. Consistency and calmness in setting rules is a good policy. Parents should discuss and reach agreement on rules before they are imposed, so that they carry through with the consequences. Rules should be consistent and include rewards and consequences. As a child displays increased responsibility, privileges should be increased to a commensurate level.

You need a driver's license to drive, a pilot certificate to fly, permits to own many types of guns, a license to hunt or fish and a license to get married. To become a parent one needs only the requisite hormones.

Time-outs

Administered correctly, time-outs are an extremely effective behavioral tool. How time-outs are taught and administered to a child determines their effectiveness. Many parents successfully employ the use of time-outs. Nevertheless, some parents report little benefit from time-outs. The difference in effectiveness has to do with how time-outs are defined and applied.

Frequently childhood misbehaviors are inadvertently reinforced or rewarded. The first sign that such behaviors are being reinforced or rewarded may be an increased frequency or incidence of the behavior. The previously discussed methods of observation can be extremely helpful in determining the elements that make up the behavior and the context within which a child expresses the behavior.

The time-out is a well established method designed to stop immediate reinforcement or reward a child might be receiving from his or her behavior. Non-reinforced behaviors eventually cease to exist. It is important to recognize that reinforcement takes place constantly on many levels and in many ways. Psychological reinforcement or reward takes place in the context of the individual. What is negative for one person may be rewarding for another. There is, for sake of example, a rewarding satisfaction when you see a reckless driver who endangered you get pulled over by the police. It can also be immediately satisfying to yell at someone with whom you are angry even if the long term consequences are ultimately unrewarding. It is in this way that a child who is in trouble with a parent may be rewarded by "getting the parent's goat", by making the parent angry and getting their full attention or otherwise irritating them.

Generally speaking, almost any type of emotional response to a misbehavior poses the danger of being rewarding. It is not suggested that a parent withhold genuine emotional responses; it is, however, suggested that a parent distinguish between an emotional reaction to a behavior and an effectively applied behavioral intervention. Emotional parental reactions are a necessary part of life and learning but they are not an effective behavioral intervention.

An effective time-out has basic rules that assist in removing reinforcing variables from the child's immediate environment. Time-outs are a particularly effective method with pre-school and school aged children. The fundamental principles of time-outs, however, can be applied to individuals of any age.

> Prominent Psychologist B.F. Skinner, condemned the overuse of punishment. He did however recognize that brief and harmless aversive stimuli can be justified when made contingent in response to self-destructive behavior when it can suppress the behavior and allow a child to develop in more adaptive ways. He also pointed out that it is a mistaken strategy to rely on punishment without exploring non-punitive methods.

Time-out Guidelines

The Setting

Time-outs should not generally be given in a child's bedroom. While removal from the general living area may remove the child from parental or sibling attention, and there are times when removal from the immediate room will be suggested, the child may feel isolated or rejected or may be rewarded by solitude, privacy and access to their toys. It is also difficult to monitor a time-out when you cannot see the child. Frequently a chair with its back against the wall in the kitchen is a convenient place for an effective time-out.

Time-outs can be effectively applied in a number of other settings as well. Observant residents of Westwood, California, may have occasionally seen the child psychiatric staff from the adjacent University of California, Los Angeles, (UCLA) Neuropsychiatric Institute, escort a group of children for walks, to ice cream shops or similar brief outings. These outings frequently include a couple of stops for a child to sit against a tree or wall for a few minutes. The inside corner or quiet area of a store will also work. When a time-out is applied in a public place it is important to not embarrass or otherwise humiliate a child to accomplish the behavioral intervention. Usually, if a parent is in fact willing to administer a time-out in a public place, a child will respond to a warning. If a child has been warned and does not comply it is **essential** that the parent follow through and administer the time-out.

Teaching a Child How To Take a Time-out

It is helpful to teach a child the elements of a proper time-out. The specific method for teaching a time-out varies slightly with the age of the child. The method suggested here can be modified as necessary. The only suggested difference of presentation is related to the age and understanding of the child and the extent or level of explanation. With all children, however, it is suggested the time-out method be presented at a time when the child is not in trouble or misbehaving. It is also suggested that the reasoning and logic behind the time-out is presented at the same time.

It will be important that a parent put the time-out presentation in their own words with a child's age and level of understanding in mind. The following is a general example of what might be said to a young child regarding time-outs.

> "Come with me a minute. I want to show you something. I need to show you how to take a time-out. You are not in trouble but I am going to start using time-outs for certain behaviors and I want to show you how they will be done. All kids require parental guidance; I did when I was a child also. All parents who love their children at times have to provide discipline. Time-outs are a better way than spanking for helping a child learn how to get along with others and to be responsible. Come with me in the kitchen for a minute. After I show you this we can play a game or something. OK, sit on the chair and don't talk. (wait for the child to be silent for about 5 seconds) OK. You can get down, you did that perfectly. A real time-out would be longer, but that is the way to do it. I will usually warn you to stop a behavior or get a time-out, but if it is a behavior that you know you shouldn't have done you may get a time-out without a warning. If you are misbehaving I will

tell you to stop and if you don't, I will give you a time-out to help you learn how to mind. A time-out means you have to sit in the chair and you can't talk and you can't play until your time-out is over. If you are talking or playing, your time-out won't start. Your time-out will begin when you are taking it properly."

Length of Time-out

A timer with a bell is a necessary piece of equipment. Without one, a parent is stuck watching a clock or relying on the child to do so. Setting the timer and not speaking to the child until the bell rings is much more effective. Generally, once time-outs are being taken properly, one minute per age of the child works well as a time-out length. A two year old would get a two minute time-out, a five year old would get a 5 minute time-out and so on. In the early stages of applying and teaching time-outs it can be helpful to apply shorter time-outs. The first parental goal should be getting proper time-out compliance from the child. A 30 second time-out done correctly will ultimately be more helpful than a 7 minute time-out that took 15 minutes of parental intervention (and reinforcement) to achieve. After 20 to 30 successfully administered time-outs the time should be increased by 30 to 60 second increments to the ultimate time the child should be receiving. If a time-out is being administered in a public place it is helpful to keep the interaction between yourself and child as much as possible. If the time-out is being taken properly it is also helpful to decrease the normal time-out as long as you have achieved behavioral control and compliance.

Refusal to take a Time-out

It is important to distinguish between a child who has learned how to take time-outs properly and refuses a time-out and a child who has not learned how to take a time-out properly. As mentioned before, a child who has been out of control for an extended period of time will strongly resist a parent's efforts to intervene. If this is the case, it is all the more important for the parent to intervene with a firm resolve and continued analysis of the problem.

For the child who generally complies with a time-out and refuses, the following is suggested. Refrain from arguing over the cause of the time-out. It is recommended **not** to double the time for non-compliance, but to remind the child that the time-out will not begin until they are taking it properly. Tell the child they owe you a time-out and all of their privileges are frozen including watching television, playing outside or seeing friends until they properly complete their time-out. If they disagree about why they got a time-out tell them you will discuss it with them once it has been properly completed.

Hopefully, these principles will be helpful. However, a parent must judge a circumstance and determine the best course for a given situation. For a child who leaves a time-out to resume the behavior they were timed out for, a longer time-out may be in order. Also, for a child who is being aggressive or persists in attempting to antagonize others, removal from the room for 15 (or more) minutes may be in order. Some childhood disorders cause a child to be more difficult or to have more difficulty complying with a time-out. Despite these difficulties, when diagnosed, treated and properly approached, most children, can benefit from time-out and other behavioral methods.

Parent Behavior During Time-outs

The parent should keep several points in mind when giving time-outs. Time-outs are most effective if given before a behavior escalates. It is particularly helpful if a parent or parents remain alert for a behavior they are wanting to extinguish and anticipate they will have an opportunity. For example, if the parent is caught off guard and irritated by a behavior, he or she may be reinforcing the behavior. Expect the behavior, have a plan of action and be resolved to have the result be the child's problem not yours. Warning the child, if appropriate, and a matter-of-fact administration of the time-out will be most effective.

It is important to minimize any possible type of attention when a child is receiving a time-out. If other children reside in a home it is helpful to tell them that speaking to someone, attempting to play or bothering someone on a time-out, will result in a time-out for themselves.

A parent should refrain from talking to a child on a time-out. Continuing to tell a child why you're angry, why they got a time out etc., will be counter productive. After the time-out is completed it can be helpful to provide any follow-up discussion. It is also helpful to minimize eye contact with the child. If the child speaks, simply remind them their time-out will begin when he or she is quiet.

Frequently a child who has caused an incident in a family will hear one parent complain to another about the behavior. It may stop a previously pleasant interaction that had been occurring between the parents. It is a very powerful intervention for the parent to instead administer the time-out and continue their pleasant interaction while ignoring the timed out child. It is helpful for the parent(s) to go on about their business and positive interactions as much as possible. For example, the parent can clean a counter or poke around in the cupboards or come in and out of the room keeping the child in the periphery of his or her vision, insuring proper compliance, while essentially otherwise ignoring the child.

The criteria for applying a time-out is suggested to **not** include parental anger. The parent may be angry about the behavior but that should not be the determinant for the time-out. The child's specific behavior should be the determinant for the time-out. A child who can push his or her parents' buttons has too much power. Ironically, while children will seek this type of power they generally don't want it. They are much more assured by the parent who can provide them structure and keep them responsible for their own behavior.

> B.F. Skinner's students
> coined the phrase
>
> "Spare the rod, use behavior mod"

Time-out Log

A time-out log can be a simple but powerful device by which to review behavioral trends and incidence with a child. This can be especially helpful if a parent is working on extinguishing a certain behavior. The time-out log is another method of making and maintaining observations. A time-out log assists in reviewing and refining a parent's use of time-out strategies.

For children who do not have any behavioral or emotional disorder and who have been taught how to take time-outs at a fairly early age, occasional time-outs and behavioral interventions usually suffice. For a child who requires occasional interventions having a time-out log can still be useful in applying a brief course of behavioral observations and interventions. For the child having frequent difficulties, a time-out log is especially helpful in reviewing, refining and analyzing behavioral strategies.

A time-out log can be custom designed. Here are some elements of a time-out log a parent might use. Appendix C has a sample time-out log for parents to photocopy.

Date:

Behavior:

Length of Time-out:

Other Consequences:

Circumstances:

Comments:

Parents Initials: (Helpful in seeing who's giving the time-outs, time of day and other trends. Initials are also helpful for parent discussions and discipline strategy sessions.)

Time-out logs should be handy but not conspicuous. As with other types of observations, parents will ruin their ability to make observations if they confront a child with their raw observations or present it to the child as if they are keeping score in some way. Interpreting a time-out log can indicate the kinds of behaviors the child has been timed out for, length of time-outs, other consequences, general circumstances and indicate who timed the child out. It is suggested that time-outs should be given only by persons with parental authority or at least the temporary equivalent like grandparents, teachers and child care persons. When reviewing a time-out log, trends should be apparent and treated accordingly.

Parental Anger

Anger is a natural emotion. We all experience anger; our own and the anger of others. Anger plays an important role in all of our lives and has the power to be constructive or destructive. Angry feelings can motivate us or, in some cases, paralyze us. If we didn't feel angry about disappointments or injustices, we would have little motivation to change or influence them. Consequently, learning ways to manage anger can be very helpful. Many people have had extremely negative experiences as the recipient of someone else's anger, often times it has been their own parent's anger. As a result, some current parents either learned poor methods of expressing anger or learned to deny their feelings of anger.

A parent's anger at a child is often born out of frustration or concern. A particular behavior may be bothersome because the parent knows that the child is well aware that the behavior causes anger in the parent. When a parent gives a child the power to anger them over a specific behavior there is an increased likelihood that the behavior will recur. It is important to analyze the behavior, the parental response and the context within which the behavior occurs in order to take that power away from a child.

There are other childhood behaviors that are unintentional and cause parent anger. It is important for a parent to examine these incidents and to become aware of what it is that angers them. If a parent is expecting too much from a child the parent may feel frustrated and angry when a child makes age normative types of mistakes or behaviors. A parent who becomes overly angry about age normative types of occurrences may set the stage for a continuation of the behavior and a power struggle. The parent can of course be effectively assertive and tell the child that he or she will receive a time-out for a certain behavior.

It is certainly difficult to know in all instances how to best handle a situation with a child. It is important to be flexible but at the same time offer guidance and structure. It is important to allow and encourage the development of independence and self responsibility in amounts with which the child can be successful; not too little, not too much. Parents have to err at times in one direction or another. While keeping a fundamental general positive and adaptive expectation of the child's behavior, it is helpful to be able to recognize when to loosen and tighten expectations.

A parent who never or rarely demonstrates anger to a child robs the child of the lessons that go with seeing a parent angry (not abusive). The child might also fear what the parent would be like if they ever did get angry. The child may feel uncared for, if their expectation is that a parent "should" get angry over a certain behavior. Children, like parents, benefit of letting off steam. This can be accomplished by a child telling about a frustration they had during the day or even more directly by the child telling a parent something they are angry about.

Explosive angry outbursts are usually only effective as a release. As such they may alert the individual to feelings of which they had not been consciously aware. If so, more direct communication may develop. Through our experiences most of us learn that a percentage of people can be intimidated by anger. There are those who then come to rely on the manipulative power of anger and intimidation. Intimidation is always negative and destructive and will ultimately push others away.

It is important for parents to listen to their children and to non-punitively acknowledge their children's angry feelings. The parent may not agree with the child or be swayed in some determination, but it is important that the child be heard. Angry feelings do not need to be expressed in an emotional tirade to be effective. Angry feelings are very effectively dissipated when stated in an effective communication. A child might be told "calm down and just tell me. I want to know how you feel." or "You need to settle down a little and then we can talk." It may be that a child will require a time-out or the child may need to leave the immediate situation to cool down before communicating effectively.

If a child is angry every time he or she doesn't get his or her own way, then a parent may realize that the child has learned to use anger to threaten and intimidate. A behavioral strategy should be developed to counter this destructive style. Intimidation by anger is maladaptive and ultimately doomed to have high social and personal costs.

Frequent or persistent childhood anger and/or complaining is usually the result of either an emotional or behavioral disorder, a learned behavior or because the child is not effectively communicating angry feelings. Learned behaviors from learning how to constructively and effectively express their anger.

> Numerous studies have concluded that spanking can further aggressive behavior and reduce self-esteem. Even though "Time-Out's" have become familiar to many mothers and early childhood educators trying to discipline children, there remain a significant number of parents who believe in corporal punishment. A recent study, directed Dr. Rebecca R. S. Socolar found that a significant number of mothers indicate that they spank their toddlers. 204 mothers were surveyed at two sites, one was an inner-city site and the other was a suburban community. Racial characteristics of the respondents were 48 percent White, 26 percent Hispanic, 21 percent Black, 4 percent classified as "Other" and 1 percent Asian. The research literature on corporal punishment does not demonstrate whether the harmful effects of spanking are a result of the act of spanking or the parental state that accompanies the spanking. Forty-two percent (approximately 85 out of the 204) of the mothers polled had spanked their young children in the week preceding the survey. The survey results further indicated that the mothers who spanked more frequently had been spanked as a child. The American Academy of Pediatrics has said corporal punishment should be discouraged in the home and prohibited in school.

Child Anger

Getting angry is like blowing air into a balloon. The more angry you get the bigger the balloon gets. If you let a little out it gets smaller. If you keep getting angry without letting it out a little at a time, it will explode. This is true for parents and children. Children, like adults, need some method (behaviors that have been reinforced to persist) can, in stable and maladaptive forms, constitute a childhood behavioral disorder. Childhood emotional and behavioral disorders need to be diagnosed by a qualified licensed professional clinician with appropriate experience diagnosing these types of conditions.

Many parents of children with emotional and behavioral disorders are frustrated and angry with their children. Identification of such a disorder allows for better understanding and the development of the most effective treatment strategies. Diagnosis can be life changing and in many cases can suggest effective treatment strategies. The methods suggested in this text can be used in conjunction with most treatment approaches. Childhood behavioral and emotional disorders will be discussed in greater detail in the following chapters.

Some parents are ultimately too angry to want a better understanding of their child. At times all parents get angry at their children. Usually, these angry periods are brief. In some families angry feelings persist and can become destructive. A child-parent war results in emotional abuse. Emotional abuse is very destructive whether from a child toward a parent or from a parent toward a child. Parents will do themselves and their children a favor by seeking a professional consultation if they feel unable to let go of their angry feelings toward a child.

Chapter Five

Adjustment Disorders

Childhood adjustment disorders will be broadly presented and discussed in this chapter. Readers are also encouraged to seek out other resources for more specific information and training. The adjustment and other disorders that will be presented are the subject of research spanning several dimensions. As such, it is helpful to keep in mind that the "naming" and identification of mental difficulties has a developmental life of its own. Differentiation of a diagnosis is a central aspect of the functions provided by a professionally trained clinician. Nothing in this book should be viewed as preparing a non-professional to make an accurate, objective or appropriate clinical diagnosis. It is the aim of this book, however, to better prepare a parent to participate in the treatment and the evaluation of treatment of a child in concert with their clinician. Frequently, several diagnoses may occur together or be very difficult to distinguish from one another. A skilled clinician with good data from a child's caretakers can generally make a comprehensive diagnosis that forms the basis of planning a treatment strategy.

Many of the behaviors and symptoms that will be discussed can be present in age normative children as well as children who suffer some degree of impairment. Frequently, the criteria for a mental disorder depends on the severity, frequency and duration of symptoms. The Diagnostic and Statistical Manual of Mental Disorders, fourth edition, (DSM-IV) is the current guide used by professionals diagnosing mental disorders. The DSM-IV essentially provides a set of diagnostic criteria professionals can utilize as a guide in clinical practice, research and education. The DSM-IV utilizes a multi-axial assessment system as a method for the clinician to code the various domains of information which are helpful to clinicians in planning treatment, predicting outcomes and as a uniform system of nomenclature.

The DSM-IV multi-axial assessment process includes five different axes on which the clinician codes various aspects relevant to an individual. It is beneficial for the parent to have a general understanding of these diagnostic domains in order to be a more informed and capable partner in the treatment process. The five axes of the DSM-IV are as follows:

>Axis I includes clinical disorders and other disorders that are a focus of clinical attention

>Axis II includes personality disorders and mental retardation

>Axis III includes general medical circumstances, illnesses or factors

>Axis IV provides a scale by which to weigh psychosocial and environmental factors

>Axis V provides a scale which can characterize the global function of the individual

A parent who suspects a disorder in their child is well prepared by conducting a preliminary assessment utilizing the methods outlined in Chapter Two and subsequently consulting their primary care physician to discuss the appropriate next step which may be some form of treatment, continued observation or referral to a more specialized resource.

It is important to understand that most often childhood disorders are complex and multifaceted. It is overly simplistic, for example, to consider all of a child's difficulties as learned. Some difficulties have biological components that play a fundamental role. It is equally simplistic to consider a childhood disorder or difficulty as wholly biological. Some disorders tend to have greater biological or learned components, however, they usually are to some degree a mixture of biopsychosocial influences. Determination of the elements causing or influencing a childhood disorder is an important facet of proper diagnosis and treatment planning. Continued parent observations (in Chapter 2) can play a critical role in the evaluation of treatment response, should a treatment course be initiated.

Adjustment Disorders

An adjustment disorder is basically a maladaptive reaction to an identifiable event, circumstance or stressor. Typically, this disorder is seen within two or three months of the precipitating event. To qualify as an adjustment disorder, the maladaptive reaction usually has not lasted over six months. When an adjustment disorder lingers on it is usually reclassified as a different type of disorder. Untreated adjustment disorders can sometimes develop into more stable or persistent difficulties. Common stressors that can result in adjustment disorders are divorce, death (although normal bereavement does not meet the criteria of an adjustment disorder) of close relative or friend, accidents or other trauma. Essentially any type of stressor can evoke an adjustment reaction or disorder depending on the stressor and the vulnerability or susceptibility of the individual. Adjustment disorders have no age boundaries and males and females are equally affected. Early identification of adjustment disorders and early interventions are especially helpful. Adjustment disorders are generally responsive to supportive measures such as play therapy or brief psychotherapeutic interventions.

The prevalence of adjustment disorders as a principal diagnosis in individuals receiving outpatient treatment varies between 5% to 20% depending on the methods and settings used. Children in foster care, maltreated children or other individuals from highly stressful circumstances may be at increased risk for adjustment and other disorders.

The personal upset or impairment in performance identified with adjustment disorders is commonly revealed as a decline in achievement at work or school and in some cases as a transient alteration in social relationships. Adjustment disorders have been associated with an elevated risk of suicide attempts and suicide. The cultural context of a person's situation should be considered in the determination of whether a response to a stressor is greater than what would be expected or otherwise maladaptive. The character, connotation, and sense of the stressors may be interpreted differently across cultures.

Stressors may occur as a natural disaster affecting many individuals, as part of an individual or familial developmental milestone such as beginning school, leaving home, marriage, parenthood, failing to meet expectations or goals, aging issues or retirement. The diagnostic criteria as defined indicate that symptoms of an adjustment disorder cannot continue for more than 6 months beyond the cessation of the stressor or its effects. Nevertheless, there are circumstances where a stressor or its effects has continuing consequences and the adjustment disorder is chronic. An adjustment disorder in which the presence of symptoms is for less than 6 months is considered an acute adjustment disorder. Adjustment disorders are usually classified according to the predominant type of maladaptive symptomatology such as anxiety, depression or behavioral features.

An Example of an Acute Adjustment Disorder

Mark was referred for evaluation and treatment by his pediatrician. Mark's father brought him to the initial visit and provided the history and current concerns. Mark's father described the reasons for seeking treatment as having to do with Mark's intense fear of cars since a recent automobile accident involving the father and Mark. Mark was a ten year old boy in the fourth grade who was described as having no previous behavioral or emotional problems and no other difficulties beyond the fear of the automobile. Mark's father indicated that he and Mark's mother were recently divorced, and that Mark spent every other weekend and Wednesday evenings with him. Mark refused to travel in his mother's car. The father was able to get Mark into the car by much coaxing, promising to drive slowly and avoiding the freeways.

Mark separated from his father without difficulty and was pleasant and cooperative throughout the evaluation. Psychological tests were administered as well as a clinical assessment. When describing the accident Mark said he had been in a head-on collision. The further description of the accident, however, revealed a surprisingly mild and fortunate event, as such things go. It turned out that the "head-on" accident was at very low speeds and no one was seriously injured. Mark's father was exiting a multi-level parking structure and struck an elderly woman's vehicle that had entered the wrong way. The elderly woman, Mark and his father all had some minor cuts and bruises but none of them required more than immediate first aid.

As Mark recounted the accident he did not appear as anxious as would have been expected given the report of his "intense anxiety" regarding automobile travel. As the clinical assessment touched on his family relationships the source of his anxiety became more clear. Mark's parents had divorced four months before the accident. Since the divorce Mark's father had moved into a small apartment and as a way to keep ownership of her home, Mark's mother shared rent with another single mother and her three children. Mark described a sudden change of lifestyle since the divorce. In the past four months both parents had become financially strapped, were unable to continue many of the normal activities which had previously been enjoyed and were now separate. Mark now shared his house with others, missed his father, and when he was with his father, missed his mother. He had fantasies of his father and mother reuniting and felt angry at both parents.

Mark's assessment revealed an intelligent, sensitive child who was diagnosed with having an adjustment disorder with anxious features. Generally speaking, Mark was psychologically healthy. Short term psychotherapy was recommended and commenced over a period of two months in which both parents were included in the first two sessions as well as the final session.

The first psychotherapy session which included both parents involved a discussion of how children feel when parents divorce and how the children frequently wish the parents to get back together, even when they know that it won't or can't happen. The discussion evolved into how Mark felt and how each of the parents felt. Finally, an interpretation was offered suggesting that the divorce had "blindsided" Mark in a way similar to the car accident; that Mark's fear was related to his vulnerability and recognition that a person may not always be as secure as they think. The therapeutic process had the desired effect with Mark rapidly losing his fear of the car and focusing his remaining sessions on adjustment issues and ways he could better communicate his feelings and needs to his parents.

How do individuals deal with chronic stressors? What strategies might an individual employ when faced with an uncontrollable persistent stressor? These are important questions because they lead us to methods by which we can better understand the role and limits of support in helping those with chronic stressors. Various studies have illustrated that methods of coping with stressors vary from information seeking to information avoiding. Distancing oneself, denial, blaming others, blaming themselves, resignation or any of the classical psychological defenses may be used or overused as an attempt to manage and cope with stress. Individual characteristics such as resiliency or vulnerability determine, in part, the reaction to or effects of stressors. Age, for example, may be seen in relationship to the ability to understand the nature of the stressors such as serious illness or the need for painful or difficult medical procedures. Gender differences of coping styles have also been noted.

> Dr. Anthony Spirito and his colleagues undertook a study to classify and codify the varieties of stressors described by children and teenagers with a broad group of chronic illnesses. They also sought to survey which conceptualizations of coping best related to the self-report of strategies used by the youth in dealing with self-reported stressors. Ninety-three male and eighty-four female subjects and their guardians consented to participate in the study. Their ages ranged from 7 to 18 years. The average age was 12.3. Each of the children or teenagers had a chronic illness for at least 1 year prior to the start of the study. Boys reported using cognitive restructuring and self-blame for the chronic illness problem more than girls. Girls reported using emotional regulation and social support more than boys. With a standard non-illness related problem, the genders used these strategies equally. Under conditions of high stress, females may find social support and other resources more readily available, allowing them to rely on emotional regulation and social support in their efforts to cope.
>
> The investigators concluded, among other things, that clinicians may find it beneficial to assimilate an assessment of children's coping strategies when they evaluate children with chronic illness.
>
> Anthony Spirito, Lori J. Stark, Karen M. Gil and Vida L. Tyc. Journal of the American Academy of Child and Adolescent Psychiatry March 1995, v34, n3, p283(8)

Obviously, chronic severe illness is a stressor that is to some degree uncontrollable. Although an individual may be able to effect some control over the illness by maintaining specific diet or medical regimens, there are elements in chronic illness that are impossible for the individual to alter. The same is true for the child in a highly dysfunctional family or a child in an abusive environment or stressed as a result of chronic poverty. The issues of homelessness as a stressor to children and adolescents was addressed by a study entitled "Constructive conflict management and coping in homeless children and adolescents. (Constructive Conflict Management: An Answer to Critical Social Problems?) by Sandra V. Horowitz, Susan K. Boardman and Irwin Redlener. The study was published in the Journal of Social Issues Spring 1994, v50, n1, p85(14).

The homeless youth study provides insight to the type and nature of stressors confronting homeless children and adolescents. Homeless families' lives are distinguished by inordinately stressful conditions, such as frequent change, discrimination, disorientation, and loss of power. As a result of homelessness, children are often rejected by classmates because of their homeless status, lack of clothing and personal belongings. Children living under conditions of homelessness are not, surprisingly, involved in more conflicts and aggression than comparably housed poor, inner-city children. Previous studies have illustrated how rejection can lead to aggression and hostility on the part of the rejected child.

Methods of conflict management vary with respect to the presence or absence of basic security. Various studies of middle-class adolescents indicate that half or more of adolescents' struggles are managed by disengagement (changing the subject or activity or one person refusing to continue the interaction); the second most probable strategy involves assertion with negotiation. Adolescents are more likely to use disengagement than negotiation to resolve their conflicts. Dr. Horowitz and her associates initiated a study of homeless youth in order to question methods for managing conflict behavior as they relate to adolescents and children.

What determines an individual's style of dealing with stress and conflict? Scientists investigating children's ability to live with environmental stress have defined numerous factors that appear to be significant. For example, dispositional attributes such as activity level and sociability, communication skills, competence and positive interpersonal relations in school. There also appears to be a protective quality for children who achieve in sports or music, who are given responsibility, or who enjoy a good relationship with a teacher. Many children, with dispositional or environmental qualities that are protective, can function well despite such adversity as being raised in a residential treatment facility, group home or foster home.

According to Dr. Horowitz's analysis of the literature, coping is thought to have two major purposes: emotion focused coping regulates disturbing emotions whereas coping that is problem-focused centers on activities designed to settle or improve the problem itself. In particular, problem-focused coping and an emotion-focused strategy are most frequently associated with better outcomes.

Coping approaches and outcomes may also be influenced by gender. Dr. Spirito's previously cited article reports that girls typically use more emotion-focused coping strategies than do boys. Girls are apparently more expressive and seek more emotional support than their male counterparts. Boys are more likely to distance themselves.

In Dr. Horowitz's study, the investigators focused on identification of the problems, conflicts, and conflict management strategies most often used by homeless adolescents; assessment of the coping ability of homeless adolescents and the relation between coping and conflict management. They also analyzed differences between homeless children who managed to achieve academically and those who reported lower achievement scores. Group differences between boys and girls relative to their coping strategies were also studied.

The initial interviews occurred when welfare hotels were being used to house homeless mothers and children in New York City. One hundred-seventy-six homeless families were included with a mother-child dyad from each. The families were from eleven different welfare hotels. According to New York City's Human Resources Administration, there were, at that time, two hundred-thirty-two homeless families in the eleven hotels who had a child between the ages of nine and fourteen. Seventy-six percent of the two hundred-thirty-two families agreed to be interviewed regarding the "problems" faced by homeless families. Follow-up interviews were completed one year later. At the follow-up interview eighty-eight percent of the families were living in permanent housing and eleven percent remained in the welfare hotels. Forty-nine percent of the children in the hotel sample were male. Sixty percent were African-American, thirty-one percent Hispanic, three percent Euro-American, and five percent were "Other". The children were asked to describe their worst problem from the preceding month. They were also asked what they did to handle the problem. Several categories were established to analyze the data: type of difficulty; strategies used to handle the problem; and the basic form of conflict management used. The four categories for the type of difficulty were: conflict with peers; problems with family; school performance and behavior problems; and fears and worries about the environment.

The investigators studying the homeless youth expected that a large number of conflicts would be associated with parents. Surprisingly, the proportion of youth reporting peer conflict was significantly greater than that for any other types of conflict, including conflict with parents. The investigators theorized that homeless children and teenagers may lack the support and parental monitoring that might result in conflict but is also necessary for the development of self and social competence.

The nature of stressors related to homelessness may inhibit the process of individuation and in some part, explain the failure of those young people to express typical adolescent behavior. A degree of conflict with parents reflects the typical process of becoming independent. Without the security or assurance required to develop autonomy, homeless youth may experience conflict with a parent as too threatening.

The homeless youth study found that homeless boys and girls differed, to a degree, in their use of coping strategies. Boys engaged in all three coping strategies to a greater extent than did girls, including the use of social support and ventilation of feelings. In problems involving peer conflict, boys used higher levels of optimistic appraisal and change than did girls. These differences were thought by the investigators to reflect the male pattern of using distracting behaviors when distressed as well as the finding that boys appeared to be more vulnerable to psychosocial stress than girls. The findings led the investigators to determine that the homeless youth interviewed were broadly dissimilar to the middle-class youth which have comprised many of the previous studies related to coping strategies. The homeless youth had both different life circumstances and used different conflict management and coping techniques.

The researchers point out that their findings suggest the importance of teaching constructive negotiation skills to disadvantaged youth. Facilitating children and adolescents to effectively cope with their lives, conflicts and social experience appears to be the most efficacious method of promoting attainment and averting problems.

An Example of an Adjustment Disorder Related to Chronic Stressors

Taylor was eight years old when he was referred for evaluation and treatment by his school psychologist. Taylor's teacher and school were concerned about the amount of school Taylor had been missing. Taylor was brought by his mother for the initial visit, and she provided the necessary background information and history. Taylor's mother indicated that she was suffering from leukemia and that she had often been quite ill over the past two years. She described Taylor as the youngest of three children. Taylor had two older sisters who had taken over many of the household responsibilities such as cooking and cleaning. Taylor's mother would undergo chemotherapy at various times and would have to be hospitalized several times a year at a facility that was approximately two hours away from the family. At the time of Taylor's initial visit his mother was between treatments and enjoying a partial remission.

It quickly became apparent that part of Taylor's difficulty in separating from his mother had to do with his fear of her impending death. Taylor's method of dealing with this conflict was to essentially deny the seriousness of his mother's health but at the same time refuse to go to school. Taylor had no behavior problems either at home or at school but was described as slow to learn. Taylor would typically complain that he had an upset stomach on school mornings. He would assure his family the night before that he would go to school but then refuse when it was time to leave the house. Taylor's father was working very long days of 14-16 hour shifts seven days a week managing a car wash. The family was unable to obtain health insurance and was overwhelmed with health care costs.

Taylor's evaluation resulted in a diagnosis of separation anxiety Disorder and adjustment disorder with mixed emotional features. An intellectual assessment demonstrated Taylor to have a lower than average intelligence quotient but no learning disability. The school accommodated Taylor's level of ability and was very supportive. It was recommended to Taylor, his parents and the school that Taylor be sent to school regardless of his complaints unless he had a temperature in excess of 101 degrees fahrenheit. It was also recommended that Taylor attend a peer-aged psychotherapy group on a weekly basis.

Treatment of Adjustment Disorders

In the previous example Taylor's adjustment disorder was due in part to the chronic stressor of his mother's terminal illness. It was appropriate to diagnose both the adjustment disorder as well as the separation anxiety disorder even though they were related. Taylor attended a peer psychotherapy group for a year and a half following his evaluation. He returned to school with minimal difficulty under the conditions defined subsequent to the evaluation. During Taylor's attendance in group, his mother was hospitalized on several occasions. Taylor received tremendous support and understanding from the group, some of whom had also lost parents. Behavioral components to Taylor's treatment included the 101 degree rule, a rule that on a day that school was missed he did not go out to play or see friends and that he completed schoolwork or reading in his bedroom throughout the day (not visiting with mother all day as he had previously). Psychotherapeutic interventions, in addition to the group, included initial individual sessions with Taylor and his mother discussing her illness allowing Taylor to express his feelings, fears and thoughts.

Adjustment disorders frequently are responsive to brief psychotherapeutic interventions. In the presence of chronic stressors supportive interventions such as group psychotherapy can be helpful. Within professional diagnostic literature, stress disorders are frequently addressed within the context of anxiety disorders. This text will consider stress related disorders in the context of adjustment.

Stress related disorders include *immediate stress reactions* in response to a traumatic event and *persistent stress reactions*. In persistent stress reactions an individual re-experiences an extremely traumatic incident with associated symptoms of elevated stimulation and attempts to avoid trauma associated stimuli. In the case of an immediate stress reaction an individual may develop anxiety, dissociative (a disruption of consciousness, memory, identity or perception of environment) and other symptoms subsequent to an extremely traumatic incident. To meet the diagnostic criteria for an acute stress disorder, the symptoms must occur within one month following an encounter with a severely traumatic stressor. These symptoms generally occur during or shortly following the traumatic event. An acute stress disorder as defined by the

Diagnostic and Statistical Manual, 4th Edition lasts at least two days and must conclude within four weeks after the end of the traumatic incident. If the symptoms persist beyond that length of time the diagnosis is changed.

Persistent stress related symptoms that meet the criteria for acute stress disorder but continue beyond one month may be diagnosed as a posttraumatic stress disorder (PTSD). The degree of severity as well as the length and type of exposure are generally the primary determinants in the development of a stress disorder. Previous and subsequent experiences, support systems, personality and psychological factors all may play a role in the development and resolution of a stress disorder.

Symptoms of stress disorders may include resignation, hopelessness and dissociative symptoms such as a personal sense of detachment or lack of emotional responsiveness. An individual may additionally feel a sense of derealization or depersonalization and symptoms of anxiety or increased vigilance. As a result, stress related disorders have the potential to impair activities previously normative for the individual. When individuals are exposed to an extreme stressor, they may experience a reduction in emotional responsiveness, difficulty in finding enjoyment, feeling unwarranted guilt, poor concentration, irritability or social withdrawal. If these symptoms are severe and continue, they may represent what can be diagnosed as a co-existing mood disorder.

In cases considered to be posttraumatic stress disorder there is generally some form of recurrent recollections and reminders of the trauma (e.g., places, people, activities) are avoided. Difficulty sleeping, irritability, poor concentration, hyper-vigilance and restlessness may also be experienced. Traumatic experiences associated with post traumatic stress disorder include direct personal experiences as well as witnessed experiences. Direct events correlated with post traumatic stress disorder include combat experiences, kidnapping, being taken hostage, terrorism, torture, personal assault and similar experiences. Witnessed events associated with post traumatic stress disorder include seeing profound harm or death of another as a result of war, disaster, accident or similar circumstances. For example, rescue workers at airplane crash sites can be traumatized by seeing body parts and some may continue to re-experience the trauma by having recurrent and intrusive memories of the situation. Anxiety and stress can be triggered by nearly anything that represents or resembles the initial trauma. As a result, individuals with PTSD may attempt to avert reflection, emotions or discussion related to the trauma. The diagnosis of PTSD can be specified by the clinician as acute (less than three months), chronic (over three months) or with delayed onset (at least 6 months between event and onset of symptoms).

Chapter Six

Disruptive Behavior Disorders

Behavioral Disorders

Behavioral disorders include those maladaptive behaviors that are socially disruptive. Attention deficit hyperactivity disorder, oppositional defiant disorder and conduct disorder are examples.

Attention Deficit Hyperactivity Disorder

Attention deficit hyperactivity disorder (ADHD) is a disorder of unclear etiology (origin or causal pathway). An additional confusion is that the symptoms associated with attention deficit hyperactivity disorder can also be the result of a variety of other conditions. Estimates of the prevalence of ADHD vary between lows of 3% to highs of 9% of all children and continuing into adulthood. Boys with this disorder outnumber girls three to one and hyperactivity is present in approximately 75-85%. ADHD has been known under a variety of names over the past twenty years. ADHD has previously been referred to as minimal cerebral dysfunction, attention deficit disorder and as hyperactivity disorder to name a few. Despite many years of research, the exact causal process resulting in attention deficit hyperactivity disorder remains obscure. The current major classification system (the DSMIV) distinguishes between ADHD that is predominantly hyperactive and impulsive as compared to ADHD that has symptoms which are predominantly related to inattention. The other primary diagnostic category of ADHD in which both hyperactivity and inattention are seen is termed combined type.

It is known that certain types of brain damage can result in symptoms associated with attention deficit hyperactivity disorder. Brain imaging studies have also demonstrated a reduced glucose metabolism in the pre-motor and pre-frontal cortex of individuals with ADHD. Increasing the availability of the neurotransmitters *norepinephrine* and *dopamine* at the neuronal synapse appears beneficial in regard to the symptoms of ADHD. While the neurotransmitter *serotonin* does not appear directly related to ADHD, it has been associated with aggression and impulsivity and may have indirect involvement in the constellation of symptoms seen in ADHD. The pharmacological treatments for ADHD primarily address the problem by either helping to release more neurotransmitter (as happens with stimulants), blocking the reuptake (thereby increasing the amount available in the synapse) of the neurotransmitter (as happens with some of the antidepressant medications) or by reducing the intracellular degradation of presynaptic neurotransmitter (as occurs when using a pharmaceutical agent to inhibit the breakdown or metabolism of the neurotransmitter). Pharmacological interventions are discussed in greater detail in Chapter 10. Figure X further illustrates these fundamental actions on neurotransmitters.

Birth trauma, genetics and biological development have also been studied as causes of and/or contributants to attention difficulties. Whatever the cause, by diagnostic definition onset of ADHD precedes age 7 and many parents report improvement, in at least some symptoms, by the time the child reaches puberty. This "improvement" of some symptoms may suggest, that the brain to some degree may have compensated for the impairment or that a level of neurological maturation has occurred that is beneficial. Attentional difficulties may or may not persist into adolescence or adulthood. Longitudinal studies have reported that approximately **70%** of school age children with ADHD have symptoms that persist into adolescence and approximately **10-20%** of those have serious impairment. The studies further suggest that approximately **30-50%** have symptoms that continue into adulthood and that approximately **30-40%** of those with ADHD generally do well as adults.

It is common to hear adults or other children refer to a child as "hyper". The current terminology is more appropriate. Hyperactivity simply means overly active and may or may not in itself mean a child has attention deficit hyperactivity disorder (ADHD). Children, however, with attention deficit hyperactivity disorder frequently demonstrate hyperactivity as one of their primary symptoms of difficulty. Hyperactivity, by itself, can sometimes be symptomatic of anxiety, illness, medication response, ADHD or simply excitement. Adults with ADHD have a similar pattern of social, psychiatric, and psychological dysfunction similar to that seen in children. Studies suggest that there is continued therapeutic efficacy from pharmacological treatment in adults with ADHD.

Difficulty with attention fundamentally impairs learning. The associated symptoms of ADHD have relatively global effects. Problems of restlessness and irritability directly influences behavior and as a result affects social relationships. These learning and social impairments, in combination with other biopsychosocial determinants become important factors related to personality development. Oppositional behavior, argumentativeness, and low frustration tolerance frequently add to the developmental difficulty of these children. The probability of having both learning disabilities and aggressive conduct disorder are significantly increased in the ADHD population, frequently leading to disruptions at home and at school. Depression, anxiety, irritability, explosiveness, substance abuse and antisocial behavior also occur with an increased frequency among those diagnosed with ADHD. When ADHD continues into adolescence and adulthood it frequently results in disorganization and diminishing productivity. The psycho-stimulants such as methylphenidate (MPH) have been the major treatments for attention deficit disorder. Side effects (decreased appetite, insomnia, the potential for increasing tics, possible over-activation and in high doses for extended periods, delaying growth rate) have prompted investigation and trials of alternative medications. Several types of anti-depressant and other medications have been found to be very effective and in some cases clearly preferable to stimulants.

ADHD occurs across the spectrum of intellectual abilities. The presence of ADHD in itself is not a reflection of intellectual ability. A child with ADHD, however, despite intellectual potential, is at high risk for impairment in the realm of academic achievement. In addition to a history of hyperactivity, children with ADHD are often more impulsive and aggressive than their same age peers. As a result, the child with ADHD is at extremely high risk for failing socially and having damaged self esteem. ADHD, like every other diagnosable mental health difficulty, may manifest as any of a broad range of impairment, from mild to severe. A mild form of ADHD can be impairing but difficult to identify.

Severe ADHD symptoms are unmistakable. The child has severely impaired attention and concentration. The child moves from one activity to another, seldom completing a task before losing interest. Often the child is hyperactive, fidgeting or in some type of constant motion. As mentioned, impulsivity and aggression are not unusual. A less obvious form of ADHD can be perplexing. Often a bright child with an unidentified mild attentional disorder will become stressed over time and as a result develop secondary psychological difficulties. In fact, children with untreated attention deficit hyperactivity disorder of any severity frequently develop significant co-existing psychological disorders. The child with an untreated attention deficit hyperactivity disorder is more likely to be rejected by others and less likely to achieve his or her potential academically. Over time, the untreated ADHD child can easily become reinforced by negative behaviors, incorporate a negative self image and become depressed, conduct disordered or otherwise maladaptive in his or her adjustment.

Treating a child with ADHD should be undertaken seriously. As mentioned, many factors should be considered. The severity and results of the disorder must be evaluated and considered in the context of all the significant factors. Pharmacological intervention is generally a very effective aspect of treatment in ADHD. Depending on the severity of the disorder and the effects it has had on a child, other interventions may also be warranted. Although many parents have a general initial reluctance to use medications with their child, in cases of ADHD a physician and parent must weigh the risks and benefits of using or not using medication.

When ADHD is diagnosed it can be helpful to begin systematic observations. Depending on the severity of ADHD or coexisting disorders, various types of medications may be suggested. It is suggested that initial treatment efforts using medications be considered as medication trials. Parental observations of the child's response to medications is helpful in determining the best approach. Many children with ADHD receiving an effective medication trial begin to have social and academic successes. Children who had previously been unhappy and disliked, frequently become more at ease and likable.

The benefit of early diagnosis and intervention cannot be overstated. Differentiating from or identification of coexisting disorders is one of the most challenging tasks confronting those concerned with the treatment of a child with attention deficit hyperactivity disorder. It is challenging because of the variable degree of severity, the dynamic developmental nature of children and the nearly countless factors that may be playing a role in any given behavioral or emotional manifestation. However, a child who has an attention difficulty is also at a higher risk for having other difficulties. Mood disorders and behavioral disorders commonly coexist with ADHD. As previously mentioned, some of these difficulties may be a result of the stress, social vulnerabilities and general environmental responses that one receives when distracted and hyperactive. On the other hand, the symptoms and course that we now call ADHD may represent a "prodromal" or early symptom pattern of another illness that only becomes clear over time. Treatment response monitoring is the most effective method of making this determination. Treatment response monitoring involves monitoring the course of symptom manifestation and tracking the progression or reduction of symptoms relative to treatment approaches. An equally important issue occurs for parents who have a *treatment resistant* child. These parents may find themselves frustrated to a degree that ultimately threatens the basic relationship they have with their child. Having a plan with contingencies for non-response or partial response can lead a parent in a way that reduces the intense anxiety that accompanies the anger and despair that parents many times feel when all of their best efforts have been ineffective.

As new disorders are presented and discussed, their relationships with previously presented disorders will be provided. For example, in the chapter dealing with mood disorders, coexisting conditions of mood disorders along with or masquerading as attention deficit hyperactivity disorder or conduct disorder will be addressed. As a parent becomes more familiar with the types and potential complexities of these difficulties, it is a natural reaction to resist the complexity. Most parents don't want their child's difficulty to be complex. With all of their own concerns parents don't need another worry, concern or expense! Parents also don't want their children to suffer from diabetes, cystic fibrosis, leukemia or other impairing and threatening illnesses. Mental disorders are much more insidious and at times just as dangerous as many of the more readily identifiable physical maladies. Parents, relatives, neighbors and friends will certainly consider a child with a serious physical illness differently than one with an emotional or behavioral disorder. The poorly understood, unknown or unpredictable is anxiety producing and can be especially frightening when a child's well being is in jeopardy. Delaying recognition or treatment until a problem cannot be ignored only increases the effort that ultimately will be required to effectively intervene.

The professional nomenclature of the diagnostic manuals simply provide a uniform criteria by which a common language is observed. Despite the value of these classification systems they do not automatically or necessarily suggest effective treatment solutions. Understandably, parents hope that a "named" illness or disorder has a straightforward, inexpensive and time limited treatment. Although most of the mental disorders are difficult to address in either a straightforward (do this) or time limited (two times a day for three months) way, it is possible to significantly reduce the cost associated with the evaluation and treatment of a child having an emotional or behavioral difficulty. Parent interventions or professional interventions augmented by parent interventions can dramatically reduce the cost of a child evaluation and ongoing treatment and treatment monitoring. Specific parental intervention methods and strategies will be discussed in the chapter "The Therapeutic Parent".

While it is helpful to consider the conceptual presentations of broad diagnostic classifications such as disruptive behavior disorders, mood disorders, anxiety disorders and others, these classifications are still merely terms used to identify similar aggregations of symptoms and are not generally distinct illnesses that necessarily have clear cut treatments. Diagnostic classifications may be misleading when they are considered as singular illnesses without dimensions. The disruptive behavior disorder categories of ADHD, oppositional defiant disorder and conduct disorder all present numerous illustrations of how a diagnostic label may be misleading.

As the previously cited study points out, there are limits to diagnostic classification. This text has been designed, in part, to prepare a parent to generally understand many of the major diagnostic classifications concerning children. More importantly, however, this text has been designed to provide a conceptual framework to understand children dimensionally, with the full consideration of biopsychosocial and developmental influences in relationship to specific observable symptoms and measurable responses to treatment. The complex and multiple issues surrounding the diagnosis of disruptive behavior disorders provide an interesting lesson that is particularly relevant to the concept of dimensionality.

Oppositional Defiant Disorder

The key quality of *oppositional defiant disorder (ODD)* is a chronic pattern of negativism, defiance, disobedience and

> A 1995 article studied the Diagnostic and Statistical Manual-Third Edition Revised (DSM-IIIR) criteria for disruptive behaviors using dimensional and categorical models. The investigators related the measures to later outcome variables which included risk of substance use, juvenile offenses and not completing school. Dimensional measures had better predictive validity than assessments based on DSM-III-R criteria. The conclusions were demonstrated for categories including Oppositional Defiant Disorder, Conduct Disorder and Attention Deficit Hyperactivity Disorder. The categorical scoring coefficients were about sixty percent of the dimensional variables. The disruptive behavior diagnostic classifications produced measures that were not optimal predictors. The analysis of classifications provided a test of the assumptions fundamental to the DSM-III-R classifications of disruptive behavior problems. One such assumption is that those meeting the diagnostic criteria are individuals having a generally similar prognosis and those who do not meet criteria share a prognosis. This study found this was not the case. Those not meeting the diagnostic criteria (Non-cases) had significant symptom diversity from no symptoms to those just at the sub-diagnostic threshold. Dimensional scaling of symptoms had clear predictive superiority over methods based on diagnostic classification.
>
> David M. Fergusson and L. John Horwood. Predictive validity of categorically and dimensionally scored measures of disruptive childhood behaviors. Journal of the American Academy of Child and Adolescent Psychiatry April 1995, v34, n4, p477(9)

hostility toward those in positions of authority. The current diagnostic criteria requires these behaviors to have persisted for at least 6 months and including the frequent occurrence of specific behaviors such as argumentativeness, fits of temper, blaming others, defiance or other non-compliance with requests or rules. Primary diagnostic considerations include the frequency of the behavior and the deviance from what is developmentally normative. This diagnostic classification is not used when the oppositional behaviors are exclusively related to the development of a mood or psychotic disorder. A diagnosis of conduct disorder frequently follows a history or earlier diagnosis of oppositional defiant disorder and when diagnosed excludes the additional diagnosis of ODD being made.

Every combat experienced parent has had the opportunity to observe negative and defiant behaviors. Transitory oppositional conduct is standard operating procedure for preschool children and teenagers. It is important to recognize these normal transitions and deal with them effectively. A parent will know that it goes beyond normative behavior if it resists resolution and remains unresponsive to parental interventions. Attention-deficit hyperactivity disorder, moody temperaments, low self-esteem and low frustration tolerance have all been associated with the diagnosis of oppositional defiant disorder. This classification may be one of the most illustrative and easiest to understand in relationship to other childhood and adolescent mental disorders. For example, it is easy to see how a hyperactive or mood disordered child can develop entrenched maladaptive styles of dealing with others. These are prime examples of situations in which parents and others can inadvertently reinforce maladaptive behaviors. The disruptive behavior disorders have an extremely high relatedness to hyperactivity and mood disorders. There are numerous variations on how these disorders can evolve and grow from initial hyperactivity or an earlier mood disorder.

Intervention strategies depend upon understanding the elements that initiate and maintain these conduct related behaviors. Harsh, inconsistent and/or neglectful parenting styles are often associated with this classification of disorder. Neglectful parents will never be motivated to utilize a text such as this. Nevertheless, parents who become frustrated and pushed away by their children, can discover themselves detached to a point of neglecting their child out of avoidance.

Baseline observations and observations of responses to interventions can assist in determining the degree to which a difficult child contributes to a maladaptive parenting style versus the degree to which a maladaptive parenting style contributes to the development of a difficult child. This distinction is suggested as a requirement to designing an effective intervention strategy, not as a way to assign or partial out blame.

An Example of an Oppositional Defiant Disorder

An oppositional defiant disorder may be primarily learned behavior or it may be initially motivated by underlying irritability associated with some degree of a mood disorder. Regardless of how an oppositional trend begins, it's maintenance and development is dependent on being reinforced and it is in this way learned. The following example presents a young boy who had no signs of mood or other disorder at the time of evaluation other than an oppositional defiant disorder.

Tim Adate
Age: 11.5

Tim's mother indicated that she had brought Tim for an evaluation because she had been requested to do so by Tim's school. Tim was present while his mother provided the background information and history. Tim's mother is an executive for a large corporation and despite having excellent insurance coverage, emphasized that she agreed to the evaluation only because the school had promised to cover the evaluation costs. As a matter of course Tim's mother was asked who Tim's biological father is, if he lives in the home, whether he is involved with Tim and whether there is any significant medical history relative to either biological parent. Tim's mother indicated that Tim's father lives in the city where they lived several years previously and immediately responded with concern, "why do you want to know who his father is?" It was explained that it is important to understand the possible significance of Tim's relationship or lack of one with a father. It is also significant from the vantage point of determining if there is any relevant medical history that might suggest biological risk. Tim's mother then stated that she didn't know anything about Tim's father's medical or family history. She stated in a matter of fact manner, in front of Tim, that she had a short lived relationship with Tim's father and that he has never been involved in Tim's life and she intends to keep it that way. She went on to deny any problems with pregnancy, delivery, early day care or preschool or early elementary school. She did admit that Tim has an explosive temper and bullying that has caused him recent school problems but that she really doesn't see it as a big problem. She suggested that the school was exaggerating the significance of this behavior. As Tim's mother openly questioned the school and teacher's credibility Tim sat across the room smiling, confident that in his mother's eyes he could do no wrong. Interestingly, near the end of the interview Tim's mother rather casually mentioned that Tim is in a class placement for emotionally and behaviorally disturbed children. This bit of information appeared incongruent with her presentation of Tim as essentially "normal".

Tim's testing reflected a bright child who feels entitled, has learned to oppose authority and has little respect for adults. He describes the father he has never met as a "dork" and "he's never sent child support". From his mother's presentation it would not be unlikely that the father, if aware of this child, knows where he is. It was impossible from the initial evaluation to determine with an assurance whether the mother was presenting the biological father in a fair manner. Despite the credibility of the mother's vague and evasive description of the father, Tim clearly felt that he had a father who never wanted him and who was not supporting him. Parent response questionnaires were consistent with the mother's presentation in that they demonstrated that the mother was significantly more defensive than most parents in completing a standardized questionnaire. The individual clinical interview with Tim revealed that he had a good sense of humor, a recognition that he "acts up" in class and knowledge that he gets away with a lot with his mother. Nevertheless, he maintained that he has an unfair teacher and excused much of his behavior problems on her. He described his goal in life is to "become rich".

Relying on conventional wisdom one would describe this child as "spoiled rotten". He is however, impaired socially and developmentally by his oppositional behavior and as such at risk for developing additional and more stable maladaptive behaviors. Tim's mental status was as follows: His affect was broad and his mood was bright. He demonstrated no signs of thought disorder and was oriented to person place and time. He demonstrated above average intelligence, no attentional difficulties and had good recall and memory functions.

Diagnosis:
313.81   Oppositional Defiant Disorder

Recommendations:
Tim's mother stated during the interview that she would consider therapy for Tim only if the school committed to cover all expenses. While she admitted that Tim had some mild temper problems, she didn't feel they were "that bad". Given Ms. Adate's resistance to treatment or even acknowledgement of Tim's difficulties, it seemed futile to suggest psychotherapy at the time. It also seemed impractical and unfair for the school to be burdened with the cost of his treatment when the mother has resources to provide treatment if she wished to. On the other hand Tim did express a need to understand more about his father and his father's family of origin. He suggested, in private, that

he frequently wonders what his father is like. Tim also had clearly adopted attitudes supplied and reinforced by his mother which have undermined the authority of the teacher and school. Tim's mother appeared to have little current difficulty with Tim because she infrequently confronted or challenged him. This maternal strategy is likely to backfire during adolescence. It appeared that the most powerful approach, if possible, would be to require Ms. Adate to participate as an aide in Tim's class for one or two mornings or afternoons a week. Since Tim has had frequent difficulties on the playground, Ms. Adate might be assigned as a playground supervisor on those days. In this way she may become more realistic about her child in the context of the other school children.

Dr. Don T. Panec

Conduct Disorders

The primary characteristic utilized for the diagnostic criteria of *conduct disorder* is repetitious and recurring behavior where the fundamental rights of others or public laws are violated. These behaviors include aggression that may result in physical harm, intentional property damage, theft and similar types of actions occurring over the previous year with at least one such behavior over the past six months. The diagnosis of conduct disorder further defines that the behavior results in significant impairment in social or academic functioning. The children and adolescents associated with this diagnosis frequently start fights and respond aggressively to others. They may bully, threaten, intimidate and may even resort to using a weapon. Unfortunately, there has been a significant increase in violent crimes and deaths among teenagers in much of the United States.

Conduct disorders represent symptoms which result in serious difficulties requiring professional assistance for diagnosis and treatment. It is important to distinguish conduct

Teen Deaths, Violent, Percent Change: 1985-91

State	Teen Violent Deaths Percent Change 1985-91
ALABAMA	25
ALASKA	8
ARIZONA	-2
ARKANSAS	17
CALIFORNIA	18
COLORADO	8
CONNECTICUT	14
DELAWARE	-30
Dist. C.	520
FLORIDA	-5
GEORGIA	8
HAWAII	-31
IDAHO	-14
ILLIN	42
INDIANA	21
IOWA	-0
KANSAS	11
KENTUCKY	5
LOUISIANA	27
MAINE	42
MARYLAND	19
MASSACHUSETTS	-11
MICHIGAN	12
MINNESOTA	-13
MISSISSIPPI	22
MISSOURI	32
MONTANA	-23
NEBRASKA	-8
NEVADA	29
NEW HAMPSHIRE	-15
NEW JERSEY	-15
NEW MEXICO	-8
NEW YORK	38
NORTH CAROLINA	3
OKLAHOMA	11
OREGON	-7
PENNSYLVANIA	6
RHODE ISLAND	-1
SOUTH CAROLINA	24
SOUTH DAKOTA	7
TENNESSEE	21
TEXAS	1
UTAH	-27
VERMONT	-16
VIRGINIA	21
WASHINGTON	9
WEST VIRGINIA	5
WISCONSIN	14
WYOMING	6
UNITED STATES	13
US WHITE	0
US AFRICAN AMERICAN	94
US HISPANIC	Not Reported

Source: KIDS COUNT DATA BOOK 1994. CENTER FOR THE STUDY OF SOCIAL POLICY

State	Teen Violent Deaths Percent Change 1985-91
NORTH DAKOTA	11
OHIO	8

Disruptive Behavior Disorders 163

disorders from certain types of mood and other disorders or coexisting disorders. The totality of the significant elements may suggest different treatment strategies and expected outcomes. It is possible to have combinations of what is currently diagnosed as ADHD, conduct disorder and depression. Children with ADHD are considered at greater risk than the general population to develop conduct and other disorders. It appears that this is particularly true among children with untreated symptoms of ADHD. Further important distinctions will be discussed in the chapter on mood disorders.

Conduct disorders are serious from the point of view that they represent stabilized anti-social behaviors such as lying, stealing, aggression and similar maladaptive behaviors. Conduct disorders are generally difficult and challenging to treat. Many children who have suffered severe deprivation, abuse or trauma develop conduct disorders. Similar to all mental states, however, there is an interdependence on biological, psychological, social and cultural determinants that play roles in the expression of these difficulties. Factors that have been associated with the development of conduct disorder include: family pathology, inconsistent parenting with harsh discipline, parental rejection, demanding infant temperament, physical and/or sexual abuse, neglect, early institutionalization, numerous changes of caregivers and large sized family.

Example of a Male with Conduct Disorder

Name: Phil A. Anger
Age: 18

Phil was referred for a psychological evaluation as part of his entering the community upon being released from a correctional facility. Phil indicated upon his arrival that he was being required to submit to this evaluation. Phil was generally suspicious and hostile in his response to even the mildest questions. When asked about his parents whereabouts and his relationship with them he angrily responded "Why do you want to know that?!" He was similarly evasive when asked about why he had been incarcerated and none of his records were available to the examiner. He indicated that he basically had broken some minor rules and was blamed unjustly for resisting various authorities. His responses were hardly believable given that the institution he was being released from was a federal correctional facility and some of his cell mates had been convicted of murder.

He was initially uncooperative and withholding of information. He asked at one point "what happens if I don't answer this, do I go back?". When asked about previous psychiatric hospitalizations he admitted that he had been hospitalized and went on to describe how a doctor "like you was asking me questions that were none of his business. I told him to shut up and he didn't listen, so I hit the jerk and they ended up putting me in hospital!" These comments were clearly meant to be threatening and intimidating. Once he realized the evaluation would not be used to send him back to prison, he was a little more forthcoming.

He described reacting aggressively to others because of justifiable threats. His statements along these lines appeared to be generally intimidating with a flavor of pride. He related some assaultive, threatening and intimidating behavior that he used before and while incarcerated, by his account, in self defense. He demonstrated no remorse for any of his actions and assumed no responsibility for any of his behavior. He proceeded by sharing very small amounts of information, typically getting angry after having said more than he intended. The pattern of his behavior began before age 12 and included staying out late at night, staying away from home overnight and truancy from school.

Diagnosis:
Conduct Disorder Childhood-Onset Type
Rule Out Antisocial Personality Disorder

Recommendations:
Although Phil has apparently earned his current freedom he appears to be at very high risk for re-offending. The supervision that has been required as part of his release is certainly in order and a rather intense vocational training program would also seem in order. It does appear, however, that Phil will be likely to have significant difficulty with those in authority. Unfortunately it appears likely that Phil may have a persistent Conduct Disorder with a high probability to develop into an adult antisocial personality disorder.

Sincerely,

Gilbert Freud, Ph.D.

Example of a Female with Conduct Disorder

Name: Anne T. Soshal
Age: 16

Anne was referred for an evaluation by the juvenile courts who were preparing to make a placement determination regarding Anne. Anne was incarcerated in the county juvenile detention facility where she had been since her most recent arrest. Anne was most recently arrested for running away from a group home placement and for grand theft auto. Anne was evaluated in an empty classroom within the jail facility. Anne was asked her age and she responded " I turned 16 yesterday, in jail! Doesn't that just suck!" Anne was very guarded and began the session by demanding to know why she was being "evaluated again". She was asked if she was aware that an evaluation had been requested for her and if she understood the nature of the evaluation. She indicated that she didn't know what the evaluation was for but it probably had to do with her appearance in court, the next week. She was informed that the court was trying to make a determination regarding her placement and had asked for a psychological evaluation in order to assist in making the determination.

Anne was then asked to complete two projective drawings. She refused. She was then asked to complete a personality inventory to which she replied " I've already done four of those ****ing things. I'm not doing anymore". And so went the rest of the responses to testing materials. Despite her resistance to tests she was talkative. She offered the information that she had been out of her home for four years, since age 12, which had previously been confirmed by her probation officer. She described having been in numerous foster placements, group homes and detention facilities. She had spent one and a half years in the last facility she had been in prior to her premature and unplanned departure. She said if it hadn't have been for her mother none of this would have happened. She was unable, however, to provide anything specific her mother had done. When asked why she had been out of her parent's home for the past four years she indicated because she had been abused and "they all hated me". When asked how she had been abused she said "in all ways, you know, I was emotionally abused and sometimes was hit". Her report of abuse did not ring true and was very vague. She denied sexual abuse and the probation officer had previously reported that her parents had exhausted every means of dealing with her and helping her to no avail.

When asked about school experiences she indicated that she hated school and that she was never liked by others. Teachers are "assholes" and kids are "jerks". When asked if she had made friends at any of the group homes or detention facilities she responded "I wasn't there to make friends". She indicated that she feels others are always out to get her. Anne stated matter-of-factly at first and then tearfully that she expected to be locked up until she is 18. When asked why she ran from her previous placement she responded, "I didn't want to be in there on my 16th birthday! Would you?!" She then indicated that she left so she could see her boyfriend. Her story then reflected an incredible story of a boyfriend who works in a carnival and with whom she had a rendezvous. In part what was incredible was that she had a boyfriend. To this point she had indicated never having a friend. The second part that was incredible was how she would locate a boyfriend after a year and a half, who spends approximately one week in each town that he passes through. Her response was that she was aware of the circuit traveled by this carnival and that it is always the same each year. According to Anne, all would be fine if the authorities would only let her be with her boyfriend and work in the carnival. After all "all I did was run away, now they're afraid that I'll just run away". When asked if she had committed any crimes she stated "No! All I did was run away! But, they are trying to charge me with stealing a car, but I didn't".

Additional interchanges resulted in her ultimately describing that she had ended up in a motel with her boyfriend, that she saw a car across from the motel and asked the motel manager if he knew whose it was and of course he did not. She then described "standing next to the car when the police came and they said I stole the car". She mentioned as an afterthought that she had the keys to the car in her pocket because she saw them in the car and didn't think they should be left in there. She then looked intensely at the examiner as if to make a quick judgement as to the examiner's gullibility quotient.

Diagnosis:
Conduct Disorder Childhood-Onset Type
Bipolar Disorder, Mixed
Borderline Personality Disorder

Recommendations:

It is recommended that Anne be held in a secure facility until a secure treatment facility can be located. Anne is a seriously mentally ill young woman, who will most probably escalate her antisocial behaviors unless a significant treatment impact can be obtained. She at this time has absolutely no insight and presents with a mixed emotional state (mood incongruent crying, temper and irritability). She denies hallucinations and does not appear delusional. Her projection of blame on others and her feeling of persecution verge on delusional.

Erika Erikson, Ph.D.

Treatment of Conduct Disordered Children

Pharmacological interventions with conduct disordered children are useful to the extent that there are co-existing disorders such as mood disorders. It is the admitted bias of the author that untreated mood and disruptive disorders, particularly when paired with significant environmental factors, are a prevalent precursor to the development of conduct disorders and *antisocial* personality. Despite this view, even in the case of a child who has a primary underlying mood disorder, if an established conduct disorder exists, medication without a significant multidimensional highly structured treatment approach has a low probability of being successful.

Cognitive behavioral and behavioral methods coupled with strategic pharmacotherapy appear to be the most effective approach to treatment. The principles and methods of cognitive behavioral therapy will be further presented in Chapter 10. The principles of cognitive behavioral therapy with an aggressive individual focus on teaching self monitoring in situations where they or others are angry. It is an important treatment goal for aggressive people to learn how to recognize their emotional reactions and feelings of anger. Behavioral methods incorporated in these treatment strategies include extinction techniques combined with positive reinforcement and controlling reinforcers that may be derived from the aggressive behavior.

Structured residential treatment facilities with transition programs into foster care or back home frequently offer the best opportunity to treat co-morbid or underlying conditions while addressing the components of maladaptive conduct. Facilities such as this can provide a structured treatment plan within the context of clear rules and consequences while holding the individual responsible for his or her actions in a secure facility.

Exercise 3

Go to Chapter 11 and locate the sample of research articles on childhood behavior disorders. Browse through the titles. The titles will give a sense of the range of research. The interested or motivated reader can take desired citations to a university library, find the reference librarian and be directed to articles of interest.

Chapter Seven

Mood Disorders

Emotional Disorders

Emotional disorders include childhood depressions and anxiety disorders. Frequently when these types of disorders appear in childhood they are interwoven, with one or the other tending to dominate.

Childhood Depression

It is difficult for many adults to accept that children can suffer from depression. Defining depression relative to adults or children can be tricky. The term "*depression*" is so commonly used in general language that it means many things to people in various contexts. The way depression is used in this text is to describe an emotional disorder of mood. There are numerous types and subtypes of depression. The interested reader is referred to the resources in chapter 11 and to their local university library for in-depth descriptions of depression and mood disorders.

While a child with an adjustment disorder may have some depressive features, a child with a major depression usually has persistent symptoms of depression. Many types of depressions have significant biological components. For example, there is a higher incidence of depression among children whose parents or grandparents have histories of depression. Depressions in some cases are precipitated by an environmental or traumatic event. In some cases major depressions appear to occur spontaneously. A major depression may include persistent symptoms of moodiness, irritability, anxiety, appetite and sleep disturbance.

It is not unusual for a depressed child to either withdraw from normative interactions or to act out with behavior. When possible, it is important to distinguish whether a child that is acting out is doing so as the result of an emotional disorder or as the result of a behavioral disorder or both. Observations can be helpful in making these distinctions. Depending on the type of depression, medication may or may not be indicated. Certain types of depressions such as those related to adjustment issues are responsive to psychotherapeutic or supportive methods while others are most responsive to combined psychopharmacological and therapeutic measures.

What causes depression? Most contemporary theories related to the biological basis of depression consider either disturbances in neurotransmitter actions, abnormalities in regulation of circadian rhythms or both as playing a fundamental role in the development and maintenance of depression or a depressive state.

Disturbances in Neurotransmitter Actions

The neurotransmitter *serotonin*, for example, is known to affect the behavior at a neuronal level of not only the central and peripheral nervous systems but also the immune, cardiovascular, renal and gastrointestinal systems. Variations in the synthesis, metabolism and transmission of serotonin has been associated with depression, obsessive compulsive disorders, aggression and learning problems. Some of the newer classes of antidepressant medications are referred to as serotonin specific reuptake inhibitors (SSRI's) reflecting the action of the pharmaceutical agents on the neurotransmitter. Figure 4 illustrates how the reuptake of serotonin occurs. The SSRI's inhibit the reuptake allowing more serotonin to remain available within the synapse.

The previous chapter suggested a relationship between aggression, depression, disruptive behavior disorders, conduct disorders and serotonin. It may be helpful to consider these relationships in this section regarding neurotransmitters and

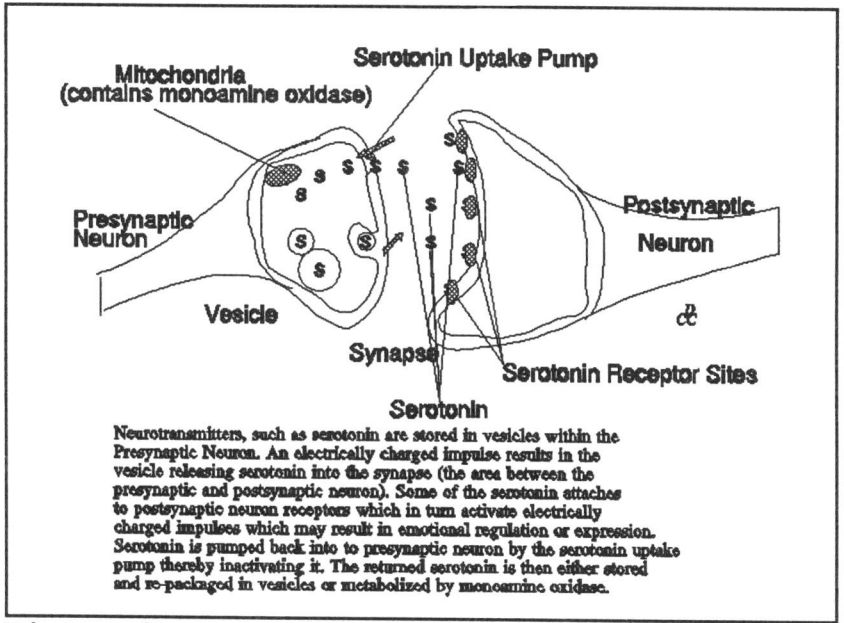

Figure 6

Neurotransmitters, such as serotonin are stored in vesicles within the Presynaptic Neuron. An electrically charged impulse results in the vesicle releasing serotonin into the synapse (the area between the presynaptic and postsynaptic neuron). Some of the serotonin attaches to postsynaptic neuron receptors which in turn activate electrically charged impulses which may result in emotional regulation or expression. Serotonin is pumped back into the presynaptic neuron by the serotonin uptake pump thereby inactivating it. The returned serotonin is then either stored and re-packaged in vesicles or metabolized by monoamine oxidase.

mood disorders. What is the relationship between mood, aggression and impulsive behaviors? While both aggressive and obsessive compulsive disorders may share a common relationship to serotonin, there are clearly different factors that result in their particular manifestations. Serotonergic neurons in general appear to play a role in delaying or inhibiting behavior. Current research is focusing on the delineation of a number of sub-types of serotonergic receptors that suggests multiple variations of serotonergic abnormalities may result in different as well as coexisting disorders. Although there are similarities, there is also evidence that there is a significant difference in serotonergic activity between obsessive compulsive disorder and the disruptive behavior disorders. Despite their differences, compulsive and impulsive behaviors can also be considered as disturbances in impulse control.

One way that the metabolism of serotonin can be measured is in the cerebral spinal fluid. Serotonin (5-HT) is metabolized and becomes a chemical called 5-hydroxyindoleacetic acid (5-HIAA). Levels of 5-HIAA in cerebral spinal fluid are regarded as an indication of central nervous system serotonin metabolism. Low amounts of this metabolite usually indicate reduced formation of serotonin. Suicidality, impulsive violence, cruelty toward animals and arson have all been associated with low concentrations of 5-HIAA in the cerebral spinal fluid. The further understanding of these neurotransmitter systems offer hope of increasingly effective interventions.

Circadian rhythms

Circadian is a term that means related to biological variations or rhythms that have a cycle of about 24 hours. Circadian rhythms help to determine how late we will stay awake and when (or in what condition) we will wake up in the morning. Jet lag is a common disrupter of biological clocks. The circadian clock regulates sleep through a process involving the neuroendocrine system. In this way, circadian rhythms regulate sleep substances such as melatonin, which in turn modulates other hormone secretion, temperature, metabolism, immunoreaction as well as learning and memory consolidation. It is thought that these "sleep substances" such as melatonin may help to normalize the human organism through the regulation of the state of vigilance.

Scientists postulate that light, directly or indirectly, activates circadian genes. Light, for example, synchronizes the circadian rhythm to the external world. It has been shown that when animals are kept in continual darkness, their circadian rhythm will persist in keeping a cycle of approximately 24 hours. Light can reset the circadian clock. Studies of how certain genes react to external stimuli, like light, may help to explain how light and other external stimuli activate neurotransmitters. Neurotransmitter and circadian theories are compatible since most neurotransmitters demonstrate a circadian regulation of their actions. The leading circadian based theory of depression suggests that circadian rhythms in depression represent a loss of stability or strength of the rhythm. According to this view, antidepressants work by

> Individuals who are blind and who do not perceive light may have intervals of insomnia in part due to the lack of light and dark cues to synchronize their circadian rhythms to a 24-hour day. In normal physiology, plasma concentrations of melatonin are expected to play a role in synchronizing the circadian rhythm and to be higher at night than during the day. A study of 11 blind patients, none of whom had the capacity to consciously perceive light, compared with six sighted subjects found that three of the 11 blind individuals had decreases in melatonin plasma concentrations, as do those who are sighted, when exposed to bright light. The eight remaining blind patients did not demonstrate melatonin plasma changes. The investigators concluded that the eyes of some totally blind persons may still communicate ample data regarding light and dark to their brains and as a result synchronize their circadian rhythms.
>
> Charles A. Czeisler, Theresa L. Shanahan, Elizabeth B. Klerman, Heinz Martens, Daniel J. Brotman, Jonathan S. Emens, Torsten Klein and Joseph F. Rizzo III. Suppression of melatonin secretion in some blind patients by exposure to bright light. The New England Journal of Medicine Jan 5 1995, v332, n1, p6(6).

reestablishing the circadian rhythmicity.

Seasonal Affective Disorder

Issues related to the effects of light and dark are directly related to what has been referred to as a *seasonal affective disorder*. The current usage is to identify a seasonal affective component as a related "specifier" of the course of the particular mood disorder. The diagnosis is made even more specific with an additional specifier of with or without full interepisode recovery.

> Dr. H.S. Akiskal at the University of California, San Diego has reported on an 11 year follow-up study of 559 patients sampled from the National Institute of Mental Health's Collaborative Program on the Psychobiology of Depression. Significant findings by Dr. Akiskal and his associates were that a Labile temperament (shifting moods), high degrees of energy and activity and excessive daydreaming and mental activity in those with major depression, defined a cyclothymic profile that is more likely to switch to a bipolar II type of disorder. He points out that despite their depression these individuals may not appear depressed. They are energetic and restless and their moods constantly change, which is more like a mixed bipolar state.
>
> Erik L. Goldman. Clinical Psychiatry News, May 1995.

Dysthymic Disorder

The basic distinction between dysthymic disorder and major depression is that dysthymia refers to a chronically depressed mood and is diagnostically distinguished as the predominant mood for at least 2 years or for a least one year in children and adolescents. Symptom free periods related to dysthymia are not expected to last longer than two months. Dysthymic disorder may be described as early onset if the onset of the dysthymic symptoms occurs before age 21 years. Individuals with early onset dysthymic disorder are also more likely to develop major depressive episodes. Dysthymic disorder frequently has an insidious early onset and tends to be chronic. Dysthymic disorder and major depressive disorder share comparable symptoms. The differences are primarily between onset, duration, persistence, and severity. Major depressive disorder generally is manifested as an episode that is clearly different from the individual's usual functioning.

Depressive symptoms are also associated with other mental disorders such as chronic psychotic disorders and schizophrenia. Depressive symptoms may also be related to a variety of medical conditions. Depressive symptoms can be due to the physiological effects of a medication and in the case of a child or adolescent who is using drugs, drug abuse. The primary depressive symptom seen in dysthymia is a generally depressed mood. Children and adolescents with dysthymia may not have the general appearance of depressed mood but express more prominently an irritable mood.

In children and adolescents a depressive mood lasting more than one year is more likely to represent the pattern associated with dysthymia. The diagnostic categories also accommodate individuals who have "double depression"; that is, dysthymia and major depression. Symptoms associated with dysthymia and a major depressive episode include:

irritability
moodiness
low self-esteem
poor concentration
difficulty making decisions
sleep disturbances
poor appetite or overeating
low energy or fatigue
feelings of hopelessness

It should be noted thst children may not "appear" sad when they are experiencing depression. They may present as more predominantly moody or irritable. As with all "disorders", the symptoms must cause significant disturbance or impairment in social, school (occupational) or other important areas of functioning. Also, the reader will note that coexisting additional diagnoses tend to be the rule and not the exception. Additionally, there are a variety of specific diagnostic sub classifications of mood disorder that will not be addressed in this general overview of mood disorders.

Major Depressive Disorder

Dysthymic Disorder precedes *major depressive disorder* in approximately 10% of the samples observed in population studies and in approximately 15%-25% of those sampled in clinical settings. Other common co-occurring disorders include anxiety disorders and obsessive-compulsive disorder. The basic feature of major depressive disorder is a clinical progression. The clinical progression of major depression is distinguished by one or more major depressive episodes. These episodes occur in the absence of other primary causes such as those that might be related to another disorder or condition. Individuals with severe major depressive disorder are at significant risk for suicide.

An Example of an Adolescent with Major Depression

Ed Depus
age: 15

Ed Depus was a 15 year old male referred for evaluation and psychotherapy by his family physician. Ed was accompanied to his first and subsequent visits by his biological father, Ron Depus. Ed's and his father's primary concern was related to depression. Ed resided with his biological mother Vera Tinse and his step father U.R. Tinse. Ed's biological parents were separated in when Ed was 5 and divorced when he was 6. Ron had regular and frequent contact with Ed and there were no ongoing conflicts of significance between the biological parents. Ed had one male sibling, Fred 18, who also was residing in his mother's home. Ed's biological father had not remarried. Ed's father operated his own small business. Ed's mother aspired to be an artist (watercolors), however, had not completed a painting project in the previous five years. Ed was described as an easy infant with unremarkable early development. Ed attended day care and enjoyed kindergarten but had experienced separation problems. His grade by grade educational adjustment was described as good throughout the years including his completion of his previous year with a 4.00 GPA. Ed's difficulties at the time of the evaluation included sleep onset insomnia, mid-night awakening, concentration difficulties, stomach aches, bossiness, irritability, daily headaches and moodiness. He had no previous psychological or psychiatric evaluations. His family history was positive for depression in the mother, maternal grandmother and paternal grandfather. There was no familial history of epilepsy, and Ed had not been known to have ever had a seizure. Approximately two months prior to the evaluation Ed's family physician began him on Zoloft 50mg once every morning and referred him for evaluation and consultation.

Ed was obviously a bright high functioning young man. He admitted to being perfectionistic and being a worry wart. He described keeping many of his angry feelings to himself and recognized difficulty working in groups or playing team sports. His primary social difficulty resided in his intolerance of other's mistakes. He recognized that he tended to be hypercritical of others and of himself. Ed described himself as hating arguments, being sensitive, being polite and mature. He described his mother as controlling and demanding. He recognized that in many ways he and his mother had similarities. Ed admitted to suicidal ideation prior to beginning the antidepressant, however, indicated no suicidal ideation or inclination at the time of the evaluation. He had felt significant but diminishing benefit since beginning the Zoloft at the 50 milligram a day dosage.

Actuarial assessment and other psychological testing demonstrated the presence of moderate clinical depression and anxiety. He appeared to be overachieving and conforming. Ed's mental status was as follows: He was very well groomed and demonstrated a mildly restricted and at times, anxious affect. His mood was described as elevated as compared to the pre-medication state, however, remained mildly depressed. There was no evidence of thought disorder, delusions or hallucinations. Ed had excellent insight and was motivated to challenge his self-demanding behaviors.

DSM-IV Diagnostic Impression:
Axis I
296.22 Major Depressive Disorder
300.02 Generalized Anxiety Disorder with obsessive compulsive personality traits
Axis II
V71.09
Axis III
None
Axis IV
Minimal
Axis V
GAF 80 current

Recommendations:
It appears that Ed will benefit from both continued biological and psychotherapeutic interventions. Based on Ed's history and assessment an increase in his medication is indicated.

Dr. I.B. Helpin

An Example of a Child with Major Depression

Anne Hadonic
age: 7.5

In describing why Anne was being seen for evaluation and treatment Anne's father, John, and her step mother, Mary, reported "We're concerned about her behavior". Anne's residence was with her biological father, step mother and 12 year old step-sister. Anne's biological parents were divorced shortly after her birth and Anne has had no contact with her biological mother. Anne's biological mother was described as having a history of bipolar disorder (or possible schizophrenia). A family history of alcoholism and other mental illness was also endorsed. The pregnancy of Anne was complicated by the biological mother having been on psychotropic medications (unspecified) until the pregnancy was confirmed. Anne was described by her father as having been born with "small fetal size". At the time of the evaluation Anne attended a local elementary school and was in the 2nd grade. John describes Anne as a normal infant and reported that she attended preschool and loved it, attended kindergarten and liked it, had problems with peers in the 1st grade and has been unhappy in the 2nd grade. Symptoms included learning difficulties, bossiness, irritability, impulsivity, difficulty concentrating, behavior problems at home and school, defiance, no friends, moodiness, inattention, frequent crying, immaturity and aggression. Anne's father indicated no history of seizures or previous medications for emotional or behavioral issues. Three years previous, Anne had a minor head injury caused by a fall off of a swing set. She hit the back of her head, was seen by a physician and had no apparent enduring ill effects. Over the year prior to the evaluation Anne's father and step mother noted increased irritability, distractibility and declining school performance.

Anne appeared appropriately groomed and displayed a depressed and guarded affect. Her facial expressions had a restricted range of expression. Her observed mood appeared congruent with the tone of the self report. Anne appeared oriented to time, place and person and reported and displayed no unusual perceptions.

Anne's content of thought centered around problems with friends and feelings of anxiety. Her recent and remote memory appeared intact and age normative. Her retention and immediate recall appeared intact as well. Anne was able to accomplish basic simple counting and calculations and demonstrated an apparent age appropriate fund of general knowledge.

Anne's actuarial and projective assessments suggested that her current general emotional and behavioral state was moderately to severely maladaptive. Anne's PIC profile demonstrated clinically significant elevations on numerous clinical scales. The configuration and degree of elevations present suggested the presence of major affective disorder, a coexisting behavioral and personality disturbance, depression, anxiety, mild hyperactivity or hypomania, possible underlying psychotic trends or borderline personality adjustment, significant withdrawal, the presence of vegetative symptoms, academic impairment, current acting out and poor social skills.

Diagnostic Impression:
Axis I
296.20 Major Depression Disorder
313.81 Oppositional Defiant Disorder
314.01 Attention Deficit Hyperactivity Disorder
Rule out
296.70 Bipolar Disorder NOS
Axis II
799.90 Diagnosis deferred
AXIS III
NONE
AXIS IV
Psychosocial Stressors:
Severity: 3-Moderate
AXIS V
Current GAF: 55
Highest GAF past year:60

It appeared that Anne would benefit from an initial antidepressant trial of imipramine with continued monitoring and evaluation of treatment response. Family issues of significance included consistency of parental direction and discipline, sibling relationships, issues related to an absent biological mother and over protective, indulging grandparents. Personality characteristics were a focus of individual psychotherapy included oppositionalism, withdrawal, avoidance, shyness, low self esteem, fear of failure, poor frustration tolerance and impulse control.

Carla Jung, M.D., Ph.D.

Cyclothymia

The disorder referred to as cyclothymia is syndrome that resembles depression and mania but without the severity, duration or the numbers of symptoms necessary to meet those diagnostic criteria. Cyclothymia has been proposed as being at least as common as bipolar disorder. Cyclothymia can be thought of as on a continuum with bipolar disorder at the upper limit and normal mood swings at the lower limit. It has been reported that many patients with bipolar disorder have had a history of preceding cyclothymia. One of the difficulties with the diagnosis of cyclothymia and as previously mentioned, the limits of diagnostic labeling, is the fact that many mental disorders present with mood swings. Defining the boundaries between depressive disorders, cyclothymia, bipolar disorder, borderline personality disorders and schizoaffective disorders is fraught with complexity, variance among professionals and in some cases, controversy. These fuzzy boundaries, the reality of our incomplete understanding and knowledge regarding these disorders, and the resulting imprecise definitions we employ require us to ultimately view treatment from a practical point of view. The degree of impairment or potential for the impairment "worsening" has much to do with designing initial treatment strategies. Response or the lack of a response to treatment doesn't necessarily confirm or discount a particular diagnosis but does provide important data from which to assess treatment response or alternate trials.

Bipolar Disorders

A major issue regarding bipolar disorder and unipolar disorders (ie. major depression) is whether they are in fact two separate disorders or variations of one. Kraepelin, in 1921, first recognized the "bipolarity" of *affective disorders* when he described the nature of manic depressive illness. Since those early conceptions of bipolar illness, there have been many refinements and attempts at greater understanding. G.L. Klerman, for example, described six variations of elevated moods to define the manic states. These included normal states of happiness and joy, elation, hypomania (a mild state of mania), non-psychotic mania, psychotic mania and delirious mania. Hypomania is a non-psychotic expansive, irritable or elevated mood. Mania is an emotional disorder typified by heightened psychomotor activity, decreased need for sleep, excitement, racing thoughts (flight of ideas) and unstable attention. Bipolar disorders have also been categorized as Bipolar I, Bipolar II and Bipolar III.

Bipolar I disorder is a descriptor of the classic manic depressive illness, in which, the individual has had at least one episode of mania with or without a history of depression. Some research definitions require that at least one depressive episode has also occurred. Increasingly, mental health professionals have found it valuable to differentiate between Bipolar I and Bipolar II disorders. Individuals with Bipolar I disorder endure episodes of depression and mania as compared to those with Bipolar II who experience brief hypomanic episodes and episodes of major depression. A criteria has been suggested that hypomania lasting at least two days can be considered a "probable" episode while hypomania lasting a week is a definite hypomanic episode. Bipolar III disorder has been used to identify a small subgroup of individuals that "appear" to demonstrate manic symptoms subsequent to treatment with antidepressant medication. It is impossible to clearly separate or assign this "polarity switch" to the effects of medication, since those with bipolar disorder may cycle to mania or hypomania even without medication. Nevertheless, antidepressant medications have been associated with "triggering" a switch from depression to hypomania or mania in a small percentage of individuals. With this in mind it is wise for those beginning an antidepressant trial to be aware of the possibility of precipitating a non-desirable elevated state. If this occurs, the prescribing physician should be consulted in order to revise or adjust the treatment approach.

Common Problems and Current Controversies

A child presenting with bipolar illness frequently becomes a complex treatment challenge. The early onset of the illness often suggests a more severe form of the disorder. As has been emphasized throughout the text, the developmental and dynamic nature of children also cause many professionals to be very cautious if not overly cautious in both the diagnosis and/or treatment of children. This has resulted in controversy among those who believe in early recognition and treatment versus those who either recognize the disorder but advise against biological treatment or those who cling to the idea that bipolar disorder is either very rare or non-existent in children. There is a presumably small number of professionals who recognize children with bipolar disorder but who choose not to accept the degree of treatment difficulty and risk associated with this population of disturbed children who are impulsive and often have poor judgement.

It was previously stated that a diagnosis cannot be confirmed as the result of a treatment response. Even so, lack of response tends to cause one to reconsider the fundamental diagnosis and treatment strategies. For example, in the case of a child who is hyperactive and has poor attention, does the child have an attention deficit hyperactivity disorder or does the child have a bipolar disorder? Does the child have an attention deficit disorder and a major depressive episode or does the child have an attention deficit disorder and bipolar disorder? It is also possible that a child has a primary disorder that has become "environmentally complicated". That is, if a child has attention deficit disorder he or she may alienate others, develop low self esteem and become dysthymic or depressed. Given successful early intervention the child would be expected to self correct many of those prior behaviors and ultimately be less depressed and increasingly less affected by the ill effects of the disorder. If that child does not respond to standard interventions, that may suggest that the initial working diagnosis was incomplete or incorrect. The bipolar disordered child is frequently a child who has not responded to numerous other treatment approaches.

Treatment of Mood Disorders

It is always desirable to utilize the least invasive, least restrictive and most effective methods when approaching the treatment of any emotional or behavioral problem. In general terms, cognitive behavioral therapy addresses the facets of depression that result in distorted self perceptions. Perceptual distortions associated with mood disorders, often have an outcome of the individual making global, negative self attributions and having low self esteem. Cognitive behavioral therapy with mood disordered children focuses on changing the way the individual looks at things (cognitive restructuring) as a method of modifying the child's distorted assumptions, perceptions and thinking. Frequently, non-pharmacological methods have been attempted (in some cases, exhausted) prior to consultation with a physician. If not, careful behavioral methods and observation will provide direction regarding whether further options such as medical consultation or pharmacotherapy are indicated.

When pharmacological methods are required, it is most effective to combine those efforts with other non-pharmacological interventions such as play therapy, behavioral approaches and cognitive behavioral therapy. Pharmacological interventions, behavioral methods, cognitive behavioral therapy and play therapy will be further described and illustrated in Chapter 10.

Test your knowledge about bipolar disorder. The answers are at the end of the chapter.

1. A survey of people with bipolar disorder by the National Depressive and Manic Depressive Association (NDMDA) found that on average respondents did not receive a correct diagnosis for:
    a. 2-6 months
    b. 1 year
    c. 5 years
    d. 8 years

2. In the NDMDA survey ___ of the respondents reported suffering their first symptoms during childhood or adolescence.
    a. 5%
    b. 18%
    c. 59%
    d. 65%

3. According to Akiskal ___ of the outpatients presenting with Major Depressive disorder develop bipolar disorder.
    a. .2%
    b. none
    c. some
    d. 20%

4. Strober and Carlson (1982) studied 60 adolescents ages 13-16 over a four year prospective study. Of the 60 adolescents ___ (___) switched from major depressive disorder to bipolar disorder during the study period.
    a. 20% (12)
    b. 10% (6)
    c. 30% (18)
    d. 5% (3)

5. Strober and Carlson (1982) determined that within their study those most likely to switch had:
   a. Rapid onset of symptoms, psychomotor retardation, mood congruent psychotic symptoms.
   b. Three generation family history of bipolar disorder
   c. medication-induced hypomania.
   d. b and c
   e. a,b and c

6. Peter Hauser and colleagues evaluated the presence and severity of attention deficit hyperactivity disorder in 18 families with a history of generalized resistance to thyroid hormone. Among the children resistant to thyroid hormone ___ and ___ of the unaffected subjects met criteria for ADHD.
   a. 46% and 5%
   b. 39% and 10%
   c. 10% and 1%
   d. 70% and 20%

7. Gabrielle A. Carlson, Shmuel Fennig and Evelyn Bromet in a 1994 Journal of the American Academy of Child and Adolescent Psychiatry report state:
   a. Bipolar disorder in youth is over-diagnosed.
   b. Oppositional defiant disorder is under-diagnosed.
   c. ECT is effective in treating acute psychotic episodes.
   d. Bipolar disorder in youth is under-diagnosed.

8. Barbara Geller and associates studied the rates and predictors of prepubertal bipolarity during follow-up of 6- to 12 year old depressed children. The results of her study included:
   a. Bipolarity rarely develops during prepubertal development
   b. Multigenerational family history was significantly associated with bipolar I and bipolarity developed at a mean age of 11.2 years.
   c. 80% with bipolar onset were prepubertal
   d. 31.7% of the children with MDD developed bipolarity.
   e. b, c and d.

9. Charles Popper, M.D., Editor of the Journal of Child and Adolescent Psychopharmacology made distinctions between ADHD and bipolar disorder. Some his distinctions included.
   a. ADHD children display "non-angry destructiveness".
   b. ADHD children usually calm down from anger outbursts and temper tantrums within 20-30 minutes. Bipolar children may continue to feel and act angry over 30 minutes and for up to 2-4 hours.
   c. Children with ADHD do not generally show dysphoria.
   d. a and b
   e. all of the above

10. Overlapping symptoms of ADHD and Mania include distractibility, physical restlessness and talkativeness. Wozniak (1993) distinguished between 44 children with mania versus 180 with ADHD. Findings included:
   a. ADHD criteria do not include a mood component.
   b. The clinical course of prepubertal mania was predominantly irritable, mixed (depression) and chronic.
   c. Children with prepubertal mania are most effectively treated psychodynamically.
   d. a and c
   e. a and b

11. The following structured interviews, tests and scales are useful in identifying and distinguishing between various childhood and adolescent psychiatric disorders, including depression, ADHD and bipolar disorder.
   a. The Personality Inventory for Children -Revised
   b. The Systematic Observation Scale
   c. Connor's Rating Scales
   d. The Minnesota Multiphasic Personality Inventory-Adolescents
   e. None of the above
   f. a, b, c and d

12. The statement that there is evidence that juvenile mood disorders may be more refractory to pharmacologic interventions than the adult disorders is:
    a. True
    b. False

13. There is documentation that there are seasonal variations in peak occurrences of Mania and Depression.
    a. Mania is most likely to occur in September
    b. Mania is most likely to occur in August
    c. Depression is most likely to occur in January
    d. Depression is most likely to occur in March
    e. a and d
    f. b and d
    g. b and c

14. Lifetime expectancy of bipolar disorders is reported as ranging from .24% to approximately 7%. Additionally,:
    a. males outnumber females 3 to 1
    b. 15 to 30 % of bipolars have onset by age 19.
    c. Females with BPD have a higher incident of ulcers.
    d. Prepubertal onset suggests a milder form of illness.

Answers to Quiz
1.D, 2.C, 3.D, 4.A, 5.E, 6.D, 7.D, 8.E, 9.E, 10.E, 11.F, 12.A, 13.E, 14.B.

Chapter Eight

Anxiety and Movement Disorders

Anxiety Disorders

Anxiety disorders can overlap and coexist with certain depressive and obsessive-compulsive difficulties. Movement disorders, such as Tourette's disorder and tic disorders have been included in this chapter due to their biological relationship to obsessive compulsive disorders. In some cases it can be very difficult to distinguish between the more dominant symptom clusters. Acute anxiety reactions, for example, may reflect the presence of an underlying major depression. Once again, this is a very complex topic that must be limited to a general discussion.

One of the most common elements of a childhood anxiety disorder is an anxious parent. It is hard not to be anxious, however, when your child complains of severe abdominal pain or demonstrates a "panic" type of reaction. If there are no medical findings a parent often becomes even more anxious. It is important to analyze any elements that may support or reinforce a child's anxieties. If a parent is quick to allow a child to stay home when ill, a child may begin to use illness as an avoidance mechanism. A visit to your physician to rule out any medical illness is the first order of business.

In the absence of medical findings, persistent school refusal is one of the most common manifestations of what is referred to as separation anxiety disorder. This disorder can be significantly impairing. It is critical that the child be placed back in school as quickly as feasible. A helpful criteria for a child who has an absence of medical findings with persistent physical complaints is to send them to school unless they have a fever.

As with all avoidance behaviors, the more something is avoided the more anxious the individual becomes. The parent who attempts to rescue their child from their discomfort will inadvertently make things worse. It can be helpful for a parent to simply, firmly and matter of factly reassure a child while expecting them to continue their normal routines. While it is important to avoid reinforcing maladaptive, anxious behaviors inadvertently, it is also important to recognize, that in some cases, children can be disturbed and anxious to a severe degree. The child who cannot return to his or her normal routines should receive a professional assessment.

What Frightens "Normal" Children

An Associated Press report of a survey by KidsPeace (U.S. Kids frightened about Future. Associated Press, Washington, May 11, 1995) reflects some significant anxieties among this national randomized sample of 1,023 children. The poll has a plus or minus 3 percentage points margin of error. The following are some of the KidsPeace Survey's findings:

65% think their parents might die.
57% fear doing poorly in school.
54% fear they may contract AIDS
53% are afraid of poverty.
51% feel they might die.
50% are afraid they will be kidnapped.
47% feel their parents may not "be available".
45% fear sexual or physical abuse.
43% fear bullies.
42% expect they won't get married or have children.
41% consider they may get involved in drugs.
40% are afraid they won't have any close friends.
40% think they may start using alcohol.
38% are afraid their parents may divorce.
38% think they might start smoking cigarettes.

KidsPeace (U.S. Kids frightened about Future. Associated Press, Washington, May 11, 1995)

Types of Anxiety Disorders

Anxiety disorders include panic disorder, agoraphobia, specific phobias, social phobia, obsessive-compulsive disorder, generalized anxiety disorder, anxiety disorder resulting from a medical condition and substance use causing an anxiety disorder. Many consider post trauma and stress reactions to be anxiety disorders as well, however, they are included in this text within the chapter on adjustment disorders.

Panic attacks are states that have a distinct duration in which a sudden onset of intense fearfulness, terror, or feelings of impending doom occur. Panic attacks are frequently accompanied by symptoms such as chest pain, choking sensations, shortness of breath and heart palpitations. The person experiencing a panic state may feel that they are going to die or that they may otherwise lose control. Agoraphobia refers to an anxiety regarding places or situations. The individual with agoraphobia may or may not also have panic attacks. Those with agoraphobia generally avoid places that may be difficult to leave or obtain help should they experience a panic attack. In panic disorder without agoraphobia there is persistent concern about and occurrence of unexpected panic attacks.

Specific phobias are characterized by significant anxiety focused on a specific circumstance or object. Phobic anxiety results in avoidance or attempted avoidance of the circumstance or object. Social phobia also leads to avoidance behaviors and is distinguished by significant anxiety provoked by exposure to particular social or performance circumstances. Obsessive compulsive disorder typically includes obsessions (causing anxiety or distress) and/or by compulsions (which tend to counter anxiety). Generalized anxiety disorder is defined as not less than six months of continuing, excessive anxiety and worry. Anxiety disorders may also be due to a general medical condition. Some anxiety disorders are a reflection of direct physiological consequence of drug abuse, a medication, toxin exposure or other substance exposure.

Anxiety disorders can also have their onset in childhood. Separation anxiety disorder is an example. Separation anxiety disorder is generally seen as anxiety related to separation from parental figures. Anxious temperaments may be seen as early as in the newborn. Shortly after birth some infants demonstrate an inclination toward anxiety and a tendancy to overreact to stimulation. Parenting practices, however, are a significant determinant as to whether those babies become anxious children and adults. As with all of the disorders, early experience and genetics interact to shape behavior for a lifetime. Innate qualities have a significant, but apparently not an overriding influence on the later development of anxiety disorders in children and adults. Jerome Kagan, Ph.D., and Doreen Arcus, Ph.D., Harvard psychologists, have examined hundreds of babies whom they have followed for up to five years. Dr. Arcus reported at an American Psychiatric Association meeting that of those parents who dictated clear boundaries on their children's conduct, none of the infants considered overexcitable as an infant showed signs of being fearful at age two. This is in contrast to the over 40 percent of other highly reactive infants that were seen at age two to be inhibited, avoidant, crying and exhibiting distress when exposed to unfamiliar objects, people or events.

At the same conference Dr. Michael Liebowitz, psychiatrist and head of Columbia University's unit on panic disorders, related that he finds that a high ratio of patients with panic disorder report having had a parent or parents who were overprotective. Both of these professionals point out the mistake of attempting to shield children from stressful situations increases the likelihood of developing an anxious child. When children are allowed to manage their own day-to-day difficulties they become more resilient and learn coping strategies. The parental balancing act is never ending with the parent having to decide when to support independence and when to provide limits. At first glance, overprotection might appear as a parent setting limits. Instead, overprotection, generally involves the parent taking responsibility for the child in ways that rob the child of the learning experience. It is a logical outcome that overprotective parents will increase the likelihood that they will parent a child who is poorly prepared for self responsibility and self confidence.

The biology of panic disorder has been extensively studied with mixed results. Much of these investigations began after it was discovered that administration of sodium lactate would induce a panic attack in 50-70% of individuals with panic disorder while it would induce a panic attack in less than 10% of healthy control subjects. Even so, lactate's relationship to panic disorder, like most everything else that will be considered in this text, it not quite that simple. Lactate is a respiratory stimulant and the hyperventilation that follows it's administration may suggest that panic disorder is related to an abnormality in respiratory function. Current respiratory hypotheses under consideration include speculation that carbon dioxide sensitivity may have a role in panic disorder and that in some individuals they are incorrectly sensing imminent suffocation. There are also noradrenergic, serotonergic, hypothalamic-pituitary-thyroid axis and other neurobiological hypotheses models that have been suggested as related to panic disorder. Despite these various hypothetical models of the biology of panic disorder, cognitive behavioral therapy has been demonstrated to reduce panic disordered individuals' panic response to lactate infusion. The effectiveness of pharmacotherapy with panic disorder has also been established for several decades.

Separation anxiety is part of normal development in children, however, lessens in late infancy and is absent in most children by the time they begin school. Some children will express this anxiety briefly and it will not persist. Younger children may cling and cry expressing fear that something may happen to the parental figure. Older children may focus on physical complaints. A pattern of several, recurring physiological complaints requiring treatment may represent a somatization disorder. Separation anxiety disorder co-exists with depression in as many as 30-70% of children.

Somatization Disorder

An Example of Somatization and Separation Anxiety Disorder

Name: Mona Lutt
age: 10

Mona Lutt is a 10 year old female referred for evaluation, treatment recommendations and psychotherapy by her family physician. Mona was accompanied to her first and subsequent visits by her biological mother, DeeDee Lutt. Mona's and her mother's primary concern is related to chronic "stomach problems" and anxiety. Mona resides with her biological mother DeeDee and her maternal grandparents. Mona's biological parents were divorced in 1991. Johnnie Lutt is Mona's biological father. For the first three years after the divorce Mona stayed with him every other weekend and one month in the summer. Over the past year, however, Mona has not wanted to stay overnight at his house. Johnnie has remarried and his current wife's name is Lorraine. Mona has a 12 year old sibling, Robyn, and 2 younger half siblings, Allen, 3 and Megan, 1 and a half. Mona states that she likes her step mother and that she enjoys visits with her father but just doesn't like to stay overnight any more. Mona's birth was a planned caesarean section, she was described as an easy infant with unremarkable early development. Mona loved kindergarten and her grade by grade subsequent adjustment was described as "okay" until last year at which time her grades went down.

Mona's current difficulties include daily stomach aches, some trouble concentrating, moodiness, she cries easily, she's demanding at home, excessive worry about her mother, at times she has a poor appetite, at times she is withdrawn, she is shy, she is a light sleeper and she sometimes fears that she is having a heart attack. Mona has attempted to spend the night with friends and has become anxious and gone home. Mona has had no previous psychiatric or psychological evaluations. Family history is positive for depression in the paternal grandfather (which was medication responsive), possible alcoholism in a grandparent, bipolar illness in a maternal nephew and, significantly, panic disorder in the maternal grandmother, three maternal aunts and in one maternal uncle. There is no familial history of epilepsy and Mona has not been known to ever have had a seizure. Mona has been prescribed medication for spastic colon. She has not been on any other medications other than for general childhood illnesses.

Mona is an obviously bright, high functioning child. She admits to being anxious and she and her mother agree that her difficulties have worsened over the past year. She currently will not sleep alone, however, and says that she wants to. She worries that her mother will be robbed at work and describes her mother as being overprotective. Actuarial assessment and other psychological testing demonstrate the presence of moderate clinical somatization and anxiety. Mona's mental status is as follows: She was well groomed and demonstrated a bright but anxious affect. Her current mood is described as euthymic and mildly labile. There is no evidence of thought disorder, delusions or hallucinations. Mona has excellent insight and is motivated to deal with her anxious behaviors.

DSM-IV Diagnostic Impression:
Axis I
300.81 Somatization Disorder
300.01 Panic Disorder without agoraphobia
309.21 Separation anxiety disorder
Rule out prodrome of depressive disorder
Axis II V71.09
Axis III None
Axis IV Minimal
Axis V GAF 80 current

Recommendations:
It appears that Mona will benefit from both biological and psychotherapeutic interventions. Based on Mona's history and current assessment it appears that she is an excellent candidate for an imipramine trial. My recommendation is to obtain an EKG, initiate an imipramine trial of 25mg at bedtime for 7 days and then 50mg each night. If this is agreeable with her primary physician, I will provide psychotherapy and treatment monitoring throughout the medication trial. Mona's small stature may tend to cause others to treat her as younger than she is. It is also likely that others within her household heighten her anxiety with their own anxiety. Mona is most probably correct in her assessment that she is overprotected. Nevertheless, Mona has certainly come to the point of being impaired.

Allison Ellis, Ph.D.

Generalized Anxiety Disorder

Generalized anxiety disorder, considering current diagnostic conventions, refers not only to conditions seen in adults, but also represents what had previously been referred to as overanxious disorder of childhood. The primary characteristic of generalized anxiety is worry that is extreme and becomes difficult to moderate. The clinical disorder is one that is present more days than it is absent and is present for at a minimum, 6 months. This worry that is excessive for the circumstance is frequently present along with further features such as difficulty concentrating, irritability, restlessness, becoming easily tired and sleep disturbances. The essential impairment that is a result of generalized anxiety disorder is due to the interference of anxious thoughts with general functioning. Children with this disorder may worry unreasonably over their performance or ability. The highlight of worry may change from one issue to another. Generalized anxiety disorder is often found co-occurring with depressive disorders and other anxiety disorders such as panic disorder or social phobia.

Obsessive Compulsive Disorder

Obsessive compulsive disorder (OCD) is distinguished by the inability to restrain intrusive, repetitive thoughts and/or actions. *Obsessions* are reappearing intrusive thoughts, ideas, urges or images. These intrusions are experienced as spontaneous and excessive. Obsessions produce anxiety because they are recognized as being unrealistic, excessive or otherwise incompatible with the individual's general view of reasonableness. *Compulsions* are repeated behaviors that are purposeful and ritualistic. Compulsions are expressed as an attempt to reduce anxiety. In most cases the individual is aware that their compulsive acts, which are frequently in response to their obsessions, are unrealistic or excessive.

Younger children experiencing OCD symptoms may not recognize that their fears are unreasonable. Their fear that a droplet of insect spray will not contaminate them or harm them once washed off, may be difficult for them to discern as they become anxious. Likewise a child who is obsessed about being separated from his or her parent may fear that harm will come to either him or her or his or her parent, if they are separated. This may present initially as a separation anxiety disorder. The features required to diagnose OCD, the presence of compulsions or obsessions, may not be obvious initially.

Frequently, a ritualistic compulsion brings about concerns and recognition of a need for intervention. Common obsessions in OCD include obsessions about contamination, cleanliness, religion, aggression and illness. Compulsive rituals may include such things as excessive washing, checking, repeating and ordering. A young person with OCD symptoms, for example, might demand that they wear a plastic glove before touching a doorknob or item that has been used by others. Some children unrealistically fear they will contract diabetes or other illness by touching or even being near someone who is diabetic or has an illness. Despite a recognition that a fear may be unreasonable, the symptoms persist and can be significantly impairing.

The complexity of mental disorders is found in most diagnostic categories. The complexity arises, in part, due to the many combinations of genetic and environmental influences. Like many other disorders there is a genetic component to OCD, although OCD is not entirely genetic. Twin studies have demonstrated that identical twins have a co-occurrence rate of approximately 50% indicating that their are additional factors beyond the genetic contribution that are at play. Early age of onset is more often associated with persons who have a family history of OCD. On the environmental side of the balance, recent studies have identified an infection-triggered subtype of OCD and Tourette's syndrome. Obsessive compulsive disorder subsequent to brain injury has also been reported.

The neurobiology of OCD is a very promising area of current investigation. Considering the neurobiology of OCD, it is interesting to note some similarity to other disorders and the rates of co-morbidity (co-occurrence) in this regard. For example, there are high rates of co-occurrence of disruptive disorders, mood disorders, anxiety disorders and tic disorders among those with OCD. There are also other neurobiological correlates among OCD, mood disorders and disruptive disorders; most notably, serotonergic functioning. Previous chapters have indicated evidence of low levels of serotonin being related to disruptive behaviors, aggression and depressive mood states. A fascinating example of the role of serotonin in OCD has been shown by the "anti-obsessional" effects of the serotonin specific re-uptake inhibitors that are independent of the antidepressant actions.

Another neurobiological area of investigation has to do with regional brain metabolism related to OCD. Current studies report a pre-frontal cerebral abnormality involved in the *neuropathophysiology* of OCD. There also appears to be a *lateralization* of the frontal cortex abnormalities. The right frontal cortex is thought to be particularly involved with the perception and reaction to negative emotions. Gordon Harris and his colleagues recently furthered the evidence of these abnormalities and pointed out that there may be a disequilibrium between right and left frontal lobe performance. OCD was correlated to right frontal overactivity, and depression was related to left hemisphere underactivity. Both of these findings may be a reflection of abnormal serotonergic functioning.

Further explorations of the neuroanatomy of OCD by Baxter, Schwartz and Bergman (1992) established significant correlations of orbital cortex activity with the caudate nucleus and the thalamus before treatment for obsessive compulsive disoder. Subsequently, the correlations were absent in those who responded to treatment. Baxter and his group also noted differences in glucose metabolism in caudate nucleus (on the right) associated with successful treatment. Additional findings continue to favor a neuroanatomical theory of obsessive compulsive disorder. Rauch, Jenike, Alpert and others (1994), reported increased relative cerebral blood flow during a symptomatic obsessive compulsive state opposed to the resting state. The increased flow was noted in the right caudate nucleus, the left anterior cingulate cortex, and bilateral orbitofrontal cortex.

It appears that obsessive compulsive disorder can also result from injuries or lesions that are confined to orbitofrontal areas of each hemisphere. An interesting case was reported by Jeffrey E. Max, Wilbur L. Smith Jr., Scott D. Lindgren, Donald A. Robin, Philip Mattheis, Julie Stierwalt and Mary Morrisey in 1995. They reported on a case of obsessive compulsive disorder following brain injury in an 11 year old child. At a three month post-injury evaluation, the child had acquired compulsive hand washing. She also engaged in other ritualistic behaviors involving counting, ordering and arranging. She became uncharacteristically ordered about her room and would become mad if items were moved or touched by others. The child became perfectionistic in schoolwork whereas she had previously been careless in her work.

After a period of a year the child was essentially free of the OCD behaviors, however, she did have persistent difficulties with aggression and *disinhibition* that was not present before her injury. Disinhibition is the inability to inhibit impulses. The classic example of disinhibition as a result of frontal lobe damage was made known by an accident that occured during railroad construction. While tamping dynamite into a blasting hole, a railway worker named Phineus Gage was struck by the tamping rod when there was a premature explosion. The tamping rod became a projectile and shot through the worker's skull and brain, exiting on the other side. Mr. Gage survived the accident, but not without a nearly total change in his personality. Mr. Gage had been well liked and moderate before his accident. Afterwards he became vulgar, impulsive and aggessive. This brings us back again to the similarities between compulsive disorders and impulse control disorders.

Many who suffer from obsessive compulsive disorder experience episodic waxing and waning of symptoms. This has also been noted in Tourette's and other tic disorders. Albert J. Allen, Henrietta L. Leonard and Susan E. Swedo, in 1995, identified a subset of children whose course of symptoms were characterized by abrupt onset succeeded by a slow decline of symptoms over months. These children displayed movements that were noted by the investigators as similar to those seen in Sydenham's chorea. It has also been reported that individuals with Sydenham's chorea often describe an appearance of obsessions and compulsions along with the movement symptoms.

Dr. Swedo reported a case in which she made the diagnosis of acute rheumatic fever with Sydenham's chorea. This included the presence of inflammation of the heart muscle, involuntary movements, incoordination and a prior streptococcal infection. She theorized that Sydenham's chorea might suffice as a physiological model for obsessive compulsive disorder. The movement disorder of Sydenham's chorea also appears related to tic disorders. Tic-like movements were observed in patients with Sydenham's over 100 years ago. Contemporary studies have discovered patients with increased tics after a community outbreak of streptococcal pharyngitis. Dr. Swedo and her colleauges have proposed a hypothesis that suggests that therapy altering immune function may benefit some children with acute and severe aggravation of obsessive compulsive disorder and Tourette's disorder.

An Example of Obsessive Compulsive Disorder

Name: Rich U. Listick
Age:13

Rich and his parents were referred for evaluation and treatment by his pediatrician. Rich's parent's inidcated that their primary concern was related to Rich being uncooperative, anxious over what they considered minor things and bizarre fears.

Rich's parent's described that Rich refused to touch doorknobs, bedsheets or many other objects without having some type of protective plastic over his hands. Rich also had many other "habits" that the family had tended to allow in order to avoid Rich's predictable, hysterical behavior when not allowed. Rich was also a compulsive handwasher. Rich had become increasingly impaired with difficulty in all domains of his life. He was not regularly attending school, he had been ostracized by most of his peers and he is became increasingly detached from his parents and siblings. Rich believed in aliens and was obsessed about alien contacts. Rich's parents were anxious, angry and confused.

Rich had been an above average student until about the 6th grade at which time his grades began declining and he became increasingly preoccupied with contamination fears. He also avoided homework but read books about aliens as quickly as he could find them. He became identified by his peers at school and within his neighborhood as "really weird". At the time of the evaluation Rich's parents were providing him with boxes of sandwich bags that served as his constant supply of plastic "gloves". They were also involved in many of his other rituals, in that they washed foods in particular ways and allowed him, in general, to maintain his compulsive behaviors.

Rich participated in an evaluation and was aware of his surroundings, aware of his difficulties and in fact recognized the irrationality of his contamination beliefs. Although he did not appear psychotic or delusional, he did indicate that he believed in aliens. The clinical assessment was made that Rich had become accustomed to eliciting dramatic responses or concerns by sharing this belief. The examiner responded by stating matter-of-factly, that he believes that while there may be life in another galaxy or universe, he has no belief and has seen no evidence that any extraterrestrial life form has been discovered. Rich argued the point weakly and ultimately reduced the certainty of his belief.

Rich's clinical assessment and testing were consistent with a diagnosis of obsessive compulsive disorder.

Diagnosis:
Obsessive Compulsive Disorder

Recommendations:
Family therapy was recommended and aimed at discontinuing any support or reinforcement for compulsive behaviors. Parents were advised to not provide him with plastic bags and to respond in a matter-of-fact manner if he brings up aliens, ghosts or similar concerns. Their response was recommended to be along the lines of "I've told you I don't share that belief; you need to complete your responsibilities

whether you believe that or not". They were then instructed to refuse to continue any debate or argument. Individual therapy was aimed at self monitoring and encouraging exposure techniques such as touching dirty objects and not allowing himself frequent handwashing. Psychiatric consultation was also recommended in order to combine a biological intervention.

Grady X. Posure, Ph.D.

Tourette's and Movement Disorders

Tourette's disorder, similar to obsessive compulsive disorder, is shaped by genetic and environmental factors. Tourette's disorder is typically diagnosed in children and frequently persists throughout the lifespan. Characteristics of Tourette's disorder include repetitious motor and vocal tics that are often combined with obsessive compulsive symptoms or symptoms of attention deficit hyperactivity disorder. Tourette's disorder and related tic disorders are, in part, inherited. Genetic transmission occurs in an autosomal dominant pattern. Fetal environmental conditions also play a role.

The median age at onset of Tourette's is 7 years of age. The prevalence is 0.3 to 0.5 per 1000 population. Male children are up to 9 times more likely to have Tourette's while adult males are about three to four times more common than females. In many circumstances the tics persist throughout life, although there is frequently a decrease in the intensity of symptoms following puberty. Tourette's disorder includes multiple motor and one or more vocal tics that occur during the course of the illness. Tics occur daily, or nearly daily, and vary in frequency over the course of at least a year. Anatomic locations, frequency and severity of tics vary over time. Tourette's disorder and related tic disorders comprise a spectrum of related disorders ranging from transient motor and vocal tic disorders to Tourette's disorder. Neuroimaging studies focusing on the basal ganglia have found preliminary evidence of subtle structural abnormalities.

A chronic motor or vocal tic is similar to Tourette's except it involves only a single motor or vocal tic. A transient tic disorder generally occurs many times a day for at least four weeks but for no longer than 12 months. The transient tic disorder is only diagnosed when there is no history of Tourette's disorder or chronic motor or vocal tic disorder.

Treatment of Tourette's and Tics

Pharmacological interventions have been available for Tourette's disorder and chronic tic disorders for the last three decades. Clinical management centers on distinguishing target symptoms. Although tics may be the most blatant indication, attention deficit hyperactivity disorder and depression may be more impairing. Tics generally respond to low doses of haloperidol or pimozide (which block dopamine and are referred to as dopamine antagonists). Clonidine has also been demonstrated as advantageous, even though it is probably less effective than the dopamine antagonists. Pharmacological interventions will be discussed more thoroughly in Chapter 10.

The Treatment of Anxiety Disorders

Behavioral theory offers a model from which to understand learned behaviors that contribute to maintaining anxious, obsessive or compusive behaviors once they begin. For example, the obsession is perceived as anxiety producing and uncomfortable. Consequently, a ritualistic behavior develops which serves to diminish anxiety. The ritualistic behavior is not potent enough to completely eliminate the initial anxiety. As a result the individual will tend to increase the frequency of the ritualistic behavior with minimal benefit in anxiety reduction. Behavior therapy utilizing procedures called graded exposure and concurrent response prevention are effective treatment methods, particularly when used in conjunction with pharmacotherapy.

Most people have had the experience of increasing their anxiety by ruminating about something. Normal behavior includes times when a feared event becomes larger than life or focused on to a point of exaggeration. A normal child whose anxiety level is escalating as he or she "works himself or herself into lather" can frequently be distracted, redirected or matter-of-factly reassured. Some parents inadvertently reinforce this type of anxious preoccupation by continuing to respond to each expressed concern. When this is the case, the parent is essentially participating in the child's anxious rumination. After an initial reassurance, a parent may refuse to maintain the anxious preoccupation. A parent may simply state in a nonjudgmental tone that it is understood that the child is anxious or worried, but it won't help by continuing to focus on the fear. Most parents can visualize a child on his way to the doctor for a blood test or injection. The more the child focuses on the procedure, the more anxious the child becomes. The child with greater than normative anxiety resulting in some type of interference or impairment may benefit from cognitive behavioral interventions.

Is there an identifiable source of the anxiety? In some cases insecurity and anxiety are related to a "point of view". Anxious preoccupation related to point of view is somewhat akin to the old sitcom plot in which each of a romantically involved couple wants to end their relationship but is intolerably anxious when they perceive being dumped first. There are numerous sources of potential misinformation and misperceptions for children as well as adults. Some anxious children may misperceive expectations resulting in unnecessary stress. While it is true that we can talk ourselves into a "tizzy", we can also use *self talk* to reduce anxiety. Relaxation methods in combination with deep breathing can also be helpful.

Relaxation and behavioral principles have been joined in a number of techniques used in treating anxiety. Imagining, for example, a feared situation from a "safe" vantage point with techniques such as *systematic desensitization* may help an individual become less sensitive to the situation's anxiety-provoking features.

Systematic desensitization is a procedure where an individual uses imagination to progress gradually through a hierarchy of anxiety-producing situations. The individual begins with the least anxiety producing, while maintaining a relaxed state, and continues on to the imagined situation that elicits the most anxiety. A procedure called self systematic desensitization has been described and basically is a self modification procedure. While systematic desensitization is not the most effective technique for overcoming phobias, it has been adapted to self management programs and may be effectively applied in cases of problematic fears that are not debilitating or severe. There are three basic phases in systematic desensitization:

1. Construction of a fear hierarchy.

2. Learning deep muscle relaxation.

3. Carrying out the steps of the procedure which involve getting into a relaxed state and then imagining the situations that have been identified in the hierarchy as the least to most anxiety producing.

Specific instructions for creating a fear hierarchy, learning deep muscle relaxation and preparation for the procedure is available in the textbook "Behavior Modification: What it is and how to do it" by Garry Martin and Joseph Pear, published by Prentice-Hall, 4th edition, 1992. This textbook also describes in detail how to utilize exposure methods.

Exposure

The primary behavioral treatment of all phobias is exposure. Indirect exposure is symbolic, as in pictures of feared stimuli or imagined as in systematic desensitization. Direct exposure may be graduated or sudden. The effectiveness of these methods has been shown to be enhanced when used in combination with several types of antidepressant medications. The idea behind the immediate return of a child with a "school phobia" (aka separation anxiety disorder or panic disorder) is sudden and continuing exposure. As related to obsessive compulsive disorder, a child with contamination concerns must come and stay in contact with the feared objects until his or her anxiety is decreased. Repeating the exposure exercise results in reduced anxiety coinciding with exposure experiences until the child no longer fears contamination from that particular object. Exposure can be set in motion in a step-by-step (graded) manner or by flooding. In gradual or graded exposure, the child classifies the symptoms from the simplest to most difficult to defy. This becomes a hierarchy from which to approach the gradual exposure.

Flooding consists of extended exposure to the most anxiety-provoking element of the hierarchy. This is done to shorten treatment and maximize benefit. One of the research findings related to exposure techniques and young patients is what constitutes exposure versus flooding. What may be gradual exposure to an adult may be flooding for the child. Since failure in an exposure task usually reinforces anxiety, it has been recommended that young persons be allowed to define and control their own exposure targets.

Response Prevention

The major underlying response prevention principle asserts that sufficient exposure relies on barring rituals or avoidance behaviors. In this way a child fearing contamination not only must touch the feared object(s) but also must resist washing until his or her anxiety diminishes. Many situations will occur throughout a day in which the child will be unable to avoid exposure. These can be targeted to be reponse prevention targets. For example, the child is handed a glass in the cafeteria and feels compelled to wash immediately. The response prevention is to not wash until the anxiety is diminished.

Extinction

Extinction is the elimination of behaviors through removal of positive reinforcement. For example, parents may ignore compulsive reassurance seeking. This technique can be effected with or without the child's participation.

Modeling

Modeling can also be an effective method for treating anxiety disorders. A parent can show how a child might deal with the given situation by using role playing and taking on the role of the child. This can be accomplished, within the role, by discussing or describing the thoughts and feelings that accompany anxiety-provoking situations. The parent can then model alternative methods of dealing with an issue. The child can further practice coping skills by using real life situations for exposure. With parental guidance, these situations can be used to dispute or correct misperceptions and help to create new response patterns. Teaching a child these concepts as a problem solving technique can help them to identify a problem, generate possible solutions, choose a solution, implement the solution and evaluate the effectiveness of the solution.

Cognitive Therapies

Cognitive therapies include techniques such as thought stopping and cognitive restructuring. Cognitive behavioral therapy techniques will be discussed further in Chapter 10, the Therapeutic Parent.

Exercise 5

Go to Chapter 11 which includes a sample of research articles on childhood emotional, depressive and anxious disorders. Browse through the titles. The titles will give a sense of the range of research. The highly interested or motivated reader can take desired citations to a university library, find the reference librarian and be directed to articles of interest.

Chapter Nine

Autism, Schizophrenia and Developmental Disorders

Autism

Autism refers to a severe form of pervasive developmental disorder characterized by a lack of awareness of the existence or feelings of others. Together autism and pervasive developmental disorder refer to a range of disorders defined by particular clinical presentations. The features of impaired social relatedness, impairment in communication and repetitive stereotyped behaviors are generally noted in autism. Autistic "thinking" refers to extreme withdrawal. Autism has been referred to by various terms over the years. Children we now call autistic have been referred to as having infantile autism, atypical children and as having childhood psychosis. The prevalence of this disorder varies from 2 in 10,000 to 5 in 10,000 depending on the diagnostic criteria used in various studies. The ratio of males to females is approximately 4 or 5 to 1. There has been no prevalence differences demonstrated between various ethnic or socioeconomic groups. The prevalence of pervasive developmental disorders has been estimated as between 10 and 15 per 10,000.

Most parents first note delays in speech, poor relatedness, other developmental delays or, in a percentage of cases, a loss of skills previously acquired. The average age at diagnosis is between 2.5 and 3.5 years of age. While children with autistic disorder have a variable distribution of abilities, approximately 20% have standardized intelligence scores within the range of mental retardation. As infants, these children are frequently described as being difficult babies, as becoming rigid when held and not being comforted by being held. There are also reports of the easy baby that was simply satisfied being left alone. Early childhood is characterized by avoidance of others, a lack of eye contact, lack of recognition of others' emotions or feelings and self stimulation. The self stimulation may present as repetitive play with objects, rocking or other repetitive movements and difficulty tolerating changes in routines. Approximately 40 to 50 percent of children with autistic disorder remain nonverbal by five years of age. Obsessive compulsive symptoms, hyperactivity, psychosis, seizures (in about 20%) and other symptoms may vary throughout development.

Studies of causation of autism have included investigations of the role of neurotransmitters. Whereas in depression, the serotonergic hypothesis basically suggests a deficit in serotonergic transmission, in autism studies have focused on the finding of increased serotonin (*hyperserotonemia*) in the platelets of autistic individuals. The finding of unusually high concentrations of serotonin in autistic individuals was first reported by Drs. R.J. Schain and D.X. Freedman in 1961 and has since been replicated by a number of research groups. Group averages of platelet serotonin in autistic individuals range from 121% to 237% of that found in normal control groups. Hyperserotonemia was seen in the unmedicated autistic groups. In the medicated autistic individuals there was a decrease in platelet serotonin levels. Despite the recognition of hyperserotonemia in autistic individuals, understanding the mechanism that results in hyperserotonemia remains elusive. George M. Anderson, William C. Horne, Diptendu Chatterjee and Donald Cohen at the Yale Child Study Center, Yale University School of Medicine, have suggested two possible causes of hyperserotonemia, 1) that platelets are exposed to an abundance of serotonin because it either has not been metabolized as usual or there has been an increased synthesis of serotonin and 2) that the platelets are handling the serotonin in an abnormal manner.

Dr. Anderson and his associates have completed studies which suggest that hyperserotonemia in autism is neither the

Developmental and Psychotic Disorders   213

result of improper metabolism nor increased serotonin production. They have come to focus their investigations on the platelet and the platelet's regulation of serotonin uptake, storage and release. As stated earlier in this text, serotonin has several sub-types of receptors; autistic subjects appear to have fewer $5HT_2$ receptors in the presence of higher 5HT (serotonin) levels. It may be that the $5HT_2$ receptors play a role in regulating the platelets handling of serotonin. These studies have the potential to direct investigators to gene probes and the chromosomal locations involved in the abnormalities which result in autism.

Schizophrenia

Childhood onset schizophrenia is rare. The criteria for diagnosis of schizophrenia is currently the same as it is for adults. The prevalence of schizophrenia, however, in adults at 10 in 1000, is approximately 500 times the prevalence in children. Estimates of prevalence in the past are unreliable due to variations in how persons were diagnosed with schizophrenia. In the past many individuals who were diagnosed as schizophrenic would now be diagnosed differently. Some of the symptoms manifested by those with schizophrenia include experiences in which the individual believes his or her thoughts are being controlled by others, auditory hallucinations, delusions, catatonia, thought disorder, incoherent speech, bizarre actions such as grimacing or stereotyped movements.

Distinctions between autism and childhood schizophrenia have long been recognized. The differences basically distinguish between children with the autistic features of input processing peculiarities and the bizarre perceptual and attention abnormalities of children with schizophrenia. Children after age five that have child onset psychosis as distinguished from autism, have symptoms that include hallucinations, thought disorder and incongruent or blunted presence.

The presence of hallucinations does not automatically suggest schizophrenia as the underlying cause. It is important in adults as well as children to determine whether hallucinations may be related to delirium, medication, epilepsy, migraine, sleep deprivation, substance ingestion or bipolar or other disorders.

> Researchers monitored 4,746 people for over 40 years. All of the subjects were born in March, 1946. The investigators concluded that the development of schizophrenia as adults may be prefaced by developmental deviations in childhood. Thirty subjects developed schizophrenia in adulthood. The findings suggested that schizophrenia was associated with certain developmental abnormalities in childhood although was not associated with lower social class. Greater percentages of those who became schizophrenic had been unable to talk, sit, stand and walk alone at age two. While five percent of the non-schizophrenic control group had speech difficulties, eleven percent of those who later became schizophrenic had speech disorders at age six. Those who became schizophrenic were twice as likely to have played in solitude as children and felt greater anxiety in groups, than controls, at 13 years. The schizophrenic subjects scored lower on educational tests at ages 8, 11 and 15 years than did controls. The researchers concluded the data suggests factors occurring early in life may predispose certain people toward schizophrenia.
>
> Source: Peter Jones, Bryan Rodgers, Robin Murray and Michael Marmot. Child developmental risk factors for adult schizophrenia in the British 1946 birth cohort. The Lancet Nov 19 1994, v344, n8934, p1398(5).

There is genetic evidence of a 50% concordance rate (co-occurrence) of schizophrenia among identical (monozygotic) twins versus an 8-28% concordance among fraternal twins (dizygotic). High risk studies include investigations of the offspring of schizophrenic parents. Research among this particular risk group is aimed at attempting to understand the interaction between a genetic risk and some other interactive factor such as viral illness during pregnancy or other factors causing a variant in neurodevelopmental processes. The risk of schizophrenia within the general population is 1%. If an individual has one parent with schizophrenia the odds of acquiring schizophrenia are 12% and with two schizophrenic parents the risk becomes 40%. Interestingly, ninety percent of schizophrenics do not have schizophrenic parents.

Many questions remain involving the relationship between childhood onset schizophrenia and the range of pervasive developmental disorders. Early symptoms of neurological illness can include incoherence, rapidly changing and inappropriate emotional states and a deterioration of performance which can appear similar to schizophrenia. In an organic brain condition there will frequently be pervasive difficulties and severe psychotic symptoms. Various investigative groups, notably those led by Dr. Gordon and also by Dr. McKenna, have identified a category of patients with incidental indications of implied developmental difficulties they have referred to as being impaired "multidimensionally".

Brain abnormalities associated with schizophrenia include frontal lobe dysfunction in schizophrenic adults. Frontal lobe dysfunction has not been scientifically evaluated in children with schizophrenia. Children's brain development, however, may yet provide important insights for schizophrenia research. Children undergoing normative development produce an excess of neurons and synapses. As they continue to mature there is a programmed cell death that results in a decrease of synapses and is referred to as *synaptic pruning*. This synaptic pruning occurs through childhood and adolescence and is accompanied by developmentally associated changes in cerebral glucose metabolism. In normative child development, cerebral glucose metabolism increases up to about age 4 and then remains relatively stable until approximately nine years of age. The acceleration in synaptic density is followed synaptic pruning and a resultant descent to adult quantities by late adolescence.

Late adolescence is also the developmental stage most associated with onset of psychosis.

Numerous studies suggest a neurodevelopmental basis for schizophrenia. A recent study of childhood onset schizophrenia reports having identified right posterior parietal hypometabolism. Currently available imaging techniques will further enable measurement of gray and white matter ratios, which will be a reflection of myelination, cortical and subcortical volumes. Adult schizophrenics have demonstrated limbic structure and associated corpus callosum abnormalities, enlarged cerebral ventricles, reduced medial hippocampal amygdala volume and smaller superior temporal gyral volume.

Social impairment, peculiar communication and odd fantasies may be seen in children with childhood onset schizophrenia but are also common traits of children with schizotypal personality disorder and those with Asperger's syndrome. Major depression can also be accompanied by psychoses (hallucinations and delusions) and misidentified as schizophrenia. As discussed in the chapter on mood disorders, early onset bipolar disorders may not be easily identified and in the past what now might be diagnosed as bipolar disorder may have been referred to as schizophrenia.

Developmental Disorders

The primary feature of developmental disorders is a predominant disturbance of the acquisition of motor skills, cognitive skills, social skills or language. Developmental disorders occur in all degrees of expression. Some developmental disorders are mild to moderate, while others are severe. Mental retardation usually suggests below average intellectual functioning and significant impairment in adaptive functioning with an onset before age 18 years. This diagnosis requires specialized assessment and clinical procedures. Mental retardation is prevalent in approximately 1% of the population.

Developmental and Psychotic Disorders

In 1992 The American Association on Mental Retardation provided an operational definition of mental retardation. "Mental retardation refers to substantial limitations in present functioning. It is characterized by significantly subaverage functioning, existing concurrently with related limitations in two or more of the following applicable adaptive skill areas: communication, self care, home living, social skills, community use, self-direction, health and safety, functional academics and leisure and work. Mental retardation manifests before age 18".

Causes of Mental Retardation

Causes of mental retardation include hereditary disorders, early alterations of embryonic development, later pregnancy problems, perinatal difficulties and acquired childhood disorders.

Fragile X syndrome is the most common known heritable cause of mental retardation. Patients and carriers of fragile X syndrome have generally been identified by use of a DNA test system. Recently a research group has developed a new test that requires only 1 or 2 droplets of blood. The syndrome called Fragile X has an incidence estimated to be between approximately one per 1200-1500 males and one per 2500 females. Fragile X is caused by a gene mutation which consists of an increase in length of a section of *trinucleotide repeats* which help determine the function of the gene. Within the normal population, it would be expected to find the number of trinucleotide repeats varying from 6 to 50. When the trinucleotide repeats exceed 50, the gene is unstable when transmitted to the next generation. In what is considered a full mutation, there is an increase beyond 200 repeats. All males with full mutations have been reported to have syndromes associated with mental retardation. In females, only about 65% with a full mutation are mentally retarded. Full mutations are associated with the subsequent absence of an encoded protein which is believed to be responsible for the mental retardation. Fragile X syndrome occurs in all studied ethnic groups.

> Food and nutrition specialists estimate that about 800 million children below the age of five years suffer from malnutrition and mental and physical retardation due to diseases such as diarrhea. Supplementary foods rich in nutritional value and easily digestible may reduce the malnutrition problems that occur when the child's food must be augmented.
>
> Source: L.T. Weaver. Feeding the weanling in the developing world: problems and solutions. International Journal of Food and Sciences Nutrition, June 1994, v45, n2, p127(8)

The discovery of Fragile X syndrome genes that become altered or mutated has resulted in illuminating concepts about gene mutation stability. The process and results of DNA (trinucleotide repeat) insertion in the chromosomes determines the probability of further alterations. The resultant dynamic mutation produces heritable erratic DNA.

Fetal Alcohol Syndrome

Fetal alcohol syndrome (FAS) is a leading preventable cause of birth defects and mental retardation in the United States. Fetal alcohol syndrome is typified by an assortment of physical and behavioral features that result from maternal alcohol consumption during pregnancy. Characteristics of FAS include prenatal or postnatal growth deficiency, characteristic abnormal facial features and central nervous system deficits. Some distinguish Fetal Alcohol Syndrome from Fetal Alcohol Effects (FAE), with the syndrome being a more severe condition with mental retardation. Fetal alcohol effects may present as less obvious, yet nevertheless significant impairments such as attention difficulties, learning disabilities or other cognitive impairment.

Developmental and Psychotic Disorders 219

Birth defects associated with Fetal Alcohol Syndrome or Fetal Alcohol Effects vary. The effects of FAS or FAE vary depending on the gestational stage when the fetus is exposed to alcohol and how long the exposure persists. Craniofacial abnormalities (dysmorphia) have been associated with early pregnancy exposure although other cognitive and behavioral impairments have not yet been correlated to a particularly critical period of pregnancy. Animal studies, given their inherent limitations, have demonstrated that early exposure, equivalent to the first trimester produces significant dysmorphia and neurological damage. These studies have demonstrated that later exposure only also results in significant effects on the nervous system. With a rat model, Miller (1992) has analyzed the consequences of exposure during the equivalent to the second trimester in humans. He consistently found a reduction of brain weight in rats exposed to alcohol both in this second trimester equivalent and in the rat's early postnatal period, which is equivalent to the third trimester in humans. In normal development during the second half of gestation, neurons in the neocortex are generated and migrate to specific brain regions. It appears that alcohol exposure influences the period and formation of nerve cell propagation, both postponing the process and changing the amount of cells that are created. In this type of alcohol exposure, cell migration patterns result in unusual cell formations in several areas in the brain, including the hippocampus, cerebellum, sensory nucleus and in the neocortex (Miller 1992).

Third trimester (equivalent) effects have been studied extensively in a rat model by West and Goodlett (1990). This period is of unique interest because it includes the brain development spurt, a period of very brisk brain development that occurs in part during the third trimester in humans. In rats the gestational equivalent occurs postnatally. Exposure to alcohol during this period leads to reductions in brain weight and head circumference and presumably with alterations in brain structure and function. The quantity of neurons in particular regions of the hippocampus and the cerebellum are also reduced. The hippocampus is known to be integral to learning and memory. The cerebellum is essentially concerned with coordinated movements and maintenance of muscle tone and equilibrium. The findings that hyperactivity and learning deficits can be observed in physically normal animals exposed to alcohol during this late gestational period suggest these anatomical changes are related to abnormal behavior later in life.

According to data obtained by the national Birth Defects Monitoring Program (BDMP) the rate of reported incidents of FAS classified among newborns in the United States during 1979-1992 increased approximately fourfold. The national Birth Defects Monitoring Program obtains its data from hospital discharge data of newborns provided voluntarily by nonfederal, short-term stay hospitals. In 1993, FAS was reported in 126 of 188,905 newborns (rate: 6.7 per 10,000). Overall, during 1979-1993, FAS was reported in 2032 of 9,434,560 newborns (overall rate: 2.2 per 10,000 births). The rate for 1993 was more than sixfold higher than that for 1979 (1.0 per 10,000 births). This increase may reflect a true increase in the number of infants with Fetal Alcohol Syndrome or an increase in the awareness and diagnosis by primary-care clinicians of FAS in newborns. Investigations are under way to better describe the extent of FAS, particularly among population subgroups at increased risk for alcohol consumption during pregnancy and for having an infant with FAS.

Down Syndrome (Trisomy 21)

Down syndrome (DS) (trisomy 21) is one of the most significant and recurrent reported birth defects among newborn infants. It also represents an important cause of mental retardation. It has been known for some time that the prevalence of DS at birth increases with increasing maternal age. Down's syndrome is a congenital condition which is characterized by mild or moderate to severe mental retardation, almond shaped eyes, a broad short skull, broad hands with short fingers and by trisomy of chromosome 21. Down syndrome was named after John Langdon Haydon, a British

Developmental and Psychotic Disorders 221

Physician who wrote a treatise on mental deficiency in 1866. The Centers for Disease Control examined data from 17 states with population-based birth defects surveillance programs to ascertain the birth prevalence of DS and describe trends in DS, within the United States during 1983-1990.

During the study period of 1983-1990 17 states reported a total of 7.8 million live-born infants, which represented 25% of all U.S. live-born infants. The combined birth prevalence rate of DS during 1983-1990 for the 17 states was 9.2 cases per 10,000 live-born infants. These rates varied among the states. For example, Kansas had: 5.9 cases per 10,000 while Colorado had 12.3 Colorado. There were also significant rate differences by racial/ethnic group. Hispanic infants had a rate of 11.8 per 10,000. White infants had a rate of 9.2 per 10,000 and black infants had a rate of 7.3 per 10,000. All racial groups demonstrated increased prevalence of Down Syndrome with increasing maternal age.

From 1983 to 1990 the general prevalence of DS for all races summed was fundamentally unchanged for infants of mothers less than 35 years of age. The rate for white infants was constant, the rates decreased for black infants from 7.1 in 1983 to 5.3 in 1990 and in Hispanic infants from 9.4 in 1983 to 6.4 in 1990. Infants of mothers aged greater than or equal to 35 years also declined significantly from 36.6 in 1983 to 25.9 in 1990. Some of these declines may be attributable to the increased use of prenatal diagnosis services.

Normalization and Community Living

There have been recent attempts to apply quality of life measurement concepts in assessing the rehabilitation outcome of persons with mental retardation and mental illness. Debate has come after the drive toward de-institutionalization of mentally retarded persons. Since that time, calls for advancement and employment of quality of life assessments have been widespread among advocates for the mentally retarded. The controversy centers around which living environments heighten life quality and which types of facilities can optimize the quality of life for those individuals who differ in functioning. It is also questioned whether the conventional institutional settings can be changed to a degree that they can offer an environment that enhances life quality for at least some individuals greater than other options. Factors that make up quality of life include such things as where individuals live and work and their ability to make decisions and have choices.

Those with mental retardation reside in a variety of placement settings. Typical settings include the family or natural home, supervised apartments, boarding homes, community training homes, community residences, and regional facilities. In the family or natural homes, clients may receive services such as case management and day programming. In supervised living, clients may reside alone or with a roommate in an apartment, rented house, or room and receive periodic monitoring, supervision, and training consistent with individual needs. In community training home settings, clients may reside with one to two peers in caregivers' personal homes.

Further movement toward normalization for the mentally retarded has been demonstrated by the increasing numbers of "self advocates". President Bill Clinton appointed a committee on mental retardation which hosted a forum called: The President's Reform Agenda and People with Mental Retardation: 21st Century Realities. The conference was held April 24-26, 1994, as a way to offer a platform for designated national leaders in the areas of mental retardation and developmental disabilities. The discussions centered on the consequences for citizens with mental retardation and developmental disabilities of reform initiatives in health care, welfare, long term care, employment, education and housing.

A representative number of self-advocates and family members of mentally retarded were included as keynote speakers and active participants in the conference. The

Developmental and Psychotic Disorders   223

self-advocates were nominated by two national self-advocate associations, People First and Self-Advocates Becoming Empowered. Secretary of Health and Human Services, Donna Shalala stressed the Administration's firmly held belief that every citizen's contribution should be prized, and quoted President John F. Kennedy's call upon Americans to "integrate people with mental retardation within our modem society...We do not have the luxury of wasting our human resources."

Several excerpts by the self-advocates and parent representatives were reported. The following excerpts are from T. J. Monroe, a Self-Advocate, Vista Volunteer with People First of Tennessee; Koquese Collins mother of an eleven year old son with Down Syndrome; Don and Dawn Merriman of Salina, Kansas; and Linda and Lincoln Charlton.

Mr. Monroe is noted as responsible for contributing leadership and technical assistance to several regional self-advocacy groups. In part, Mr. Monroe states:

"I know you are experts in this field because of your schooling, training, family and professional experiences. I am also an expert in this field because of my first hand experience: living in institutions and the community; fighting for a good education; getting a real job; searching for good health care; struggling to pay my bills; looking for long term support; and speaking up for my needs and my rights to lawmakers. I think what we need to do is bring together professionals' knowledge and self-advocates' personal experience. This way, we can build a plan for action that solves the real problems people have. Self-advocates want to become empowered and have a voice in solving the problems they experience. Together with professional and government resources, we can make it work."

Ms. Collins' comments included the following excerpt:

"When I received a call from the Director of the ARC in Detroit asking me if I would be willing to speak on my experience as a single parent of a child with a disability, my initial response was why me? Shouldn't you find someone better qualified to speak before such an important audience? But then I realized that my experiences as a parent of a child with a disability, though in many ways similar, were indeed, uniquely different from the experiences of parents of children who are without special needs."

"You have an enormous responsibility, for you will help shape the services, supports and ultimately the very quality of life afforded my son Brian and others like him into the twenty-first century and beyond. I could not allow an opportunity to speak on behalf of the Brians, the Sarahs, and the Jasons -- the people with disabilities -- to simply pass me by. "My son, Brian is 11 years old, has Down Syndrome, and is classified as educably mentally impaired and trainable mentally impaired. But more importantly, Brian is an active, compassionate and extremely friendly young man. I am constantly amazed by this child who in so many ways is wise beyond his years. Brian is the third of my five children. His siblings are without disability. Brian realized he is different, as do his brothers and sister. In our family though, Brian's disability has really become secondary. He is my son, a brother, playmate, friend, family."

"I guess you could characterize our household as an inclusive environment that works. Our dynamic, of course, is not without difficulties. I dream of the best futures possible for all my children. I fear, however, that ignorance, bias and the inability to see people with disabilities as people first, not Brian's disability itself, will stall Brian. Today, I sit before you in an attempt to ensure that doesn't happen."

Developmental and Psychotic Disorders

Don and Dawn Merriman are involved in numerous advisory, planning councils, and legislative advocacy. They are the parents of a 14-year-old son, Craig. Comments shared by Mr. and Mrs. Merriman follow:

"We are here today because we are parents of a 14-year-old son named Craig. He is our only child, and we are proud parents. In files and on paper you will see words like profoundly retarded, cerebral palsy, seizure disorder, nonverbal and severe and multiple disabilities. This is how the systems that provide services to Craig describe him. As parents and people who are close to Craig, you will hear us describe him in a very different manner. Craig has a zest for life like no one else we know. He loves doing anything with his dad, loves race cars, being outside shooting baskets, riding in convertibles and trucks, the Three Stooges, and going to middle school dances."

"Life with Craig has never been dull. In his first 14 years of life he has spent more time in hospitals having surgeries and tests and medical procedures than most people will spend in a lifetime. Our world quickly became one of hospital emergency rooms, frequent hospital stays, orthopedic surgeries, blood levels, special education and fear of what tomorrow might bring."

"One of our major accomplishments is being here at this convention today. We dream of a day when the gaps are eliminated, and there is truly a continuity of services. We dream of a day when families are asked, "Tell us what you need. We dream of the day when people really listen. We know that when people listen change can and does become a reality."

Linda and Lincoln Charlton are from Bel-Air, Maryland and are parents of a two year-old daughter, Kaitlin Aubrey, born with Down Syndrome. Their comments:

"Two years ago, we became the first-time parents of a baby girl, Kaitlin Aubrey, who was born with Down Syndrome. While this was a heartbreaking and unanticipated outcome, we're grateful for the tremendous support we received, from family, friends, health professionals and educators, as we ourselves become 'educated' on what it means to have a child with special needs...a continual learning process."

"Katie has always been an alert child...ever watching all that goes on around her. She began early intervention services at three months of age and now also receives speech therapy during which she is also learning sign language. She has been in good health overall these past two years. While it's still too early to know what level she will function at in later years, we try to set no limits for her, and give to her the same experiences we would to any child of ours."

"She loves people, music and animals and is very social. While we read a lot about Down Syndrome, mental retardation and other disabilities to learn what others have experienced, how they've handled different situations, etc. our best coping mechanism seems to be Katie herself. Her smiles, good nature and continued progress enable and encourage us to keep working with her to master different skills. Like all parents, we want the best for our daughter. Our hope for Katie is that she will grow up feeling very much loved by us, the rest of her family and friends. However, we also worry about her future...her acceptance in the community, the schools she will one day attend, and much later, employment opportunities."

"From a philosophical standpoint, having a child with special needs changes one's priorities; from a practical standpoint, it can also have an economic impact. And emotionally, there will always be some sadness about what 'won't be' for Katie and for us, but as we move forward that is no longer the first concern. As I have observed people with disabilities who have attended the Forum, I keep wondering in my head what my daughter will be like at their age, and if she too might one day attend such an event or be a self-advocate. I've learned to keep my expectations high for her."

On August 26, 1994 President Clinton announced the appointment of Ann M. Forts of Center Harbor, New Hampshire, as a member of the President's Committee on Mental Retardation (PCMR). Ms. Forts is the second self-advocate to serve as a member of the President's Committee on Mental Retardation and the second self-advocate appointed by the President to serve on the Committee. The President praised the contribution that Ann Forts will make as a self-advocate on the PCMR Board:

> "Ann Forts represents the goal of my administration in meeting the needs of citizens with disabilities. By listening to citizens with disabilities, as experts about their lives and what they need to live healthy and productive lives, we will be able to pursue ourcommon vision of moving from exclusion to inclusion, from depend ence to independence, from paternalism to empowerment. I look forward to the insight and wisdom Ann Forts will share with the members of the President's Committee on Mental Retardation."

As part of a growing recognition of the needs of the mentally retarded, leisure services for mentally retarded people are being modified to apply to new definitions of mental retardation. For example, services are now aimed at empowering people and increasing their support levels instead of restricting them based on assumptions of learning limitations. Families, along with the advocacy movement, have influenced the development and direction of services to include normalization, participation, choice and integration. Mental retardation and other mental impairments present important social issues relative to individual rights and the right of these individuals to live as normal a life as possible and in the least restrictive environment that is practical.

An Example of a Child with a Developmental Disorder

Name: Wanda Newhouse
age: 7-4

Tests administered
Mental and Neurological Status Examination
Personality Inventory for Children-Revised (PIC-R)
House Tree Person Projective Drawing
Draw a Person Projective Drawing
Structured Play Evaluation
Kaufman Brief Intelligence Test (K-Bit)

Summary of Findings and Clinical Impressions:

Wanda Newhouse was a 7 year, 4 month old female referred by M. Smith, County Social Worker. County Social Services had legal custody of Wanda and there was a high probability that she and her sibling might require out of home placement in the near future. Dr. R.U. Sickly was Wanda's pediatrician and Mr. Smith authorized the release of copies of the evaluation and consultation regarding diagnostic evaluation and possible treatment strategies to both himself and to Dr. Sickly. Wanda was presenting with significant and chronic emotional, behavioral and developmental difficulties. At the time of the evaluation Wanda was residing with her mother, Mary Contrary and brothers, Jeff age 4 years and Ike age 2 years. Her step father had recently left the home. There had also been an on-going paternal rights issue, in that, Wanda's mother has not allowed Wanda's biological father visitation rights. Additionally, Wanda's mother had not been cooperative with past social service department recommendations. Since a court determination giving legal custody to the county, the mother expressed a greater willingness to cooperate with the social services department.

An initial history was provided by Wanda's mother with additional information provided by Mr. Smith. Wanda's mother reported that during the pregnancy with Wanda she had a "tear in the placenta" which required her to be limited to bed rest from 5 months up to the delivery. She described a difficult delivery with labor starting on Wednesday and the delivery occurring on Saturday with the use of forceps. She described Wanda as a fussy, colicky infant. As a toddler she described Wanda as "disinterested in toys" and "hyper". Wanda reportedly walked at 9 months and began verbalizing single words at 10 months. Wanda's speech development was described as delayed from that point on. At age three years she was hard to understand and continued to demonstrate immature language. Mr. Smith reported that Mary previously refused to allow Wanda to receive recommended psychotropic medications, however, when Mary provided the history she stated otherwise.

Difficulties reported by Wanda's mother at the time of the evaluation included aggression, violence (she had gone after her mother with a knife and had threatened to kill her), screaming, crying, impulsive, bossy, behavioral and learning difficulties at school, hyperactivity, defiance, irritability, enuresis (2-3 times a week), destructiveness, withdrawal, overeating and oppositional behavior. Wanda was being retained in the first grade. The mother stated that Wanda had never been on any medication other than for typical childhood illnesses but stated that she has tried to get her on Ritalin. Mary denied a family history of bipolar illness, depression or other mental illness, which appeared inconsistent with the mother's reported history of multiple on-going problems with various agencies.

Assessment:

Wanda was right handed, sighted with her left eye and appeared significantly developmentally delayed. Wanda had to open her eyes and catch herself when asked to close her eyes with her feet together for a Romberg test. She also had difficulty standing on one foot, had saccadic eye movements and demonstrated very immature visual motor integration.

Wanda's most notable features were immature language, mood lability and some perseveration. Wanda's assessment continued over two sessions. At the second session Wanda was brought by Mr. Smith, who informed the evaluator that the mother had given Wanda one of her brother's methylphenidate doses because she felt Wanda was getting "hyper". The dose was given to Wanda at approximately 10:00 am and the evaluator saw Wanda at 2:00 pm. It was possible the dose had worn off by the time she had been seen, however, no difference was noted between either of the two sessions. This brought up the issue of the mother giving the child medication that had not been prescribed for her. Between the previous reports of the mother resisting medical interventions and the occurrence of her administering a non-prescribed medication, Wanda's mother presented as a potentially unreliable caretaker in regard to providing medication consistently and as prescribed.

Due to Wanda's apparent limitations, the Kaufman Brief Intelligence Test was administered as an alternative to a more comprehensive intellectual assessment. Wanda's verbal standard score was 46, her performance standard score was 79 and her composite standard score was 59 plus or minus 8 points with 95% confidence. The difference between verbal and performance was significant at .01. Wanda's Personality Inventory for Children-Revised scores were as follows:

Scale Name	Corrected Raw	T-Scores	
LIE	2	38	
FREQUENCY	19	137	*
DEFENSIVENESS	5	11	
ADJUSTMENT	41	107	*
ACHIEVEMENT	15	69	
INTELLECTUAL SCREENING	15	60	
DEVELOPMENT	12	73	*
SOMATIC CONCERN	10	69	
DEPRESSION	28	95	*
FAMILY RELATIONS	13	69	
DELINQUENCY	25	116	*
WITHDRAWAL	11	84	*

ANXIETY	17	88	*
PSYCHOSIS	23	133	*
HYPERACTIVITY	19	83	*
SOCIAL SKILLS	18	78	*

DSM-IV Diagnostic Impression:

Axis I
311.00 Depressive Disorder NOS (rule out bipolar disorder)
314.01 Attention Deficit Hyperactivity Disorder, Combined Type
307.6 Enuresis (nocturnal)

Axis II
317.00 Mild Mental Retardation
315.31 Mixed Receptive-Expressive Language Disorder
299.80 Pervasive Developmental Disorder NOS

Axis III
Soft Neurological Signs
Rule out seizure disorder

Recommendations:

It appeared that Wanda would benefit from both biological and psychotherapeutic interventions. Based on Wanda's history and assessment, it appeared that issues of treatment strategies and treatment compliance might be significant. The elements of significant aggression, distractibility, agitation and psychotic features may have represented a depressive state that was more typical of a bipolar spectrum illness or a prodrome of bipolar illness, than simply depression and attention deficit hyperactivity disorder. Charles Popper, M.D., Editor of the Journal of Child and Adolescent Psychopharmacology made distinctions between ADHD and bipolar disorder. Some of his distinctions included: ADHD children display "non-angry destructiveness", ADHD children usually calm down from anger outbursts and temper tantrums within 20-30 minutes, bipolar children may continue to feel and act angry over 30 minutes and for up to 2-4 hours and children with ADHD do not generally show dysphoria. Additional studies have pointed out that the clinical course of prepubertal mania is predominantly irritable, mixed (depression) and chronic. At the time of the evaluation it was premature to make the bipolar diagnosis and therefore it was not made. However, treatment response and continued monitoring were recommended as methods to make further diagnostic distinctions.

Wanda's presentation was further complicated by her mixed receptive expressive language disorder. It was unknown to the evaluator whether Wanda has had an EEG, MRI or other assessments for organic neurological involvement. If not, it was recommended that there be consultation with Dr. Sickly to determine the most appropriate course of further evaluation. After Dr. Sickly has had an opportunity to receive the evaluation and provide whatever further assessment he deemed necessary.

Brenda Shelter, Ph.D.
Child Clinical Psychologist

Chapter Ten

The Therapeutic Parent

A child's most motivated therapist can be a parent. The parent has the most invested, the most at stake and usually the most durable relationship. Certainly, most professional therapists care about their patients, however, ultimately even the child in therapy will need to move on and separate from a professional therapist. While professional therapists can play a life changing role with children, their part is transitional.

The therapeutic parent can work independently or in league with a professional therapist, depending on the nature and stage of a child's difficulties. A parent whose child is receiving medication may find it most effective to monitor a child's response to medication while providing some form of targeted therapeutic intervention. In this way the parent can work in collaboration with the prescribing physician providing treatment response documentation as well as other therapeutic interventions.

Several therapeutic techniques have been demonstrated as highly effective interventions when utilized by prepared and motivated parents. These techniques include behavior modification, cognitive-behavioral therapy, systematic desensitization, exposure techniques and play therapy. These techniques have the further advantage of being highly compatible with one another as well as beneficial in league with appropriate pharmacological interventions. The overview of interventions provided is presented in the order of biological interventions, behavior modification, cognitive behavioral approaches and play therapy. The optimal intervention strategy will incorporate the appropriate combination of elements from each of these techniques.

This chapter will also provide an overview of psychopharmacological treatment strategies and issues so that parents can better understand the logic that results in certain pharmacological approaches. This information is provided in order to assist the parent in becoming a better informed observer of treatment response. The better informed parent will be a more valuable and effective member of the treatment team.

Biological Interventions

Biological interventions refer primarily to the utilization of medications or *pharmacotherapy* but also include interventions such as *phototherapy* (bright light therapy). The explosion of information in neuroscience has ushered in a new age of biological interventions and hopes for profound changes in how many mental disorders are conceptualized and treated. Advances in neuroscience and biological psychiatry have dramatically altered the treatment of mental disorders. Despite these achievements many controversies and biases remain related to the utilization of biological interventions.

There are those who fear the use of any medication to the degree that they can be referred to as pharmacophobics. Nevertheless, individuals with extremist views that resist any type of biological intervention are few. There are many, however, who generally resist the idea of using medication with children. On the basis of common sense most can agree that a child or an adult should not be on an *unnecessary* medication. The argument may then go to the issue of what demonstrates necessity. There are those who believe that no individual should take medicine. There are those who state unequivalically that they disagree with the use of medications *in children*. On the other extreme, there are those who expect medications to be the complete solution to a childhood difficulty. The diligent reader of this book will realize that neither extreme is supported or promoted by this text.

Pharmacotherapy with children should not be entered into lightly or discounted without thorough assessment, planning, and measurable goals. In part, the aim of this text is to assist the parent in becoming a true partner in the treatment and evaluation process of a child with a mental disorder or potentially impairing difficulty. As with all pharmacotherapy, whether with adults or with children, risks must be weighed against the benefits. The risks, however, are not all related to the effects of medication. Some risks may be related to a decision not to use medication. While an emotional or behavioral problem may not be life threatening or overwhelming in a young child, the effects of untreated conditions can ultimately be life threatening and most certainly can have enduring negative effects.

A Role Playing Exercise

In this exercise the parent is asked to assume the role of the primary care physician. For the sake of the example, let's say that you specialize in family medicine, have had several children as patients that you have treated through the years with either stimulant or antidepressant medications. Let's also assume a generally common attitude that while you are not against medication when needed for a child, you are also not quick to offer medication as a quick fix for behavioral problems or emotional immaturity. Imagine yourself having arrived at the office on Monday at 8:30 AM after completing hospital rounds. You have 15 patients scheduled in the morning and 15 scheduled for the afternoon. In your morning schedule is six year old Stevie and his mother who is concerned about Stevie's behavior. Stevie has been observed by yourself and the office staff as behaviorally difficult, when brought in for his well child care or illnesses. Stevie's mother tells you that he is hitting his sister, that he won't mind at home and that he is frequently getting in trouble in school. She asks if he is hyperactive or if you can give him some medicine to make him behave. Given your experience and knowledge, you refer Stevie and his mother to a psychologist for an evaluation.

In the afternoon you have David and his mother, Irene, scheduled. David is 11 and his mother has expressed concern about David's irritability, moodiness and sleep difficulties. When David and his mother arrive, Irene presents a concise history, a summary of possible environmental factors, a summary of David's current symptoms, their duration and her attempts to intervene. She concludes that she has done what she can environmentally, has been conducting behavioral observations and is conducting weekly play therapy sessions. She believes that a medication trial might also be in order. She wants your opinion regarding the trial of an antidepressant medication.

The point of this exercise is to illustrate the physician's point of view in assessing and deciding what should occur in a situation such as this. There are some very conservative physicians who will simply tell a parent that the child will outgrow the behavior or otherwise dismiss medication as an option. There are others who simply don't want the additional responsibility or liability of having a child on medication. The majority of primary physicians wish to help but are in a position of being unable to provide adequate medication monitoring and therefore may be reluctant to prescribe. The option of psychiatric, psychological or frequent visits may be recommended, however, these options also involve significant expense.

The parent can play an important role both in reducing cost and ensuring quality of care by active participation in the **on-going** evaluation and treatment of their child. Parents and individuals are no longer the passive health care consumers they once were. Parents are increasingly recognizing that they are not required to be passive consumers of medical treatment or education. When individuals become increasingly involved and self responsible for health care they become better informed and educated about health care quality, access and other health care issues. As such parents can play an active, effective and critical role in the process of health care reform.

How to Approach Your Physician

Chapter one provided the basic rationale and steps in preparing for a medical consultation. The reader who has read the previous chapters will now have a deeper appreciation of how much material can actually be brought to the physician's attention during a consultation. It is very understandable that a parent may see their physician with the idea of "just discussing their concerns" and seeing what the doctor thinks. The problem with this approach is that it may result in the parent forgetting to relate important facts or in the physician getting only a section of relevant information. This approach also does little to prepare the parent for a discussion of further assessment or treatment options. Most physician's will be very reluctant to initiate treatment in an ill defined situation. On the other hand, carefully defining the problem can help the physician help you.

Consultation Preparation Tips

1. Utilize and complete the history, systematic observations and assessment materials provided in this book.

2. Initiate and continue sound behavioral interventions related to the problem areas.

3. Consider the treatment approaches presented in this text and determine specific models that you can use or inquire about within the consultation.

4. Be clear in identifying the symptoms of concern, their duration, development and ways in which they impair or threaten to impair the child.

5. Be prepared to receive a referral for a more specialized consultation if necessary.

6. Do not hesitate to say what you think, express what you feel or to obtain a second opinion if you wish.

7. It may also be helpful to make a **copy** of all of your documentation and send it to the physician prior to the consultation. There will be a good chance the physician will at least be able to scan it prior to your meeting and as a result have more time available to discuss the important issues. It is also advisable that you bring a copy of the documents in case the copy sent to the physician is unavailable.

8. Finally, make sure you keep a complete copy of all of your materials. This will alow you to compare post treatment changes, as well as a method of providing data to others when or if needed.

When a parent has demonstrated an ability to work as an evaluation and treatment partner by making pretreatment assessments and providing ongoing treatment related observations, a physician can be assured that the necessary monitoring of medications and response to medications will be done systematically. In this way a parent can assure the safety of a medication trial and quality treatment response data by which the physician and parent can evaluate the benefit of the treatment.

Frequently Prescribed Psychotropic Medications for Children

Psychotropic medication simply refers to drugs that affect the emotions and behavior of individuals. There are a variety of classes and types of medications that have such effects. This text will provide a general description of the more commonly used *psychoactive* medications that are used with children. This description is provided to allow the parent to have a more informed position from which to discuss medications and medication responses with their physician. This information will in no way prepare a lay person to make independent decisions regarding medication selection, dosing or adjustments. These decisions **must** be made in consultation with a physician who will be aware of the medical context of the ultimate decision. On the other hand, a parent who is informed about the medication being utilized and the alternatives is better prepared as a partner in medication decisions and evaluating medication response both for desired and undesirable effects. There are numerous books and software currently available that provide various degrees of depth regarding medication. One relatively inexpensive CD ROM program that is widely available is called "Pharm Assist".

In describing frequently prescribed medications there has been no attempt to be all inclusive. The drugs being discussed are being presented solely as an overview and based on their frequency of use in the child and adolescent populations.

Stimulant Medications

Brand Name   Generic Name

Ritalin   methylphenidate
Dexadrine   dextroamphetamine
Desoxyn   methamphetamine
Cylert   pemoline

The nervous system is a made up of two primary divisions: The central nervous system and the peripheral nervous system. The central nervous system, which includes the brain and the spinal cord, is the control center for the entire system. Central nervous system (CNS) stimulants are drugs that act on the central nervous system and are comprised of three primary groups 1) Psychomotor Stimulants 2) Convulsant and 3) Respiratory Stimulants. Psychomotor stimulants include such drugs as nicotine, caffeine, cocaine and amphetamines to name a few. Convulsant and respiratory stimulants are both used to stimulate respiration in cases of overdose of CNS depressants.

Psychopharmacologic interventions are increasingly being utilized successfully in the treatment of children. Methylphenidate, a stimulant, is the most widely utilized psychoactive drug in childhood psychopharmacology (DeVane, 1990). Children with attention deficit hyperactivity disorder

(ADHD) tend to respond favorably to stimulant drugs, frequently with reduced activity levels, reduced aggression and improved performance on attention related tasks (Campbell & Werry, 1986; Gadow et al., 1990). In children with ADHD, methylphenidate has also been shown to improve vigilance aspects of sustained attention (De Sonneville, Njiokiktjien & Hilhorst, 1991). There is a significant number of children, however, who have either a short-lived positive response to stimulant medications, a poor response or difficulty with side effects.

The side effects associated with stimulant medications include the possibility of increased activity levels, increased aggression, decreased appetite, sleep disturbances and depression. Generally, if a child is going to respond to a stimulant medication with increased activity and aggression, it is seen immediately within the first dose or first few doses and can be stopped accordingly. Most of the stimulants have a relatively short *half life*; that is, the length of time that it takes half of the active drug to be metabolized and disposed of by the body. As such, if there is an undesirable initial response, the stimulant can be immediately discontinued and the medication effects will last for no more than a few hours. The more common response when used with a hyperactive child, is a reduction of activity and aggression and improvement in attention span. Despite an initial positive response to a stimulant medication continued treatment with a stimulant may result in diminished benefit or the development of problematic side effects. That is not to say that stimulant medications cannot and have not been used for numbers of years with high effectiveness, but it is important for the physician and parent of a child receiving a stimulant to be alert for potential of diminishing benefits or untoward effects.

There are a few common problematic circumstances associated with stimulant medications that will be described. There are many instances where stimulant medications are very effective and can be used for extended periods of time without any difficulty. There are, nevertheless, several types of possible difficulties. For example, some children respond favorably to stimulant medication for a period of several weeks, months or even years but then become extremely moody, irritable and depressed. Some begin to manifest tics or may have significant sleep and/or appetite problems. When these types of problems occur they must be evaluated in the context of seriousness or potential seriousness in order to determine whether the treatment should proceed, be adjusted or changed.

As was discussed in the section on disruptive behavior disorders, it is common for a child with a disruptive behavior disorder to also have a mood disorder. A co-existing mood disorder may be apparent from the outset or it may only become apparent after some period of positive treatment response, partial positive response to treatment or poor response. Stimulants may elevate the mood in the very short term but generally are more likely to worsen an existing mood disorder over time. When a disruptive behavior disorder fails to be responsive to stimulant medication or when there are problematic side effects or a co-existing mood disorder, antidepressant medications are frequently excellent alternatives. In fact, many professionals prefer the antidepressant medications as the initial medication trial for a disruptive behavior disorder.

One advantage and disadvantage of stimulant medications has to do with their short half life. Since the stimulants are metabolized quickly, most formulations require frequent dosing in order to maintain effectiveness. A common dosing strategy would be a single dose of Ritalin either two or three times a day. This would normally be given to children in the morning, at noon and after school. Many children are uncomfortable receiving medication at school. Alternatives are a slow release formulation of Ritalin called Ritalin SR, a time release spansule of Dexadrine or the administration of antidepressant medication that requires less frequent dosing. These alternatives have advantages and disadvantages as well. The Ritalin SR is available only in a 20 milligram form. The Dexadrine spansule, which is also slow release is available in 5 milligram, 10 milligram and 15 milligram doses. The slow release stimulants may be able to be given either once in the morning or in the morning and after school thus avoiding an in-school administration. Many of the antidepressant medications can be given either once or twice a day and can also be administered away from school.

A common medication administration question is related to administration of medications on evenings, weekends and holidays. In regard to stimulant medications, there are some who recommend administration only on school days. With the exception of a very mild attentional difficulty without hyperactivity this approach can be problematic. The child who truly benefits from a stimulant medication continues to be impaired as the medication is metabolized and eliminated. Such a child will be more likely to have difficulty attending to or completing homework, interacting within the family and with non-school social interactions. It is not uncommon to see a child who is receiving an effective stimulant dose at school having serious problems at home with this approach. In the case of antidepressant medications it is important that the medications not be skipped, in order to maintain therapeutic blood plasma levels of the medication. If a dose is missed, it is less immediately noticeable than the missed stimulant dose because regular daily dosing and a longer half life cause the medication to maintain a more consistent and enduring plasma level. This is not to suggest that periods or trials off of medication are not appropriate. The effective use of "medication holidays" will be discussed in a following section on evaluation of treatment response.

Antihypertensive Medications

Brand Name	Generic Name
Catapres	clonidine
Tenex	guanfacine

Antihypertensive medications are generally used to treat high blood pressure, vascular headaches, congestive heart failure or dysmenorrhea (painful menstruation). These medications have been recently popular as alternatives to stimulant medications with hyperactive children. This class of medication has also been used for some time with those diagnosed as having Tourette's disorder.

Clonidine works by stimulating alpha-adrenoreceptors in the brainstem which stimulates the dilation of blood vessels. Clonidine is available in a slow release patch under the brand name of Catapres-TTS. Clonidine is effective within approximately 3 hours. Tenex (guanfacine), used primarily for the treatment of high blood pressure, affects the sympathetic nervous system causing a drop in blood pressure. Approximately one week should be allowed for this drug to take effect. Tenex has been suggested by some as an alternative to clonidine due to a longer half life and therefore a longer period of action between dosing. In the case of clonidine, it may cause very low blood pressure if used with alcohol or nitrates. In terms of Tenex, the use of non-steroidal anti-inflammatory medications such as ibuprofen may diminish the effectiveness of the medication. In both clonidine and tenex, other drugs may add to central nervous system depression and lowered blood pressure. Both of these medications are sedating and have the potential to worsen depression.

Antidepressant Medications
(To name just a few)

Tricyclic Antidepressants
Brand Name   Generic Name

Tofranil   imipramine
Elavil   amitriptyline
Pamelor   nortriptyline
Norpramin   desipramine

Other
Wellbutrin   buproprion

Serotonin Specific Reuptake Inhibitors (SSRI's)
Brand Name   Generic Name

Brand Name	Generic Name
Zoloft	sertraline
Paxil	paroxetine
Prozac	fluoxetine
Serzone	nefazodone
Luvox	fluvoxamine

Antidepressant medications include those described as tricyclic antidepressants, those described as serotonin specific reuptake inhibitors and other newer antidepressant medications that have varying specificity upon specific neurotransmitter receptors or receptor subtypes.

The tricyclic antidepressant medications have a long history of use in treating children. Tofranil (imipramine), for example, has been used for decades with children presenting with enuresis (bedwetting). Combining the antidepressant medications with behavioral methods has increased the effectiveness of both approaches. It has been suggested that there may be a sub-group of children with ADHD that respond better to tricyclic antidepressants than to stimulants and that this group may demonstrate higher levels of anxiety and/or depression. Co-morbidity (other co-existing disorders), anxiety and depression also need to be considered in children who are presenting with inattentive or disruptive behaviors. There has been an increasing tendency to utilize antidepressant medications in the treatment of numerous psychiatric disorders in children. Antidepressants are also indicated in a number of pediatric conditions in addition to depression including migraine, obsessive-compulsive disorder, separation anxiety, enuresis, school phobia, conduct and attention deficit disorders.

Despite the effectiveness of tricyclic antidepressants they appear to be particularly helpful in some types of disorders and less helpful in others. They also have a higher side effect profile than the newer classes of serotonin specific reuptake inhibitors. Tricyclic antidepressants will lower the seizure threshold of an individual prone to seizures and are usually best avoided in individuals with cardiac arrhythmias or other heart conditions. On the other hand, side effects are usually minimal or nonexistent in the lower range of dosages and therapeutic plasma levels have been established which can be monitored if necessary.

The most commonly used tricylic antidepressant medications are closely related to one another. Imipramine, for example, is metabolized in the body to become desipramine which is also psychoactive. When a blood level for imipramine is measured, both the level of imipramine and desipramine are summed to calculate the plasma level. Desipramine is also available as an antidepressant and for many, until recently, has been a first choice of treatment for a child with ADHD and depression. Desipramine alone is slightly more stimulating than imipramine and for that reason has appeared to have been an effective agent both for the treatment targets of attention difficulties and depression. A recent retreat from using desipramine (in those under 12 years of age) has occurred due to a handful of sudden deaths of children that had been receiving desipramine. Given the numbers of children that have successfully been treated with desipramine it appears that these few unusual and unexpected deaths could have occurred even if the children had not been on medication. Nevertheless, there has been no similar reports associated with the other antidepressant medications, and as a result clinicians are prescribing desipramine to young children with decreased frequency. Generally speaking, desipramine is somewhat more stimulating and amitriptyline is somewhat more sedating as compared to imipramine.

Monoamine Oxidase Inhibitors (MAOIs) are a separate class of antidepressant medication that has been demonstrated to be highly effective with certain types of depressions. The MOAIs currently available in the United States require rather strict dietary restrictions and avoidance of certain other drugs to be used safely. Due to these limitations the MAOIs are less commonly used with children. There are new classes of MAOIs that have been developed that are termed "reversible" MAOI's and are proported to not require the dietary restrictions of the original formulations. One such drug, moclobomide, is currently available in Canada.

Advantages of Tricyclic Antidepressants

1. Extensive experience of safe and effective use in children and adolescents. It should be noted, however, that as is the case with most medications, most of the psychotropic drugs do not have specific Federal Drug Administration endorsement of use in children due to the absence of studies with children. Therefore, with many psychotropic medications, as with many other pharmacological formulations, they are used in children and adolescents "off label".

2. Patents have expired and have made relatively inexpensive generic formulations available.

3. Meaningful plasma levels have been established which can aid treatment monitoring.

Disadvantages of Tricylic Antidepressants

1. Can be lethal in overdose.

2. Side effects are few at low doses but are common at higher doses.

3. Ineffective in some children and adolescents.

4. Generally require a 3-4 week period of administration prior to full therapeutic effect.

The serotonin specific reuptake inhibitors have been demonstrated as highly effective in the treatment of depression. These clinical trials have necessarily been made as compared to the previously established effective antidepressant medications.

Advantages of Serotonin Specific Reuptake Inhibitors

1. Generally safer in accidental or intentional overdose.
2. Some types are effective in 1-2 weeks (Zoloft).
3. Have very few side effects.
4. Are effective with once a day dosing.
5. Some types have no active metabolite reducing possible problematic interactions with other medications. (Zoloft and Paxil)
6. An additional benefit of Zoloft and Paxil is a faster elimination time.

Disadvantages of Serotonin Specific Reuptake Inhibitors

1. Are patented, and as "Brand" medications, are more expensive.

2. Some have a long half life causing them to take longer to be effective and longer to be excreted from the body. This is the case with Prozac which, when metabolized, results in the production of an active metabolite which can then interact with other medications and increase the total time of active medication elimination.

3. All antidepressant medications have the potential ability, in an apparently small percentage of persons, to "activate" them to an undesirable degree. While to a lessor degree this may be a desired effect, some individuals have been reported to have become *hypomanic* (mildly manic) or *manic* subsequent to treatment with antidepressant medication. The term bipolar III (see the Chapter on Mood Disorders) has been used to describe the individual that has this "activated" mania or hypomania subsequent to antidepressant treatment. This

reaction does not necessarily mean the medication must be stopped. In some cases lower dosages may result in this problematic activation being reduced or eliminated. In cases where a full-fledged mania results, the medication is most often discontinued while the manic state is managed by other medications.

4. In cases of an untoward or undesirable effect occurring several weeks after treatment with a long half life SSRI (e.g. Prozac) then it will take several weeks to completely eliminate the active drug from the body.

Mood Stabilizers and Anticonvulsant Medications

Brand Name	Generic Name
Eskalith	lithium carbonate
Tegretol	carbamazepine
Depakote	divalproex

Mood stabilizers include medications such as lithium carbonate and several of the anticonvulsant drugs. Lithium has long been the first treatment of choice in the treatment of the manic episodes of bipolar disorder. In recent years there has been an increasing trend toward treating those with bipolar disorder with anticonvulsant medications. This trend has been observed in the treatment of children as well as adults. In the case of bipolar disorder or temporal lobe epilepsy, or in a depressed individual with vulnerability to seizures, anticonvulsant medications have frequently been helpful. As with all disorders there are varying degrees of severity. In the most severe forms of bipolar disorder, it is often difficult to maintain a positive treatment response with only one medication. It is becoming more common to see a *polypharmacy* (the utilization of more than one medication at a time) approach in an attempt to stabilize the difficult to treat patient.

Neuroleptic Medications

Brand Name	Generic Name
Thorazine	clopromazine
Haldol	haloperidol
Mellaril	thioridazine
Stelazine	trifluoperazine
Navane	thiothixene
Clozaril	clozapine
Respirdal	respirdone

Neuroleptic medications are also known as antipsychotic medications, however, their use is not solely limited to psychotic conditions. Essentially, there are six classes of antipsychotic medications currently available in the United States. These are the phenothiazines, butyrophenones, thioxanthenes, dibenzoxapines, dihydroindoles and a new class referred to as atypical neuroleptics. The discovery of the neuroleptic drugs in the 1950's has reshaped the treatment of mental disorders and ushered in the era of biological interventions. The development and use of neuroleptic medications reduced the need for long term custodial care for many people. In addition to the neuroleptic's antipsychotic characteristics they have also been found to also be helpful in Tourette's Disorder (haldol), stabilization of manic patients and in some cases reduction of severe anxiety. The neuroleptic drugs generally have in common a characteristic action of antagonizing (blocking) the neurotransmitter dopamine. Similar to serotonergic receptors, dopamine has multiple *dopaminergic* receptor sub-types. The specificity of action at certain dopaminergic receptor sub-types is the characteristic of the atypical neuroleptics that presumably results in fewer long-term side effects and the preferential response demonstrated by some. The potential side effects with neuroleptic medications are numerous and will not be considered here. Nevertheless, there are many situations in which the neuroleptic medications add significant benefit to the armament used to treat resistant or serious disorders.

Antihistaminic Medications

Brand Name Generic Name

Benadryl   diphenhydramine

There are many antihistaminic medications available. Many such as Benadryl are now available over the counter. These have been used over a short term to assist anxious children to sleep. They are mildly sedating (for most) and safe when used as directed. As with all medications, the use of antihistamines should be discussed with your physician to ensure their proper application.

Evaluation of Medication Response

A positive medication response does not necessarily confirm that a given diagnosis is correct. On the other hand, a non-response or poor response may suggest that the diagnosis is incomplete or incorrect. The significance of proper differential diagnosis is underscored by audits of patient charts within two separate general hospital clinics that found only 51.5 percent of the children being treated with psycho-stimulants met the assessment criteria for attention deficit disorder (Jensen et al., 1989). The authors concluded that the initial assessment, follow up care and the overall quality of care in the diagnosis and treatment of attention deficit disorder had been found inadequate in approximately two thirds of the cases. Subsequent to initial identification, continued evaluation is required in order to provide effective on-going treatment.

The significance of early identification of psychiatric and psychological difficulties rests in the expanded options and opportunities for treatment. With recognition of the role of pharmacological treatments with children, the role of observing, measuring and documenting response to psychopharmacologic interventions has become increasingly important. For example, prior to initiating treatment with psychoactive agents, baseline assessments should be made to identify target behaviors of most concern.

A potential difficulty of attributing medication effects when they are not medication related is an illustration. Research addressing the adverse side effects of methylphenidate among mentally retarded children with ADHD demonstrated the importance of obtaining baseline information on potential positive and negative effects of medication (Handen et al., 1991). Many alleged side effects (while receiving placebo) may have been primary or secondary effects of ADHD. While the development of motor tics and social withdrawal were noted as possible adverse side effects within the population, the children responded to the stimulant medication at similar rates to nonretarded peers. The authors concluded that optimal clinical practice must utilize assessment of all primary and secondary effects of ADHD before the initiation of a stimulant trial in order that side effects can be assessed within the first week of treatment and periodically afterwards (Handen et al., 1991).

In addition to behavioral monitoring, some medications lend themselves to objective plasma level monitoring. Evidence that monitoring plasma methylphenidate concentrations is therapeutically helpful is weak (DeVane, 1990). On the other hand, monitoring plasma levels of imipramine and other tricyclic antidepressant is valuable. Broad inter-individual variability of tricyclic antidepressant plasma levels (Prescorn & Simpson, 1982) poses potential risk for the unmonitored patient while offering a rational dosing strategy in the patient receiving plasma level monitoring (Prescorn et al., 1989). Tricyclic antidepressant induced CNS toxicity is a common adverse effect of inpatient TCA treatment because the early stages of toxicity can appear as a worsening of depression (Prescorn & Jerkovich, 1990). Therapeutic drug monitoring of TCAs should assist, not replace, clinical judgement (Prescorn & Jerkovich, 1990).

C. Lindsay DeVane (1990) points out,

"The symptom overlap among various mental illnesses and the broad effects of psychoactive drugs often give the false appearance of an empirical approach to pharmacotherapy in clinical psychopharmacology.

A desirable approach is to identify target symptoms prospectively, select an appropriate psychoactive drug to treat those symptoms, and monitor treatment outcome. By combining an understanding of the time course of drug responses in the body with an appreciation for objective changes in laboratory test results and subjective changes in mental status that drugs can cause, one can objectively monitor psychoactive drug therapy to optimize patient outcome"(p. V).

Nelson and Mazure (1990) describe the construction and validation of an empirically derived scale, the TRIM, designed to rate tricyclic antidepressant response in major depression. Depression scales designed to measure global change in the depressive state, such as the Hamilton Rating Scale for Depression (HAM-D) and the Montgomery Asberg Depression Scale (MADS) were demonstrated as limited in measuring psychopharmacologic treatment response. TRIM scores were significantly correlated with desipramine and hydroxydesipramine levels while the MADS scores and Hamilton Rating Scale scores were not (Nelson & Mazure, 1990).

Nelson and Mazure (1990), point out,

"Rating scales designed to be more sensitive to specific pharmacologic profiles might help to define types of antidepressant effects. They might also help to detect more subtle drug effects, distinguish drug-related improvement in the presence of other symptoms, or determine true differences between drugs that global scales might fail to detect"(p. 253).

Since the majority of prescriptions for psychoactive drugs are written by general medical practitioners and nonpsychiatric physicians (Devane, 1990; Prescorn & Jerkovich, 1990) co-treating psychologists and **parents** are increasingly required to contribute to the psychopharmacological treatment evaluation data base. While the need for distinguishing psychopharmacological treatment response is critical in pharmacological research, the need is equally compelling in the more common treatment settings with out-patient children. Whereas the TRIM was empirically derived in an inpatient setting with trained observers and established inter-rater reliabilities, many clinical settings providing treatment to children receiving psychoactive drugs rely on un-defined anecdotal information regarding treatment response.

The Systematic Observation Scale (SOS) (Duke, 1988) and the Personality Inventory for Children (PIC) (Lachar, 1982) offer compatible, objectivity-enhancing methods for pre and post psychopharmacologic treatment observation and evaluation. The Personality Inventory for Children is an objective multidimensional measurement of affect, behavior, ability and family function, which is applied in the assessment of children from preschool through adolescence (Lachar, 1990). The PIC serves as both an actuarial pre-treatment diagnostic tool as well as a post-treatment repeated measurement indicating treatment associated change. Convergence and concurrent validity of DSM-III diagnosis and the Personality Inventory for Children have been demonstrated (Kline, Lachar & Gdowski, 1988). The PIC has also been demonstrated as useful in differential diagnosis including differentiating children with mania from children with attention deficit disorder (Nieman & DeLong, 1987), identifying children with somatoform disorders (Pritchard et al., 1988), and in assessing the psychological functioning of children who have recurrent migraine (Andrasik et al., 1988). The Personality Inventory for Children has been demonstrated as robust in terms of the predictive accuracy of the PIC scales. Even in cases of maternal psychopathology, PIC scale co-variations with independent behavior ratings from parents, teachers and clinicians were similar (Lachar, Kline and Gdowski, 1987).

There are no guarantees when a child begins a medication. There are children who are in need of a biological intervention that respond well to an initial medication trial and those who have a poor or inadequate response. As mentioned, there are risks associated with both a decision to use or not use a medication. As a child grows older the stakes increase. It is a very personal and important decision that a parent must make together with a trusted physician.

Behavior Modification

The definition of Behavior Modification and some basic techniques of behavior modification have been introduced in Chapter Four "Love and Discipline". It is worthwhile to incorporate behavioral techniques and principles into most other interventions. To review:

> *Behavior modification is defined as any procedure that reduces or suppresses an undesirable behavior or increases the likelihood or frequency of a desired behavior. There are both positive and negative forms of behavior modification. Corporal punishment is a form of positive punishment. Negative punishment is the condition where something desired is taken away (freedom, privileges etc.). Both positive and negative punishment are methods of suppressing an unwanted response. Reinforcement is the alternative where the goal is to increase the probability of a desired behavior. There are also positive and negative forms of reinforcement. Praise for a job well done is an example of positive reinforcement.*

Experiments with positive and negative punishment have clearly demonstrated the effectiveness of behavior modification methods with both humans and animals. The power of *negative punishment* is unquestionable, however, negative punishment results in side effects while suppressing other behaviors. An early experiment illustrates the point. In 1953 there was a study where spider monkeys were trained to press a switch for food. After the monkeys learned the switch pressing behavior the experimenters positioned a snake in the monkeys' cage whenever they grasped for food. The monkeys, who are frightened of snakes, stopped pressing the switch for food. As a result these monkeys developed many difficulties which included a breakdown in social relationships, sexual disorders and weight loss. Most of these unfortunate monkeys acquired neurotic and psychotic symptoms similar to those seen in humans, including the development of facial and other tics, hallucinations and asthma.

A very intensive and highly structured form of behavior modification has been used with autistic children. It demands comprehensive behavioral observations and recording in order to evaluate progress. This form of behavior modification is provided on a one-to-one basis and to be effective requires the coordinated training of all involved with the child so that the reinforcements are consistent. The reinforcements used include such things as smiles, pats on the back, food, praise or tokens. The treatment process begins as is suggested for all treatment approaches described in this text. The first step is the assessment, observation and baseline documentation of each significant biopsychosocial variable or domain. Then in each domain prioritized objectives to be modified are defined. Each domain's priority objective is focused on repetitiously until mastered. At that point the next objective is defined.

In the case of the autistic child, it is critical that the child is paying attention in order to learn. The behavior of looking at the parent or therapist and listening is *shaped* through reinforcement. Undesirable behaviors such as inattentiveness is modified or *extinguished* by non reinforcement. The following are examples of behavioral techniques:

Prompting- the parent or therapist might prompt the child to look at the speaker's eyes when spoken to. Once the child learns to look with the prompt, the parent or therapist works toward reducing the frequency of the prompt so that the child looks at the speaker without the prompt.

Modeling- the parent or therapist completes an action the child is requested to do. The parent might model petting a kitten as a method of teaching the child how to pet the kitten. After the child learns to respond to the request to pet the kitten, modeling is reduced (faded).

*Generalization-*refers to teaching the child to generalize behaviors to other similar situations. For example, looking at other people when they speak to him or her or petting other pets.

Behavior modification is effective for many children who suffer from functional nocturnal enuresis (night-time bed-wetting). The primary behavior modification treatment used for enuresis is called alarm therapy. Approximately 10 percent of five-year-olds and 5 percent of 10-year-olds suffer from nocturnal enuresis. The bedwetting alarm arouses the child when it senses wetness. Before using alarm therapy it is important to observe and evaluate the child's patterns of wetting for two to four weeks. Fourteen consecutive dry nights are considered by most to be a therapeutic response. Relapse may be defined as two wet nights within the same time period. Common reasons for a relapse or failure include family stress, poor housing, or behavioral problems. Observations should continue for several months after the child has succeeded in staying dry.

Cognitive Behavioral Interventions

Cognitive-behavioral therapy, abbreviated as CBT has been effectively employed with numerous childhood disorders including attention deficit hyperactivity disorder, aggression, depression and anxiety. Cognitive-behavioral therapy has been shown to be very effective, particularly when coupled with an appropriate pharmacological intervention.

> Drs. Kane and Kendall identified four children with over-anxious disorder. They provided these children with between 16 and 20 individual, hour-long cognitive behavioral therapy sessions. The treatment was centered around identifying emotions and thoughts connected with anxiety-provoking situations, then producing and evaluating a plan to handle the situation. The techniques of modeling, role playing, relaxation techniques and reinforcement helped the children acquire these skills. Once the basic skills were learned, they were practiced in anxiety-provoking situations. Parent's, independent clinician's ratings and child self-reports all evidenced improvement of specified behaviors.
>
> Kendall, P. C., Kane, M., Howard, B., & Siqueland, L. (1989). A social information processing model of social competence in children. In M. Perlmutter (Ed.) The Minnesota Symposia on Child Psychology: Vol. 18.147-158.

Current CBT with children has increasingly involved parents and other members of the child's family in the implementation of the treatment procedures. A family perspective of CBT attempts to secure the gains that can be had by including those most significant within the child's interpersonal and social context. When a parent involves other significant family members and possibly in consultation with a therapist, the family members can offer positive feedback for change, change their own perceptions and in some cases modify their expectations about the child as well.

Cognitive behavioral therapy (CBT) uses both behavioral interventions and cognitive interventions to create modifications in behavior, thinking (cognitions) and feelings. As such, this therapeutic approach addresses both environmental factors and the individual's inner feeling and thinking states. CBT lends itself well to the therapeutic parent since much of the way it has been practiced with children and adolescents is ultimately recommended to be applied by a parent. Many parents will find no difficulty in understanding and applying the principles established by CBT. Some parents wishing to assume this type of therapeutic role may find it useful to utilize a professional therapist knowledgeable in cognitive behavioral techniques to serve as a guide and consultant.

Basic Principles of Cognitive Behavioral Therapy

CBT centers on:

> How human beings respond to their interpretations of experiences instead of the environment or experience itself.
>
> How their thoughts and behaviors are related.
>
> Combining changes in thinking with behavioral interventions as a method of helping to change or restructure misinterpretations, distortions or inadequate perceptions.
>
> Constructing a fresh, more adaptive ability to understand and interact with the environment.

While the guiding principles of cognitive behavioral therapy are somewhat unconcerned with the role of genetics, biology or previous experiences, that is not to say that these elements are insignificant or unimportant. This text strives to emphasize the continuing inescapable interaction of the multiple factors that weigh on each individual circumstance. In fact, the understanding of contributory elements prepares a parent undertaking a therapeutic role with the necessary frame of reference required to effectively utilize a therapeutic change technique such as cognitive behavioral therapy. The aim of this technique with a child will be to assist in developing new coping strategies and understanding experiences in new ways. An example of showing someone how to look at something in a new way is illustrated by the metaphor of whether the glass is half empty or half full. Common statements identifying distorted perceptions are statements such as "Everyone hates me", "I'm ugly", "I'm stupid" and the like.

To effectively employ a CBT strategy a parent must seek to recognize distorted perceptions, evaluate them and develop ways to help the child view these feelings in another way. In doing this it is important to keep in mind that the obvious statement may not be the most significant distortion. For example, when the child says "No one likes me" it may not be a distortion or at least it may not be the most critical distortion. Maybe it is true that few people like the child. If that is the case, it is likely that a more significant distortion lie in the child's belief of why no one likes him or her.

A large portion of the benefit of CBT consists of linking emotional states with the new ways of considering experiences. This can be accomplished by first guiding a child through the types of situations being considered before they occur, and when possible, during the time the situation occurs. An example might be a child who says "None of the kids like me so they didn't pick me for either of the baseball teams". The therapeutic response would be to first find out more about the circumstances. For the sake of this example there were two teams to be made with 9 players each and 20 children hoping to be selected. Reviewing these elements with the child may help the child see that the particular rejection was not as personal as he or she may have experienced. On the other hand if it was, there would be further elements to consider. Whatever the circumstances, it can be helpful to introduce the idea of looking at circumstances in different ways in a non-threatening, supportive context away from the emotional event. After the child has begun to exercise the skills of "cognitive restructuring" it will be important for those skills to be practiced in situations that have stimulated previously distorted feelings.

CBT has been used effectively with an assortment of childhood disorders. This chapter will briefly consider parental applications with attention-deficit, depression, anxiety, aggression and pain.

In 1995 Dr. Phillip Kendall reported on a randomized clinical trial of anxiety disorders in youths. The young subjects had 16 to 20 sessions of individual cognitive behavioral therapy. The participants were either assigned to immediate treatment or to an 8-week wait-list preceding treatment. The treatment process trained the subjects in the use of cognitive methods of anxiety management, behavioral relaxation and provided practice building skills. The treatment included (1) identifying anxious feelings and physical reactions to anxiety, (2) identifying thinking patterns and thoughts in anxiety-provoking situations, (3) problem solving techniques and the development of coping plans, (4) evaluation and self reward. During sessions one through eight the basic concepts were taught. During the remaining sessions each participant practiced the coping skills with actual anxious arousal.

The first half of the treatment model was focused on communicating acceptance to the child, promoting the therapeutic relationship and building basic skills. The investigator concluded that the inclusion of the exposure process is essential. It is also suggested that exposure is optimal subsequent to acquiring coping skills in the framework of a positive relationship.

Kendall, Philip C. Cognitive-behavioral treatments. (Special Issue: Psychosocial Treatment Research) by Philip C. Kendall and Susan M. Panichelli-Mindel. Journal of Abnormal Child Psychology Feb 1995, v23, n1, p107(18)

Aggression

There are many possible reasons a child might be aggressive. In order for a therapeutic intervention to be effective it will be important to address each of the contributants to the aggression. In addressing the thinking and behavior of aggressive children it can be helpful to consider some elements common to aggressive children. Aggressive children have been shown not to use all of the information available to them when they make decisions and to show a slanted recollection of hostile signals. In uncertain circumstances, they ascribe others' behaviors as malicious. In turn, they may then justify an aggressive act. Aggressive children have also been shown to have limited problem solving abilities and to respond with impulsivity and aggression to frustrations. The principles of cognitive behavioral therapy with an aggressive child focus on the child learning better how to monitor him or herself in situations where they or others are angry. Aggressive people benefit from learning how to recognize their emotional reactions and feelings of anger. Behavioral methods include extinction techniques combined with positive reinforcement and controlling reinforcers that may be derived from the aggressive behavior.

Depression

Similar to its utilization in anxious and aggressive disorders, cognitive behavioral therapy treats the aspects of depression that results in the individual having distorted self perceptions. These distortions frequently result in a child making global, internal attributions for negative situations or events. Depressed children often have low levels of social and academic self confidence as well as a general sense of low self-esteem. Cognitive behavioral therapy with depressed children focuses on *cognitive restructuring* as a method of modifying the child's distorted assumptions, perceptions and thinking. Education about thoughts and feelings, relaxation techniques and social skills can all be useful.

Smart Parenting

Attention Deficit Hyperactivity Disorder

ADHD involves hyperactivity (heightened motor activity), impulsivity, and deficits in attention. Additionally, ADHD is often associated with aggression and conduct problems. ADHD has been characterized by deficiencies in problem solving, in modulation of behavior, and in overall self-control and regulation. Hyperactive children do not focus on tasks and have difficulties paying attention when there are distractions -- especially when the distractors are appealing. Douglas (1980) described these children as unable to "stop, look, and listen" and as having inefficient problem-solving skills (Tant & Douglas, 1982).

Various medications may be helpful and their effectiveness augmented by utilizing elements of cognitive behavioral therapy. By itself CBT is limited in its ability to influence the symptoms of ADHD. The limits of CBT can be reduced by including medication in concert with a selection of behavioral and cognitive components, designed for the specific needs of the child.

Pain and Learning Disabilities

Two types of techniques in CBT used for chronic pain are pain perception regulation and pain behavior regulation. Pain perception management uses muscle relaxation, deep breathing and imagery. Pain behavior management identifies and seeks to modify social and environmental influences that are associated with pain and rehabilitation. An example is frequently used to reduce children's pain. Children are taught to relax through contemplative breathing and through imagery of pleasing and distracting scenes. In a variation of that imaging technique, a child is asked to imagine the opposite of what they feel. For example, if a child feels burning pain, their imagery might be playing in snow or swimming in a pool. In these ways CBT can be used to moderate the stress and pain faced by children who are chronically ill.

The research literature supports the notion that CBT is an effective treatment method, particularly with certain childhood disorders. CBT is compatible with other treatment approaches and as such it can be applied in conjunction with other behavioral methods, biological interventions and play therapy methods.

Play Therapy

Parents have demonstrated their ability to be effectively trained as non-professional therapists in play therapy techniques. Dr. Lillian Stover, with others pioneered what has been referred to as filial therapy. In numerous studies parents have displayed that they can not only be effective therapists for there own children but that they generally also feel closer to their children as a result. There are other situations where "non-traditional" therapists have also been shown to be highly effective. Community mental health centers frequently utilize very effective para-professional counselors and therapists who are generally supervised by professional staff. The parent who is able to appreciate the tone and purpose of this book should have no diffculty becoming a very effective parent-therapist for their child. Being an effective parent-therapist also means knowing when to get professional assistance and consultation.

The effective parent therapist must keep in mind that play therapy is not the same as playing with their child as they might in other circumstances. There are important methods and sometimes subtle differences that can make the difference between whether or not a parent is effective as a play therapist. This chapter will present and discuss a basic play therapy method for parents.

What age children are appropriate candidates for a play therapy approach? In most cases, children between the ages of two and twelve tend to be the best candidates. The older children tend to benefit from a somewhat different approach although the fundamental principles are the same.

What types of problems will this technique benefit? To some degree, play therapy is an approach that can benefit to some degree a child with nearly any type of difficulty. As long as the parent can assume a therapeutic role (this will be addressed), this method can usually be helpful and relationship enhancing.

The Basic Therapeutic Commitment

It is suggested that the parent wishing to undertake this method commit themselves to a minimum of twelve sessions. It is further suggested that the sessions be scheduled weekly for 30 to 45 minutes. Younger children typically do better with the 30 minute time frame. The sessions should be stopped on time. Even if parent and child are having a great time, the session should stop at the end of the time. It will allow the child and parent to better look forward to the next scheduled play session.

The Therapeutic Environment

The therapeutic environment includes the demeanor and attitude of the therapist as well as the physical surroundings. It is essential that the parent therapist have an accepting attitude. The play therapy environment should be an exceptional setting in that the parent refrains from criticism, judgement, providing direction, asking questions or reacting personally to events in the session. It is important that the child be able to work through conflict through creative play. This process, in the presence of a warm, accepting and reflective parent, lends itself to increased self awareness and helps develop greater independence and adaptivity.

One of the most difficult habits for most parents to break is to not ask questions. The child, for example, may be sitting on the floor pretending to be cutting the head off of a doll. If the parent says "Why are you cutting the head off of that doll?" the child may say "I don't know". It may be true that the child doesn't know when a parent asks a question. Children frequently avoid the parent's ability to judge their response by saying, "I don't know". If instead, the parent simply reflects, "You want to cut off that doll's head", the child may or may not respond, but the process (unlike with the question) is not stopped. If the child were to respond to the reflective comment they might say "Yes, the bad guy is cutting off all of the kids heads". If that were the child's response it might demonstrate anxiety the child is expressing and feeling. When anxious feelings are expressed in a secure setting they are better dissipated.

Learning how to reflect feelings well, takes practice. Even experienced therapists using this technique must guard against over direction or intrusion. Usually asking a child a direct question will stop the creative process. A few examples of reflection may be instructive. Keep in mind that the therapeutic parent is attempting to facilitate and understand the expression of their child's feelings and conflicts. The parent should not try to interpret their insights to the child directly. The parent who recognizes that a child's play is suggesting a particular conflict and who interprets that directly to the child will cause the child to close that window that allows the parent to see. That is not to say that the parent can't assist in their child's discovery and recognition of their feelings; they can.

Many times children distance themselves from their feelings by attributing them to play figures or toys. The child who feeds the doll, may be demonstrating a nurturing attitude or identifying with the baby. The parents' reflective responses might be "The baby feels better now", "the baby was hungry". Children, upon hearing reflective responses often will acknowledge the reflection and add to it. The child might respond by saying "Yes, the baby was very hungry, mother was busy with the other children and forgot to feed her". An effective added reflection might be "Sometimes the baby feels left out when mother is busy". It should be noted that this reflection is very different than the parent saying "Sometimes you feel left out when mother is busy". If the child is expressing feelings at a distance through toy objects the parent should reflect those feelings on the toy objects also. If the child adds, "Sometimes I feel left out too", the parent can reflect more directly "Sometimes you don't get what you need when mom (or dad) is busy."

If this type of reflection seems odd to you stay with it, try it and you will better understand. While actively listening and watching the child a parent should not feel compelled to talk through the whole session. Apart from the reflective methods, children benefit from the parental closeness and attention. If the child is coloring or doing something quiet the parent should remain interested and comment on the colors or process.

It is important to expect and accept aggressive feelings in a play session. This is not to say that aggression is encouraged outside of the play sessions, however, everyone has aggressive feelings. In the play session context it will be counter productive for the parent to say "Don't hit that doll, you don't want to be mean to that kid". If a parent makes these types of remarks, the child's aggressive feelings may be inhibited in the play sessions and not given an opportunity for expression. More productive statements are illustrated by the parent who reflects the following types of statements: "You're mad at that guy", "You like to pound him", "It feels good to get your anger out", "He's angry at his mom".

Frequently, in response to the preceding types of reflections, children will tell you if you are on the right track or not. Children will often respond spontaneously to a reflection by clarification. For example, referring to the play context, they might say "Yeah, he took my friend's books" or "He always picks on that other boy" or "They won't let this kid play". When non-critical, accepting reflections are made the process will continue productively whether the reflection is accurate or not. The reflection becomes not only a method of demonstrating your interest but also a method of providing a sense of personal involvement. With a non-judgmental reflection, the child will feel someone has attempted to understand his or her feelings.

Getting Started

Several guidelines are helpful in preparing to conduct play sessions. The therapeutic parent must understand and be able to assume a therapeutic role. The play therapy sessions should be scheduled on a weekly basis at a regular time. The play therapy sessions should be protected from the potential interruption of doorbell, phones, siblings and others. A regular place within the home should be decided as the area for the play sessions. A wide mix of expressive play materials should be available. Ideally, this play session area will offer a comfortable flat floor space in which the child and parent can sit with play materials spread out. The child should go to the bathroom prior to the beginning of the play session. If a play session has to be canceled for some reason it should be rescheduled.

The parent considering these guidelines will note that many of these suggestions are also found in a professional therapy relationship. A child will feel the caring that is part of a session that is scheduled and treated with importance.

Play Materials

It is recommended that the parent put together a playset of materials that are available to the child only during play sessions. In this way the playset maintains a certain value that differs from normal toys. It also helps in keeping an adequate playset from becoming fragmented and with lost pieces.

Generally speaking, relatively inexpensive toys can be used for play sessions. Older children will often gravitate toward art materials and games, however, parents are often surprised when their older child enjoys some mild regression and plays, in play sessions, with toys long given up. It can be helpful to purchase some of these items at garage sales or second hand stores. There should be no concern about breakage. Cheap, expendable toys should be part of the playset. Some items that are very helpful are not necessarily cheap but a parent should feel free to build up a playset over time.

Playsets can grow as the parent and child gain more experience together in this method.

A dollhouse is a nice piece to have in a playset. Other play materials that are helpful include a set of family figures, a toy gun, a rubber knife, aggressive and non-threatening animal figures (dinosaurs, lions, tigers, sharks, deer, cows, horses etc.), toy soldiers, tanks, planes, cars, policemen, people figures (Fisher-Price little people are very durable and versatile), a bop bag, a baby, a baby bottle, play handcuffs, paper for drawing, crayons, clay, puppets and blocks. These are just a few ideas of helpful play materials. A parent should feel free to creatively design a play set as they become more familiar with the principles of the procedure. Inexpensive plastic baskets are ideal for holding playset materials.

Assuming a Therapeutic Role

The therapist's behavior is a critical element in terms of the effectiveness of this procedure. First and foremost, a parent must be prepared to separate angry feelings they may have toward the child and seek to better understand and help the child by use of this method. The parent must also understand that there will likely not be a large, immediate positive benefit from a particular play session. On the other hand, many parents report feeling closer to their children almost immediately after starting weekly play sessions. When provided consistently, play sessions are a therapeutic process that builds with time.

In the early sessions parents may feel unsettled and uncertain about the process. Parents frequently feel in the early stages of play therapy that nothing is happening, that all they are doing is playing. They may feel they are having no particular new insights about the child's problems or symptoms. Most children between the ages of 3 and 7 enter into imaginative play very easily. Although many parents do see immediate symbolic and imaginative play, others may not. Some parents may observe repetitive play with no apparent meaning. During these initial sessions it is very easy for a parent to feel anxious and ineffectual. It is most often the case, however, that more is occurring than meets the eye. Many young children seen by professional therapists demonstrate this initial, normally unexpected unimaginative play which may be related to environmental exposure to disorganization in their lives and their attempts during play to order their lives. Many children, however, also demonstrate this need to remain reality fixed and ordered as a way of dealing with their internal anxiety and disorganization.

In some cases, children who are preoccupied by inner turmoil devote many of their internal resources to basic adaptation and have little energy left to apply to imagining. Some children appear satisfied repetitiously doing the same things in play. Despite the appearance otherwise, repetitive play, in this context, is therapeutic. A parent or therapist can look upon repetitive play as a child's way of mastering or rearranging their world. Repetitive play is play that is completely under the control of the child. Even in symbolic and imaginative play it is common for a child who has been traumatized to repetitively reenact a play scene. A reduction of repetitive play or repeated symbolisms may suggest a reduction of anxiety and a greater feeling of control by the child. The regularity and stability of the weekly play sessions can play a role in helping a child feel the security of order and support.

It is all too easy for a parent or psychotherapist to maintain an expectation of what they feel should be occurring during a play session. If a parent or therapist feels anxious due to a lack of what they feel is transpiring, they will most likely communicate that anxiety at some level. Another important concept to keep in mind when conducting play therapy with a child is that even though a play expression does not have obvious symbolic meaning does not mean that it is not symbolically meaningful. An example would be the child who is pretending to be a mouse and is saying "squeak, squeak, squeak" over and over. The lack of obvious meaning to "squeak, squeak, squeak" does not necessarily mean that it is not significant. This example also lends itself to the previously recommended technique of avoiding questioning a child. Should the parent ask the child "What is that mouse squeaking about?" the child's response will almost certainly lead to more questions which have a high probability of closing the window to the meaning of this child's play. On the other hand if the parent speculates the reflection "That mouse is squeaking, he wants to find his friend" the child is more likely to respond with a clarification such as "no, he is mad because his mother told him to come inside!" or some other such revelation. In this way, even though speculative, a reflection by the parent or therapist does not derail the creative process, whereas a question usually will.

In the play therapy context, the stability and consistency of the setting, and the attentiveness and neutrality of the parent or therapist allows the child to develop a more stable model which can be internalized and developed. In being attentive and empathic, the parent communicates understanding, love and support. The consistent availability of the parent within a therapeutically sensitive situation frequently allows an anxious or internally focused child to become comfortable enough to enter into imaginary play in a way that had previously been unavailable to him or her. By following the child's play session lead, the parent is able to deepen the connection with a child. Parents are, after all, translators of cultural experience, their own and that of their children. By examination of themselves and in seeking to better understand their children, parents demonstrate and model putting meaning into words.

To potentiate a therapeutic process a parent must: 1) let the child direct the play session; 2) avoid giving the impression of shaping or expecting certain play session behavior and 3) be warm, friendly and accepting. It also helps to dump the toy and materials selection out on the floor in front of the child and parent. The child should be told he or she can play with whatever he or she would like. Once a child has experienced one or two play sessions the child will not require any start-up direction. The parent should tell the child that the only rule is that the child cannot be destructive or hurtful. If the child is destructive or hurtful the session will be terminated for the day. The next scheduled session should occur as scheduled, without recrimination or reference to the preceding week. Once the basic limit of no destructive or hurtful behavior has been expressed, it should not be brought up again until the limit needs to be set.

The therapeutic parent's job is to better understand the child, to reflect the feelings the child expresses and to follow the child's lead in play. These recommended methods apply solely in the context of play sessions. The child should be free to express him or herself as freely as possible within the play setting. The parent will need to consciously refrain from directing the process or asking questions. The parent should sit at the same level as the child and in close but not oppressive proximity. Looking at the child, watching the child and actively listening and reflecting carefully to the child are all important aspects of this procedure.

Permissiveness and Limit Setting

As you will see it is critical to allow the child to direct the session, however, it is equally critical to place some limits. Essentially, anything should be acceptable short of actual destructive or hurtful behavior. Methods of reacting to undesirable but acceptable play session behaviors will be discussed. Parents should be prepared to expect that all children will, in some form, test the play session limit. Testing the limits usually precedes a deeper level of therapeutic process. An example of how this might occur can be illustrated by the following dialogue of a parent using a non-directive play therapy approach and effectively setting and utilizing the limits established for the play session technique.

An Example of Setting Play Therapy Limits

The child has fifteen minutes of a very positive and productive play session and then begins hitting a doll with a toy metal gun. The parent says "You are angry at that guy". The child says "He's stupid! He is picking on all of the other kids" The child throws the doll at the wall. The parent says "It looks like you don't like him" The child throws the gun at the doll and hits the wall. The parent says "You hit the wall with your gun, that can damage the wall, if you throw anything more at the wall we will have to stop for today" The child throws another toy at the wall. The parent says " Ok, that's all for today we will have our regular play session next week."

The previous illustration may seem simple and obvious at first glance, but it is an important stage of the process. Once a limit has been carried out by the parent it demonstrates a deepening level of the process.

The Therapeutic Process

It is difficult and unnecessary to completely understand every element of what is therapeutic about the play therapy process. Nevertheless, it can be helpful to understand some of what makes this apparently simple process so powerful. It should also be recognized that the parent who follows these guidelines will increasingly gain insight and appreciate the complexity of the method as they gain experience.

Foremost, a parent is taking and protecting time to devote to the child. Even though this is (and should be) an unspoken element, the child recognizes this at some level. Additionally, the parent who listens and reflects to the child what they feel the child is expressing gives the child a genuine feeling that they are attempting to understand their feelings, even if they don't fully understand the child's feelings.

It is therapeutic for the child to have a setting in which he or she can express his or her anxiety, aggression, rage, love, loneliness or other emotions without fear of reprisal. It is therapeutic for a child to realize that his or her parent can recognize and accept that he or she have aggressive feelings.

Having and expressing aggressive feelings is different from acting them out. Frequently when children are anxious they reenact an anxious theme over and over until the anxiety is dissipated. Sometimes this process occurs over many weeks. Depending on the circumstances, sometimes even longer.

Initial sessions typically include testing limits. As sessions proceed, the child frequently demonstrates enough trust to regress in the session. Even older children may express fantasy play, baby talk and nurturing behavior (feeding dolls etc). Play therapy as an avenue for expression and protected time with the parent is supportive and relationship building. Again, the parent who does not typically allow baby talk, should not interfere with it's expression in the context of a play session. It is completely consistent for that parent to not allow baby talk outside of a play session.

As play sessions continue they frequently become more reality oriented. Usually parent and child feel considerably closer than prior to the sessions.

Exercise 5

Go to Chapter 11 which lists available play therapy books and samples of research articles on play therapy. Browse through the titles. The titles will give a sense of the range of research. The highly interested or motivated reader can take desired citations to a university library, find the reference librarian and be directed to articles of interest.

The methods and information provided in this book provide the parent with the potential to take on significant responsibility in league with their health providers. There will most certainly be those who will not have the desire or may not have the ability to utilize the information and methods offered. On the other hand, a parent who assumes a positive and active treatment understanding and treatment role will reap many rewards while also recognizing the limitations of treatment in given situations. A basic understanding of the common pharmacological agents used with children will assist the parent in communicating with the prescribing physician as well as preparing the parent to be a better observer of biological treatment response. These descriptions are meant as a general introduction and should not be considered as advice specific to any particular child.

This text encourages users to liberally consult the literature. When a parent is frustrated with a behavior it will help to seek further information or assistance.

Chapter Eleven

Resources

The aim of this chapter is to provide an overview of various resources. Included are citations of contemporary articles, toll free phone numbers for help, samples of research literature, titles of other related books and an additional bibliographic references. In addition to the resources listed in this chapter, most communities have regional or county wide medical and psychological associations which can provide referrals and direction. Many states and counties can also provide assistance or direction through agencies devoted to mental health, developmental disabilities and other human services. The information resource centers of most communities are their public libraries. Periodicals and inter-library loans are just a fraction of what most libraries can provide. Reference librarians can be an enormous help in locating or obtaining materials and information. Librarians are especially helpful in locating books that are out of print or not readily available. Some older book titles have been included in this chapter even though they may be out of print or not easily located. The older titles were included because they may be available in particular libraries and they also illustrate how many special circumstances are dealt with by various parenting books.

Widely available quality resources that are frequently overlooked include popular magazines such as "Parents Magazine", "Family Circle", "Good Housekeeping", "McCalls" and others. These magazines frequently offer excellent articles that are focused on common parenting issues. There are also many articles of interest available for general readers, within professional journals such as the Jouranal of the American Medical Association. A selection of particularly interesting contempory articles illustrates the abundance and practical advice provided by these magazines and journals.

Interesting Readings

40 ways to help your child succeed: tips from top principals. (school children) by Angela Ebron and Ann Matturro

>Family Circle Sept 1, 1995, v108, n12, p65(2)

>Tips are provided for helping children with homework, taking tests, school activities, motivation, peer pressure, and class participation. Advice was gathered through interviews of school principals throughout the US.

Adolescent medicine.(Contempo 1995) by Michele D. Wilson and Alain Joffe

>The Journal of the American Medical Association June 7 1995, v273, n21, p1657(3)

Attention-deficit disorder: born to be hyperactive?(Grand Rounds at the Clinical Center of the National Institutes of Health) by Alan J. Zametkin

>The Journal of the American Medical Association June 21, 1995, v273, n23, p1871(4)

Ben Wicks' born to read: literacy begins at home.(Includes information on Born to Read Day)(Special Advertising Supplement) by Diane Forest

>Maclean's April 24 1995, v108, n17, pS1(4)

Books, J.T., and me. (education of handicapped children) by Beth Porter Persinger and Judith Kent

>The Reading Teacher May 1995, v48, n8, p660(1)

Burning their bridges: disordered attachment and foster care discharge. by Rose Marie Penzerro and Laura Lein

> Child Welfare March-April 1995, v74, n2, p351(16)

Carly's race: the author, inspired by her daughter's example, keeps on running. by Kathy Kennedy-Steffen

> Runner's World Sept 1995, v30, n9, p32(1)

A championship idea: making sports more fun for families. (includes tips on what do do if your child does not seem to enjoy sports) by Ron Taffel

> McCall's Sept 1995, v122, n12, p120(2)

Classroom idea-sparkers. by Jenny Wojcik

> Childhood Education Spring 1995, v71, n3, p160G(4)

Cochlear implants and hearing aids. (Editorial) by Donald F. Moores

> American Annals of the Deaf July 1995, v140, n3, p245(2)

Cognitive profiles of reading-disabled children: comparison of language skills in phonology, morphology, and syntax. by D. Shankweiler, S. Crain, L. Katz, A.E. Fowler, A.M. Liberman, S.A. Brady, R. Thornton, E. Lundquist, L. Dreyer, J.M. Fletcher, K.K. Stuebing, S.E. Shaywitz and B.A. Shaywitz

> Psychological Science May 1995, v6, n3, p149(8)

Community-based schools: can technology help transform schools into real community centers? (includes related articles on Carrollton, GA school district's experience with telecommunications technology and use of freenet local BBSes) by Robert Gebeloff

> Electronic Learning Jan 1995, v14, n4, p26(7)

Company culture and men's usage of family leave benefits in Sweden. by Linda Haas and K. Philip Hwang

> Family Relations Jan 1995, v44, n1, p28(9)

Community adapted aquatics programming: need and necessity. (aquatic programs for disabled children)(includes glossary) by Jonathan Nessel

> Parks & Recreation June 1995, v30, n6, p48(5)

A death in the family: how children grieve and how you can help them heal. (includes related articles) by Adele M. Brodkin and Melba F. Coleman

> Instructor (1990) April 1995, v104, n7, p27(3)

Defining the "multi-" in "multicultural" through children's literature. by Lara L. Hillard

> The Reading Teacher May 1995, v48, n8, p728(2)

Developing power in linear measurement. by Sydney L. Schwartz

Teaching Children Mathematics March 1995, v1, n7, p412(5)

The discipline wars: when dad and mom undermine each other, kids get caught in the cross fire. (includes related articles on spanking and myths about discipline) by Roberta Israeloff

Parents Magazine August 1995, v70, n8, p119(4)

Earth-loving ideas. (children's environmental projects) by Barbara Hall Palar

Better Homes and Gardens April 1995, v73, n4, p198(4)

Educating through literature: flying lessons from 'Maniac Magee.' (teaching literature to children) by Irene Rosenthal

Language Arts Feb 1995, v72, n2, p113(7)

Encouraging young children's thinking skills with Logo. (Logo computer language) by Nicola J. Yelland

Childhood Education Spring 1995, v71, n3, p152(4)

Everybody's doing it. (saying no to children)(Parenting; includes related article) by Lawrence Balter

Ladies Home Journal March 1995, v112, n3, pS6(3)

The fall and rise of marriage: rebuilding commitment in a

culture of divorce.(Editorial) by Karen L. Maudlin and Michael G. Maudlin

    Christianity Today May 15 1995, v39, n6, p14(2)

Fat, thin, short, tall: help your child feel good about herself.(includes related article) by T. Berry Brazleton

    Family Circle Feb 21 1995, v108, n3, p42(2)

Five spiffy kids creativity programs. (draw and paint software) (includes related article on system requirements) (Software Review)(Evaluation) by Donna Cazet

    Technology & Learning Jan 1995, v15, n4, p6(4)

For the good, the true, and the beautiful: Northern children's magazines and the Civil War. by James Marten

    Civil War History March 1995, v41, n1, p57(19)

Four children; tight budget.(resources and ideas) by Kathy Fite

    Countryside & Small Stock Journal March-April 1995, v79, n2, p72(1)

Fun-filled facts: learning games for kids. (After Hours) (Software Review) (Evaluation) by Barry Brenesal, Charles Taft and J.W. Olsen

    PC Magazine Feb 21 1995, v14, n4, p365(2)

Getting in sync with school. (children becoming accustomed to kindergarten)(As They Grow: 5&6 Years)(includes related information) by Anne Cassidy

>Parents Magazine Sept 1995, v70, n9, p84(3)

Getting kids to listen: the real reason many preschoolers can't pay attention. (includes related article on teaching children to remember)(As They Grow: 3 & 4 Years) by Jane M. Healy

>Parents Magazine August 1995, v70, n8, p70(3)

The good marriage.(Column) by Judith Wallerstein and Sandra Blakeslee

>Family Circle July 18 1995, v108, n10, p136(1)

Guides for moms and their mates. (five books that help parents rear and understand their children)(Brief Article)

>People Weekly May 15 1995, v43, n19, p40(1)

Handling a biter: help your toddler use her words instead of her teeth. (includes related article on identifying causes of biting) by Cathy Rindner Tempelsman

>Parents Magazine May 1995, v70, n5, p50(2)

He said, she said.(parental arguments about child rearing)(includes related article on mixed marriage parents) by Nancy Hall

>American Baby June 1995, v57, n6, p76(5)

A healthy appetite. (feeding children) by Diane Welland

    Parenting June-July 1995, v9, n5, p190(1)

Help kids cope with their feelings. (pre-school children) by Robert A. Furman

    Education Digest April 1995, v60, n8, p23(5)

Helping your child - and you - get a good night's sleep.(Protecting Your Child's Health) by Paula Siegel

    Good Housekeeping Sept 1995, v221, n3, p157(2)

Help your child handle strong feelings. (includes related articles) by Debra Kent

    Working Mother July 1995, v18, n7, p56(5)

Home-style number sense: families activities that build math skills. (includes related article) by Dorothy Rich

    Instructor (1990) April 1995, v104, n7, p23(2)

How to love your kid's pals. (includes related articles on teaching children how to be assertive and dealing with an undesirable friend) by Ron Taffel

    McCall's June 1995, v122, n9, p102(2)

How to bring out the best in your child. (promoting positive qualities) by T. Berry Brazelton

>Family Circle June 27 1995, v108, n9, p35(3)

How friends can help you become a better mom. (mothers' social support networks) by Linda Bernstein

>McCall's July 1995, v122, n10, p80(2)

"I hate you!" (how to help children resolve disputes) by Ruth Mason

>Parents Magazine July 1995, v70, n7, p72(2)

"I'm so fat!" When kids hate their bodies. (includes related article) by Eva Pomice

>Redbook April 1995, v184, n6, p182(4)

Improving the life prospects of children: a community systems approach. by Craig Shields

>Child Welfare May-June 1995, v74, n3, p605(14)

Inclusion: what does the law require? (inclusion of disabled children in regular classrooms) (In the Classroom)

>NEA Today March 1995, v13, n7, p10(2)

Industry debates responsibility issue. (children's television issues) by Steve Coe

>Broadcasting & Cable June 19 1995, v125, n25, p23(3)

Internet-based learning? Mostly students use the Net to socialize.(Research/Center for Children and Technology) (includes brief glossary) by Kallen Tsikalas

    Electronic Learning April 1995, v14, n7, p14(12)

Is self-esteem an important outcome in hyperactive children? by Cheryl Slomkowski, Rachel G. Klein and Salvatore Mannuzza

    Journal of Abnormal Child Psychology June 1995, v23, n3, p303(13)

It's a scary world: parents have to face some ugly facts to deal with their children's fears. (includes information on what to tell children)(Cover Story) by Russell Watson

    Newsweek May 1 1995, v125, n18, p53(1)

Keeping your baby safe from disease. (includes related article on vaccines for infants up to 12 months old)(As They Grow: 0 to 12 Months) by Katherine Karlsrud

    Parents Magazine July 1995, v70, n7, p57(2)

Kids' health & safety. (taking medicine, kitchen hazards, sleepwalking, activities, door alarm, x-rays, shoes, rabies, bicycle rides)(includes related articles on children's health and safety) by Amy Sunshine-Genova and Maija Johnson

    Parents Magazine May 1995, v70, n5, p19(3)

Kids explore heritage through writers workshops and professional publication. by Melissa R. Lobach

The Reading Teacher March 1995, v48, n6, p522(3)

Kids: back to school. by Barbara Hall Palar, Mindy Pantiel, John Rosemond, Shannon Maughan and Debra Solberg Gibson

Better Homes and Gardens Sept 1995, v73, n9, p222(16)

Latino educators devise sure-fire K-12 dropout prevention programs. by Roberto Rodriguez

Black Issues in Higher Education June 1 1995, v12, n7, p35(3)

Leave your kids alone. (when to supervise toddlers)(Kids' Behavior) by Nancy Samalin and Catherine Whitney

Parents Magazine April 1995, v70, n4, p36(3)

"Less" can be "more" in the promotion of thinking. (thinking and decision-making in social studies) by Dwayne G. Olsen

Social Education March 1995, v59, n3, p130(5)

"Let's pretend!" (children's make-believe games)(includes related article on parents' responses)(As They Grow: 2 Years) by Bernice Weissbourd and Bill McCoy

Parents Magazine July 1995, v70, n7, p64(3)

Make a giant insect collage. (art and nature study project; includes related article) (Column) by Mary Parks

Instructor (1990) March 1995, v104, n6, p36(1)

Men as teachers: a self-help program on parenting for African American men. by Jay Fagan and Howard Stevenson

>Social Work with Groups Wntr 1995, v17, n4, p29(14)

"Mine!" Can you really teach your toddler to share? (As They Grow: 2 Years) by Patricia Henderson Shimm and Kate Ballen

>Parents Magazine August 1995, v70, n8, p67(2)

Money matters. (teaching children about finance)(includes related articles on lessons from everyday life and allowances) (As They Grow: 7 to 10 Years) by Janet Bodnar

>Parents Magazine May 1995, v70, n5, p68(3)

Mother stress: how to get dad to share the parenting.(includes related information on new fathers) by T. Berry Brazelton

>Family Circle July 18 1995, v108, n10, p22(2)

Neat tricks. (getting children to help with cleaning)(As They Grow: 3 & 4 Years) by Jennifer Cadoff

>Parents Magazine May 1995, v70, n5, p62(2)

The new summer camp. (educational camps)(includes directory of camps) by Candyce H. Stapen

>Better Homes and Gardens April 1995, v73, n4, p34(2)

New kid on the block. (children's adjustment to a change in residence) by Janine Pouliot

Woman's Day June 6 1995, v58, n10, p84(1)

No time for tears.(parents help their sick sons) by David Greising

Business Week May 22 1995, n3425, p92(3)

Our future depends on how we treat America's children.(Special Report)(Column) by Richard B. Stolley

Money May 1995, v24, n5, p153(1)

Parents and schools: will more parental involvement help students? by Charles S. Clark

CQ Researcher Jan 20 1995, v5, n3, p51(17)

Parent resources.(agencies that help parents)

American Baby April 1995, v57, n4, p58(1)

Put your last-born first (sometimes): how you can keep your second child from feeling second-best. (includes related article on spending time with children) by Patricia McCormick

Parents Magazine July 1995, v70, n7, p115(3)

Reality check: kids' looks matter. (helping children who are unhappy with their appearance; includes methods for boosting a child's self-esteem daily) by Ron Taffel

McCall's July 1995, v122, n10, p82(3)

Single mothers with custody following divorce. (Single Parent Families: Diversity, Myths and Realities, part 1) by Linda D. Ladd and Anisa Zvonkovic

>Marriage & Family Review Spring 1995, v20, n1-2, p189(23)

Stepping into another's shoes: simple ways to help nurture students' sense of empathy. (The Caring Classroom) (Column) by William J. Kreidler

>Instructor (1990) March 1995, v104, n6, p26(2)

Stumbling blocks or stepping stones? (how parents can help children overcome academic problems)(includes a related article on dealing with teachers) by Debbie Goldberg

>Family Circle Sept 1 1995, v108, n12, p58(2)

Suicide among children, adolescents, and young adults - United States, 1980-1992.(From the Centers for Disease Control and Prevention)

>JAMA, The Journal of the American Medical Association August 9 1995, v274, n6, p451(2)

Support for children of divorce. by Adele M. Brodkin and Melba F. Coleman

>Instructor (1990) Jan-Feb 1995, v104, n5, p30(2)

Taking nature's cure: do expensive therapy camps help or hurt troubled teens?(includes related article on 'escorts' who forcibly take children to camps at the request of parents) by Betsy Carpenter

    U.S. News & World Report June 26 1995, v118, n25, p54(5)

Teasing hurts! teach your child coping strategies that really work.(includes related information) by Lawrence Kutner

    Parents Magazine Sept 1995, v70, n9, p89(2)

Teen idols: celebrity crushes actually help your child learn about love.(As They Grow: 11 to 13 Years)(includes related information) by Richard M. Lerner and Cheryl K. Olson

    Parents Magazine Sept 1995, v70, n9, p91(2)

That scaredy-cat stage. (children's fears) by Harriet Brown

    Parenting June-July 1995, v9, n5, p183(1)

Toddler math: your child's skills get a boost when she can count on your involvement. (includes related article on recommended books)(As They Grow: 2 Years) by Jon Spayde and Bill McCoy

    Parents Magazine June 1995, v70, n6, p74(3)

Understanding ADHD. (attention deficit hyperactivity disorder)(Includes a directory of where to find help) by Laurie C. Williams

    Essence July 1995, v26, n3, p102(2)

Weathering life's bad days. (teaching children to cope)(child care: ages 5 & 6) by Salley Shannon

> Parents Magazine March 1995, v70, n3, p88(2)

"What happens when we die?" (helping children cope with death)

> Woman's Day June 27 1995, v58, n11, p114(1)

When kids hate the doctor: the best way to help them cope. (includes bibliography and related article on giving children shots) by Susan King

> Redbook July 1995, v185, n3, p150(2)

When a child has trouble learning. by Loraine Stern

> Woman's Day August 8 1995, v58, n13, p86(1)

Why preschoolers want to be little helpers and how to help them help you. (As They Grow: 3 & 4) by Lawrence Kutner

> Parents Magazine Feb 1995, v70, n2, p77(2)

Why kids collect: all that stuff gives them a sense of order and ownership. (includes related article on game called POG)(As They Grow: 7 to 10 Years) by Rosemary Black

> Parents Magazine July 1995, v70, n7, p74(2)

Winning and losing: learning to do both with grace boosts kids' self-esteem. (includes related article on how to modify games for players of various skill levels) by Carol Krucoff

Parents Magazine July 1995, v70, n7, p43(2)

Organizations

The Mental Health Association

Each October for the past several years thousands of Americans have congregated in hospitals, auditoriums and on college campuses to talk about sadness, anxiety and loss of interest. The national event is part of a now annual National Depression Screening Day. This is a public education program sponsored by the National Mental Health Association (NMHA). The NMHA is based in Alexandria, Va. and is primarily an education and advocacy organization committed to providing information that mental illness is treatable and not disgraceful. NMHA sends out free informational publications to anyone who calls its toll-free information number. Additionally, the NMHA lobbies Washington lawmakers in order to ensure that treatment of mental illness will be covered in health-care reform plans. Tipper Gore, is a NMHA group volunteer and NMHA supporter. Most communities have local Mental Health Associations.

CH.A.D.

Chad is an organization that exists at the national level and within many local chapters. The acronyn CH.A.D.D. stands for Children and Adults with Attention Deficit Disorders. This support organization beagan in 1987 as the initiative of a group of parents and professionals. The organization now has over 600 local chapters and over 25,000 members. The organization interacts on the local, state and national level to sponsor parent support groups, organize educational forums and impact educational policy. Members of CH.A.D.D. receive a regular newsletter, a magazine style publication with features regarding recent research and developments, a series of fact sheets regarding educational rights and medical management. Interested individuals may join CH.A.D.D. by writing:

Children and Adults with Attention Deficit Disorders
499 N.W. 70th Avenue, Suite 109
Plantation, FL, 33317
or calling: 305-587-3700

Toll Free Help Numbers

Social Security Administration
800-772-1213

Coalition for Persons
with Disabilities/Autism and
Cerebral Palsy 800-342-4587

National Council on Alcoholism
800-622-2255

AIDS Hotline
800-342-2437

Alliance for the Mentally Ill
800-950-6264

Al-Anon Headquarters
800-356-9996

Allergy and Immunology
800-822-2762

Alzheimer's National Office
800-621-0379

American Cancer Society
800-283-7800

Arthritis Foundation
800-283-7800

Better Hearing Institute
800-424-8576

National Library for the Blind
& Handicapped
800-424-9100

Breast cancer Support
800-221-2141

Cancer Information Service
800-422-6377

Child Help U.S.A.
800-422-4453

Childfind of America Inc.
800-426-5678

Children and Youth with Disabilities
800-999-5599

Children's Hospice International
800-242-4453

Cleft Palate Foundation
800-242-5338

Cocaine Hotline
800-262-2463

Consumer Health Information
800-821-6671

Covenant House (Crisis line for kids)
800-999-9999

Cystic Fibrosis Foundation
800-344-4823

Deaf Crisis Center (TDD)
800-446-9876

Deafness Research Foundation
800-525-3323

Juvenile Diabetes Foundation
800-223-1138

Down Syndrome Society
800-221-4602

Dyslexia Society
800-222-3123

Epilepsy Foundation of America
800-332-1000

Head Home Runaway Hotline
800-448-4663

Huntington's Disease
800-345-4372

American Kidney Fund
800-638-8299

Lupus Foundation of America
800-558-0121

National Down's Syndrome Society
800-232-6372

Parents Anonymous National Office
800-421-0353

Runaway Hotline
800-231-6946

Runaway Switchboard
800-621-4000

Tough Love International Inc.
800-826-0826

Family Medical Books

The American Medical Association Family Medical Guide

New Family Medical Guide.

Family Medical Guide.

Family Medical Software

Life Form (Health and Fitness)- Fitnesoft

Mosby's Medical Encyclopedia- Softkey

Body Works-Softkey

Pharmassist-Softkey

Parenting Books

Dinkmeyer-don.
The Parents Handbook. Systematic Training for Effective Parenting.

Dinkmeyer-don. Sr.
Title: Parenting Young Children. Helpful Strategies Based on Systematic Training for Effective Parenting (Step).

Parrish-j-kip.
Successful Parenting. A Common-Sense Guide to Raising Your Teenagers.
Forward by: Cosby-Bill.

Resources

Washington-steward.
Parenting.

Giddan-norman.
Parenting Through the College Years.

Meeks-carolyn-a.
Prescriptions for Parenting.

Coplen-dotty-t.
Parenting a Path Through Childhood.

Silberman-mel.
Confident Parenting. Solve Your Toughest Child-Raising Problems

Manginello-frank-p.
Your Premature Baby. Everything You Need to Know about the Problems, Treatment, & Parenting.

Christopherson-edward-r.
Beyond Discipline. Parenting That Lasts a Lifetime.

Kimball-gayle.
Fifty-Fifty Parenting. Equality in Current Family Styles.

Peters-ruth-a.
Who's in Charge? A Positive Parenting Approach to Disciplining Children.

Siegel-stephanie-e.
Parenting Your Adopted Child.

Sammons-william-a.
Self-Calmed Baby. A Liberating New Approach to Parenting Your Infant.
Forward by: Brazelton,T. Berry. (CONTRIBUTOR)..

Walker-peter.
Natural Parenting. A Practical Guide for Fathers & Mothers: Conception to Age 3.

Shalov-jeanette.
You Can Say No to Your Teenager. And Other Strategies for Effective Parenting in the 1990's.

Popkin-michael.
Active Parenting. Teaching Courage, Cooperation & Responsibility.

Spock, Benjamin.
Dr. Spock on Parenting. Sensible Advice for Today.

Dinkmeyer-don. Sr.
Parenting Teenagers. Systemic Training for Effective Parenting (STEP).

Helmstetter-shad.
Predictive Parenting. What to Say When You Talk to Your Kids.

Spock-benjamin.
Dr. Spock on Parenting.

Mckay-gary-d. Systematic Training for Effective Parenting

Clarke-p.
To a Different Drumbeat. A Practical Guide to Parenting Children with Special Needs.

Partridge, De Garcia, Priscilla.
Guilt-Proof Parenting.

Ikeler, Bernard.
Parenting Your Disabled Child.

Weinhaus-evonne.
Stop Struggling with Your Child. Quick-Tip Parenting Solutions That Will Work for You & Your Kids Ages 4-12.

Goldstein-robin.
More Everyday Parenting. The Six-to-Nine-Year-Old.

White-joe.
What Kids Wish Parents Knew about Parenting.

Stahl-philip-m.
Children on Consignment. A Handbook for Parenting Foster Children & Their Special Needs.

Cline-foster.
Parenting with Love & Logic.

West-kenneth.
The Twenty-One Deadly Myths of Parenting & 21 Creative Alternatives.

Finston-peggy.
Parenting Plus. Raising Children with Special Health Needs.

Jason-janine.
Parenting Your Premature Baby.

Goldstein-robin.
Everyday Parenting. The First Five Years.

Carroll-david-l.
Spiritual Parenting.

Newman-susan.
Parenting an Only Child.

Hughes-barry-k.
Parenting a Child with Traumatic Brain Injury.

Firestone-r-w.
Compassionate Child-Rearing. An In-Depth Approach to Optimal Parenting.

Cohen-miriam-g.
Long-Distance Parenting. A Guide for Divorced Parents.

Rickel-annette-u.
Teen Pregnancy & Parenting.

Silverstein-herma.
Teen Guide to Single Parenting.

Bigner-jerry-j.
Parent-Child Relations. An Introduction to Parenting.

Papernow-patricia.
Step Parenting. Stages of Development in Remarried Families.

Osborne-philip.
Parenting for the '90s.

Stern-phyllis-m.
Pregnancy & Parenting.

Sammons-william-a.
Self Calm Response. A Liberating New Approach to Parenting Your Infant.

Lansky-vicki.
Koko Bear's Big Earache. A Practical Parenting Read Together Book.

Mccoy-kathleen.
Solo Parenting. Your Essential Guide.

Payne-arlie-j.
We're Driving Our Kids Crazy. The Shift to Non-Guilt Parenting.

Olkin-sylvia-k.
Positive Parenting Fitness.

Bell-roselyn. (Editor).
Title: The Hadassah Magazine Jewish Parenting Book.

Loring-gloria.
Parenting a Diabetic Child. A Practical, Empathetic Guide to Helping You & Your Child Live with Diabetes.

Bowser-benjamin-p. (Editor).
Black Male Adolescents. Parenting & Education in Community Context.

Wilmes-david-j.
Parenting for Prevention. How to Raise a Child to Say No to Alcohol and Drugs, for Parents, Teachers, & Other Concerned Adults.

Relief-society-staff.
Parenting from A to Z. An Encyclopedia for Latter-Day Saint Families.

Adams-dan.
The Child Influencers. Restoring the Lost Art of Parenting.

Ehrensaft-diane.
Parenting Together. Men & Women Sharing the Care of Their Children.

Westlake-helen-g.
Child Development & Parenting.

Hetherington-mavis. (Editor).
Impact of Divorce, Single Parenting & Stepparenting on Children.

Helmstetter-shad.
Predictive Parenting. What to Say When You Talk to Your Kids.

298   Smart Parenting

Books on Child Development

Sears, William.
Your Baby. The first twelve months.

Bremner, J. Gavin.
Infancy.

Smith, Peter, K.
Understanding Child Development.

Sawyers, Janet, K.
Helping Young Children Develop Through Play. A practical guide for parents, caregivers, & teachers.

Rogers, Cosby, S.
Play In the Lives of Children.

Bailey, Rebecca, A.
The Dynamic Infant.infant & toddler development.

Gottfried, A.E. (EDITOR).
Maternal Employment & Children's Development.

Rathus. Spencer, A.
Understanding Child Development.

Damon, William. (EDITOR).
Child Development Today & Tomorrow.

Gonzalez, Mena, Janet.
Infancy & Caregiving.

Elkind, David.
Hurried Child. Growing Up Too Fast Too Soon.

McLoyd, Vonnie, C. (EDITOR).
Responses of Children & Adolescents to Economic Crisis.

Lewis, Michael. (EDITOR).
Infant Stress & Coping.

Valsiner, J. (EDITOR).
Child Development in Cultural Context.

Malatesta, Carol, Z.
The Development of Emotion Expression during the First Two Years of Life.

Wells, Carolyn.
Seven Ages of Childhood.

Rubinstein, Mark.
The Growing Years. The New York Medical Center's Guide to Your Child's Emotional Development from Birth to Adolesence.

Kuppuswamy, B.
A Textbook of Child Behavior & Development.

McGhee, Paul, E.
Humor & Children's Development. A Guide to Practical Applications.

White, Burton, L.
The First Three Years of Life.

Siegler, Robert. (EDITOR).
How Children Discover New Strategies.

Brazelton, T. Berry.
What Every Baby Knows.

Biracree, Tom.
Parent's Book of Facts. Child Development from Birth to Age Five.

Barton, James, P.
Title: Milestones in Child Development. Conception to Seven Years.

Appleyard, J. A.
Title: Becoming a Reader. The Experience of Fiction from Childhood to Adulthood.

Abrams, Berenda.
Title: Toys for Early Childhood Development.

Schickedanz, Judith.
Title: Understanding Children.

Lidhoo-Motilal.
Title: Child Rearing & Psycho-Social Development.

Ames, Louise, B.
Questions Parents Ask. Straight Answers from Louise Bates Ames, Ph.D.

Seifert, Kelvin.
Title: Child & Adolescent Development.

Large, Martin.
Who's Bringing Them up? Television & Child Development. How to Break the T. V. Habit.

Smith, Peter, K.
Understanding Children's Development.

Berk, Laura, E.
Child Development.

Mussen, Paul.
Child Development & Personality.

Bax, M. (EDITOR).
Title: Child Development & Child Health.

Ames, Louise, B.
Title: Your Nine Year Old.

Greenspan, Stanley.
Title: The Essential Partnership.

Dworetzky, John, P.
Title: Introduction to Child Development.

Beaty.
Title: Observing Development of the Young Child.

Westlake, Helen, G.
Title: Child Development & Parenting.

Humphrey, Joy, N. Child Development During the Elementary School Years.

Dugan, Timothy, F. (EDITOR).The Child in Our Times. Studies in the Development of Resiliency.

Play Therapy Books

Schaefer-Charles-E. Handbook of Play Therapy. JAN, 1983. Wiley.

YAWKEY-THOMAS-D. (EDITOR). Child's Play & Play Therapy. 1984.TECHNOMIC.

Krail-V. A Play Therapy Primer. Therapeutic Approaches to Children with Emotional Problems.1989. Human-Sci-Pr.

Axline-Virginia-M. Play Therapy. DEC, 1981.

Schaefer-Charles. Therapeutic Use of Child's Play. 1989. Aronson.

Kissel-Stanley. Play Therapy. A Strategic Approach. SEP, 1990.C-C-Thomas.

Schaefer-Charles-E. Game Play. Therapeutic Uses of Childhood Games.MAR, 1986.Wiley.

Samples of Research Articles Observational Methods

Kline-Rex-B. Maltz-Andrew. Lachar-David. Spector-Steve. et al.Differentiation of infantile autistic, child-onset pervasive developmental disorder, and mentally retarded children, with the Personality Inventory for Children. J Amer Acad of Child & Adolescent Psychiatry. 1987 Nov Vol 26(6) 839-843.

Keenan-P-A. Lachar-David. Screening preschoolers with special problems: Use of the Personality Inventory for Children J School Psych.1988 Spr Vol 26(1) 1-11.

Kline-Rex-B. Lachar-David. Sprague-Donna J. The Personality Inventory for Children (PIC): An unbiased predictor of cognitive and academic status. Jour. of Ped. Psych. 1985 Dec Vol 10(4) 461-477.

Lachar-David. Gdowski-Charles-L. Snyder-Douglas-K. Consistency of maternal report and the Personality Inventory for Children: Always useful and sometimes sufficient: Reply to Cornell. Jour of Consult & Clin Psych. 1985 Apr Vol 53(2) 275-276.

Lachar-David. LaCombe-James-A. Objective personality assessment: The Personality Inventory for Children and its applications in the school setting. School Psychology Review. 1983 Fall Vol 12(4) 399-406.

Voelker-Sylvia. Lachar-David. Gdowski-Charles-L. The Personality Inventory for Children and response to methylphenidate: Preliminary evidence for predictive utility. Journal of Pediatric Psychology. 1983 Jun Vol 8(2) 161-169.

Fleming, W. G. The observation of educational events. MEDICAL EDUCATION, 1990 Mar. 24(2). P 190-203.

Blom, S.D., Lininger, R.S., Charlesworth, W.R. Ecological observation of emotionally and behaviorally disordered students: an alternative method. AMERICAN JOURNAL OF ORTHOPSYCHIATRY, 1987 Jan. 57(1). P 49-59.

Fossi, L., Faravelli, C., Paoli, M.The ethological approach to the assessment of depressive disorders. JOURNAL OF NERVOUS AND MENTAL DISEASE, 1984 Jun. 172(6). P 332-41.

Gleason, John J.Meaning of play: Interpreting patterns in behavior of persons with severe developmental Anthropology & Education Quarterly. 1990 Mar Vol 21(1) 59-77.

Notarius, Clifford, I., Markman, Howard J.Coding marital interaction: A sampling and discussion of current issues. Special Issue: Coding marital interaction. Behavioral Assessment. 1989 Vol 11(1) 1-11.

Horwitz, R.I., Viscoli, C.M., Clemens, J.D., Sadock,R.T. Developing Improved Observational Methods for Evaluating Therapeutic Effectiveness. AMERICAN JOURNAL OF MEDICINE, 89:5. NOVEMBER 1990. P 630-8.

Behavioral Strategies and Interventions

Erhardt-D. Baker-B-L. The effects of behavioral parent training on families with young hyperactive children. JOURNAL OF BEHAVIOR THERAPY AND EXPERIMENTAL PSYCHIATRY, 21:2. JUNE 1990. P 121-32.

Miller-Gloria-E. Prinz-Ronald-J. Enhancement of social learning family interventions for childhood conduct disorder.Psychological Bulletin. 1990 Sep Vol 108(2) 291-307.

King-Neville-J. Ollendick-Thomas-H. Children's anxiety and phobic disorders in school settings: Classification, assessment, and intervention issues.Review of Educational Research. 1989 Win Vol 59(4) 431-470.

Calvert-Susan-C. Johnston-Charlotte. Acceptability of treatments for child behavior problems: Issues and implications for future research.Journal of Clinical Child Psychology. 1990 Mar Vol 19(1) 61-74.

Sullivan-Kathryn-A. A cognitive-behavioral intervention for impulsive, attention deficit disordered children.DissertationAbstracts International. 1989 May Vol 49(11-A) 3314.

Butler-Gillian. Issues in the application of cognitive and behavioral strategies to the treatment of social phobia. Special Issue: Social phobia.Clinical Psychology Review. 1989 Vol 9(1) 91-106.

Childhood Behavior Disorders

Kellmayer, John Educating chronically disruptive and disaffected high school students. In: NASSP Bulletin Jan 1995, v79, n567, p82(6)

Barber, Stephen Educating Disruptive Children: Placement and Progress in Residential Special Schools .... Times Educational Supplement Jan 6 1995, n4097, pA16(1)

Hanna, Gregory L. Title: Whole blood serotonin and disruptive behaviors in juvenile obsessive-compulsive disorder. Journal of the American Academy of Child and Adolescent Psychiatry Jan 1995, v34, n1, p28(8)

Fergusson, David M. Predictive validity of categorically and dimensionally scored measures of disruptive childhood behaviors. Journal of the American Academy of Child and Adolescent Psychiatry April 1995, v34, n4, p477(9)

Batz, Jeannette. Girls with ADD. (Attention Deficit Disorder) COPYRIGHT K-III Magazine. 1995

Robert D. Hunt, Amy F.T. Arnsten and Matthew D. Asbell. An open trial of guanfacine in the treatment of attention-deficit hyperactivity disorder. American Academy of Child and Adolescent Psychiatry 1995.

Biederman, J., Milberger, S., Faraone, S. Guite, Warburton, R. Associations between childhood asthma and ADHD: issues of psychiatric comorbidity and familiarity. American Academy of Child and Adolescent Psychiatry 1994

Clikeman, Filipek, Biederman, Steingard, Kennedy, Renshaw and Bekken. Attention-deficit hy. peractivity disorder: magnetic resonance imaging morphometric analysis of the corpus callosum. American Academy of Child and Adolescent Psychiatry 1994.

Adelman, H.S., Taylor, L. Intrinsic motivation and school misbehavior: some intervention implications. JOURNAL OF LEARNING DISABILITIES, 1990 Nov. 23(9). P 541-50.

White, A.G., Bailey J. S. Reducing disruptive behaviors of elementary physical education students with sit and watch. JOURNAL OF APPLIED BEHAVIOR ANALYSIS. 1990 Fall. 23(3). P 353-9.

Cooper-L-J. Wacker-D-P. Sasso-G-M. Reimers-T-M. Donn-L-K. Using parents as therapists to evaluate appropriate behavior of their children: application to a tertiary diagnostic clinic. JOURNAL OF APPLIED BEHAVIOR ANALYSIS. 1990 Fall. 23(3). P 285-96.

Rubin-K-H. Mills-R-S. Maternal beliefs about adaptive and maladaptive social behaviors in normal, aggressive, and withdrawn preschoolers. JOURNAL OF ABNORMAL CHILD PSYCHOLOGY. 1990 Aug. 18(4). P 419-35.

Berden-G-F. Althaus-M. Verhulst-F-C. Major life events and changes in the behavioural functioning of children. JOURNAL OF CHILD PSYCHOLOGY AND PSYCHIATRY AND ALLIED DISCIPLINES. 1990 Sep. 31(6). P 949-59.

Brumback-R-A. Weinberg-W-A. Pediatric behavioral neurology: an update on the neurologic aspects of depression, hyperactivity, and learning disabilities. NEUROLOGIC CLINICS. 1990 Aug. 8(3). P 677-703.

Fauber-R. Forehand-R. Thomas-A-M. Wierson-M. A mediational model of the impact of marital conflict on adolescent adjustment in intact and divorced families: the role of disrupted parenting. CHILD DEVELOPMENT, 1990 Aug. 61(4). P 1112-23.

Barkley-R-A, Fischer-M, Edelbrock-C-S, Smallish-L. The adolescent outcome of hyperactive children diagnosed by research criteria: I. An 8-year prospective follow-up study. JOURNAL OF THE AMERICAN ACADEMY OF CHILD AND ADOLESCENT PSYCHIATRY. 1990 Jul. 29(4). P 546-57.

Paniagua-F-A. Morrison-P-B. Black-S-A. Management of a hyperactive-conduct disordered child through correspondence training: a preliminary study. JOURNAL OF BEHAVIOR THERAPY AND EXPERIMENTAL PSYCHIATRY. 1990 Mar. 21(1). P 63-8.

Laite-G-E. Galvin-M-R. Conduct disorder: a review. INDIANA MEDICINE. 1990 Mar. 83(3). P 172-9.

Weiner-I-B. Distinguishing healthy from disturbed adolescent development. JOURNAL OF DEVELOPMENTAL AND BEHAVIORAL PEDIATRICS 1990 Jun. 11(3). P 151-4.

Brand-H-J. Crous-B-H. Hanekom-J-D. Perceived parental inconsistency as a factor in the emotional development of behaviour-disordered children. PSYCHOLOGICAL REPORTS. 1990 Apr. 66(2). P 620-2.

Dadds-M-R. Sheffield-J-K. Holbeck-J-F. An examination of the differential relationship of marital discord to parents' discipline strategies for boys and girls. JOURNAL OF

ABNORMAL CHILD PSYCHOLOGY. 1990 Apr. 18(2). P 121-9.

Haynes-N-M. Influence of self-concept on school adjustment among middle-school students. JOURNAL OF SOCIAL PSYCHOLOGY. 1990 Apr. 130(2). P 199-207.

Elster-A-B. Ketterlinus-R. Lamb-M-E. Association between parenthood and problem behavior in a national sample of adolescents [see comments]. Pediatrics. 1990 Jun. 85(6). P 1044-50.

Pehrson-K-L. Parental self-assessment and behavioral problems of preschool children. MILITARY MEDICINE. 1990 Apr. 155(4). P 148-52.

Thompson-R-J Jr. Lampron-L-B. Johnson-D-F. Eckstein-T-L. Behavior problems in children with the presenting problem of poor school performance. JOURNAL OF PEDIATRIC PSYCHOLOGY. 1990 Feb.15(1). P 3-20.

Reid-W-J.Crisafulli-A.Marital discord and child behavior problems: a meta-analysis. JOURNAL OF ABNORMAL CHILDPSYCHOLOGY.1990 Feb. 18(1). P 105-17.

James-A. Taylor-E. Sex differences in the hyperkinetic syndrome of childhood. JOURNAL OF CHILD PSYCHOLOGY AND PSYCHIATRY AND ALLIED DISCIPLINES. 1990 Mar. 31(3). P 437-46.

Adelman-H-S. MacDonald-V-M. Nelson-P. Smith-D-C. Taylor-L. Motivational readiness and the participation of children with learning and behavior problems in psychoeducational decision making. JOURNAL OF LEARNING DISABILITIES. 1990 Mar. 23(3). P 171-6.

Nussbaum-N-L.,Grant-M-L, Roman-M-J., Poole-J-H., Bigler-E-D. Attention deficit disorder and the mediating effect of age on academic and behavioral variables JOURNAL OF DEVELOPMENTAL AND BEHAVIORAL PEDIATRICS. 1990 Feb. 11(1). P 22-6.

Heath-C-T Jr. Wright-H-H. Batey-S-R. Attention deficit hyperactivity disorder: does it affect adults too?

SOUTHERN MEDICAL JOURNAL. 1990 Dec.(12). 1396-401.

Calis-K-A. Grothe-D-R. Elia-J. Attention-deficit hyperactivity disorder. CLINICAL PHARMACY. 1990 Aug. 9(8). P 632-42.

Wolraich-M-L. Lindgren-S. Stromquist-A. Milich-R. Davis-C. Watson-D. Stimulant medication use by primary care physicians in the treatment of attention deficit hyperactivity disorder. Pediatrics. 1990 Jul. 86(1). P 95-101.

Biederman-J. The diagnosis and treatment of adolescent anxiety disorders. JOURNAL OF CLINICAL PSYCHIATRY. 1990 May. 51 Suppl. P 20-6; discussion 50-3.

Weinberg-W-A. Brumback-R-A. Primary disorder of vigilance: a novel explanation of inattentiveness, daydreaming, boredom, restlessness, and sleepiness. JOURNAL OF PEDIATRICS. 1990 May. 116(5). P 720-5.

Author: Pelham-W-E Jr. McBurnett-K. Harper-G-W. Milich-R. Murphy-D-A. Clinton-J. Thiele-C.
Methylphenidate and baseball playing in ADHD children: who's on first? JOURNAL OF CONSULTING AND CLINICAL PSYCHOLOGY. 1990 Feb. 58(1). P 130-3.

Campbell-L-R. Cohen-M. Management of attention deficit hyperactivity disorder (ADHD). A continuing dilemma for physicians and educators. CLINICAL PEDIATRICS. (Phila). 1990 Mar. 29(3). P 191-3.

Cooper-L-J. Wacker-D-P. Sasso-G-M. Reimers-T-M. Donn-L-K. Using parents as therapists to evaluate appropriate behavior of their children: application to a tertiary diagnostic clinic. JOURNAL OF APPLIED BEHAVIOR ANALYSIS. 1990 Fall. 23(3). P 285-96.

Laite-G-E. Galvin-M-R. Conduct disorder: a review. INDIANA MEDICINE. 1990 Mar. 83(3). P 172-9.

Keltner-B. Keltner-N-L. Farren-E. Family routines and conduct disorders in adolescent girls. WESTERN JOURNAL OF NURSING RESEARCH. 1990 Apr. 12(2). P 161-70; discussion 170-4.

Children's Emotional Disorders

Ackerson-L-M. Dick-R-W. Manson-S-M. Baron-A-E. Properties of the Inventory to Diagnose Depression in American Indian adolescents.JOUR. OF THE AMER ACAD OF CHILD AND ADOLESCENT PSYCHIATRY. 1990 Jul. 29(4). P 601-7.

Alnaes-R. Torgersen-S. Parental representation in patients with major depression, anxiety disorder and mixed conditions.ACTA PSYCHIATRICA SCANDINAVICA.1990 Jun. 81(6). P 518-22.

Anderson-R. Depression in childhood. 2. A psychoanalytic approach.BMJ.1990 May 12. 300(6734). P 1261-2; discussion 1260.

Auchter-U. Anxiety in children--an investigation on various forms of anxiety. ACTA PAEDOPSYCHIATRICA.1990. 53(1). P 78-88.

Author: Hughes-P-M. Lieberman-S. Troubled parents: vulnerability and stress in childhood cancer.BRITISH JOURNAL OF MEDICAL PSYCHOLOGY.1990 Mar. 63 (Pt 1). P 53-64.

Baker-J-E. Family adaptation when one member has a head injury.JOURNAL OF NEUROSCIENCE NURSING.1990 Aug. 22(4). P 232-7.

Ballenger JC, Reus VI, Post RM (1982). The "atypical" presentation of adolescent mania. Am J Psychiatry 139:602-606

Barkley-R-A. McMurray-M-B. Edelbrock-C-S. Robbins-K. Side effects of methylphenidate in children with attention deficit hyperactivity disorder: a systemic, placebo-controlled evaluation.PEDIATRICS.1990 Aug. 86(2). P 184-92.

Bassuk-E-L. Rosenberg-L. Psychosocial characteristics of homeless children and children with homes.PEDIATRICS.1990 Mar. 85(3). P 257-61.

Bell-Dolan-D-J. Last-C-G. Strauss-C-C. Symptoms of anxiety disorders in normal children.JOURNAL OF THE AMERICAN ACADEMY OF CHILD AND ADOLESCENT PSYCHIATRY.1990 Sep. 29(5). P 759-65.

Bendor-S-J. Anxiety and isolation in siblings of pediatric cancer patients: the need for prevention.SOCIAL WORK IN HEALTH CARE. 1990. 14(3). P 17-35.

Berman-M-H. Taming the tot: how to handle the difficult pediatric patients.DENTISTRY.1990 Apr. 10(2). P 16-20.

Bernstein-G-A. Garfinkel-B-D. Borchardt-C-M. Comparative studies of pharmacotherapy for school refusal.JOURNAL OF THE AMERICAN ACADEMY OF CHILD AND ADOLESCENT PSYCHIATRY. 1990 Sep. 29(5). P 773-81.

Bernstein-G-A. Svingen-P-H Garfinkel-B-D. School phobia: patterns of family functioning.JOURNAL OF THE AMERICAN ACADEMY OF CHILD AND ADOLESCENT PSYCHIATRY. 1990 Jan. 29(1). P 24-30.

Bertagnoli-M-W. Borchardt-C-M. A review of ECT for children and adolescents.JOURNAL OF THE AMERICAN ACADEMY OF CHILD AND ADOLESCENT PSYCHIATRY. 1990 Mar. 29(2). P 302-7.

Biederman-J. Rosenbaum-J-F. Hirshfeld-D-R. Faraone-S-V. Bolduc-E-A. Gersten-M. Meminger-S-R. Kagan-J. Snidman-N. Reznick-J-S. Psychiatric correlates of behavioral inhibition in young children of parents with and without psychiatric disorders.ARCHIVES OF GENERAL PSYCHIATRY.1990 Jan. 47(1). P 21-6.

Biederman-J. The diagnosis and treatment of adolescent anxiety disorders.JOURNAL OF CLINICAL PSYCHIATRY.1990 May. 51 Suppl. P 20-6; discussion 50-3.

Black-B. Robbins-D-R. Panic disorder in children and adolescents.JOURNAL OF THE AMERICAN ACADEMY OF CHILD AND ADOLESCENT PSYCHIATRY. 1990 Jan. 29(1). P 36-44.

Black DW, Winokur G, Bell S, Nasrallah, Hulbert J (1988). Complicated mania: comorbidity and immediate outcome in the treatment of mania. Arch Gen Psychiatry 45:232-236

Bowen-R-C. Offord-D-R. Boyle-M-H. The prevalence of overanxious disorder and separation anxiety disorder: results from the Ontario Child Health Study.JOURNAL OF THE AMERICAN ACADEMY OF CHILD AND ADOLESCENT PSYCHIATRY. 1990 Sep. 29(5). P 753-8.

Deblinger-E. McLeer-S-V. Henry-D. Cognitive behavioral treatment for sexually abused children suffering post-traumatic stress: preliminary findings.JOURNAL OF THE AMERICAN ACADEMY OF CHILD AND ADOLESCENT PSYCHIATRY. 1990 Sep. 29(5). P 747-52.

Bowring MA, Kovacs M (1992). Difficulties in diagnosing manic disorders among children and adolescents. J Am Acad Child Adolesc Psychiatry 31:611-614

Bradley-S. Wachsmuth-R. Swinson-R. Hnatko-G. A pilot study of panic attacks in a child and adolescent psychiatric population.CANADIAN JOURNAL OF PSYCHIATRY. REVUE CANADIENNE DE1990 Aug. 35(6). P 526-8. PSYCHIATRIE.

Brennan-J. Andrews-G. Morris-Yates-A. Pollock-C. An examination of defense style in parents who abuse children.JOURNAL OF NERVOUS AND MENTAL DISEASE.1990 Sep. 178(9). P 592-5.

Bromet EJ, Schwartz JE, Fennig S et al. (1992). The epidemiology, of psychoses: the Suffolk Country Mental Health Project. Schizophr Bull 18:255

Brophy-C-J. Erickson-M-T. Children's self-statements and adjustment to elective outpatient surgery.JOURNAL OF DEVELOPMENTAL AND BEHAVIORAL PEDIATRICS.1990 Feb. 11(1). P 13-6.

Bruder-G. Puig-Antich-J. Berger-Gross-P. Ausubel-R. Auditory perception and lateralization in prepubertal children with depressive and nondepressive emotional disorders. JOURNAL OF THE AMERICAN ACADEMY OF CHILD AND ADOLESCENT PSYCHIATRY.1987 Mar. 26(2). P 197-202.

Buhrmester-D. Intimacy of friendship, interpersonal competence, and adjustment during preadolescence and adolescence.CHILD DEVELOPMENT.1990 Aug. 61(4). P 1101-11.

Buist-A-E. Dennerstein-L. Burrows-G-D. Review of a mother-baby unit in a psychiatric TRALIAN AND NEW ZEALAND JOURNAL OF PSYCHIATRY.1990 Mar. 24(1). P 103-8.

Cadman-D. Boyle-M. Offord-D-R. The Ontario Child Health Study: social adjustment and mental health of siblings of children with chronic health problems.JOURNAL OF DEVELOPMENTAL AND BEHAVIORAL PEDIATRICS.1988 Jun. 9(3). P 117-21.

Campbell-S-B. Ewing-L-J. Follow-up of hard-to-manage preschoolers: adjustment at age 9 and predictors of continuing symptoms.JOURNAL OF CHILD PSYCHOLOGY AND PSYCHIATRY AND ALLIED1990 Sep. 31(6). P 871-89. DISCIPLINES.

Carlson, Gabrielle A., Shmuel Fennig and Evelyn J. Bromet. The confusion between bipolar disorder and schizophrenia in youth: where does it stand in the 1990s? American Academy of Child and Adolescent Psychiatry 1994

Carlson GA, Davenport YB, Jamison KR (1977). A comparison of outcome in adolescent and late-onset bipolar manic-depressive illness. Am J Psychiatry 134:919-922

Carlson GA (1990). Child and adolescent mania: diagnostic considerations. J Child Psychol Psychiatry 31:331-341

Carlson GA, Strober (1978). Manic depressive illness in early adolescence: a study of clinical and diagnostic characteristics in six cases. J Am Acad Child Psychiatry 2:511-525

Chang-P-N.Psychosocial needs of long-term childhood cancer survivors: a review of literature.PEDIATRICIAN.1991. 18(1). P 20-4.

Chellappah-N-K. Vignehsa-H. Milgrom-P. Lam-L-G. Prevalence of dental anxiety and fear in children in Singapore.COMMUNITY DENTISTRY AND ORAL EPIDEMIOLOGY.1990 Oct. 18(5). P 269-71.

Comings-D-E. Comings-B-G. A controlled family history study of Tourette's syndrome,

I: Attention-deficit hyperactivity disorder and learning disorders.JOURNAL OF CLINICAL PSYCHIATRY.1990 Jul. 51(7). P 275-80.

Costello-E-J. Janiszewski-S. Who gets treated? Factors associated with referral in children with psychiatric disorders.ACTA PSYCHIATRICA SCANDINAVICA.1990 Jun. 81(6). P 523-9.

Cotterill-J-A. Psychophysiological aspects of eczema.SEMINARS IN DERMATOLOGY.1990 Sep. 9(3). P 216-9.

Cowen-E-L. Pedro-Carroll-J-L. Alpert-Gillis-L-J. Relationships between support and adjustment among children of divorce.JOURNAL OF CHILD PSYCHOLOGY AND PSYCHIATRY AND ALLIED DISCIPLINES.1990 Jul. 31(5). P 727-35.

Curry-J-F. Craighead-W-E. Attributional style in clinically depressed and conduct disordered adolescents.JOURNAL OF CONSULTING AND CLINICAL PSYCHOLOGY.1990 Feb. 58(1). P 109-15.

Der G, Gupta S, Murray R-M (1990). Is schizophrenia disappearing? Lancet 1:513-516

Dietrich-D. Berkowitz-L. Kadushin-A. McGloin-J. Some factors influencing abusers' justification of their child abuse.CHILD ABUSE AND NEGLECT.1990. 14(3). P 337-45.

Dilsaver-S-C. Jaeckle-R-S. The naturally occurring rhythm of blues: winter depression.OHIO MEDICINE.1990 Jan. 86(1). P 58-61.

Dobson-P. Enuresis. Bedwetting--the last taboo.NURSING STANDARD.1990 Jul 25-31. 4(44). P 25-7.

Downey-J. Bidder-R-T. Perinatal information on infant crying.CHILD: CARE, HEALTH AND DEVELOPMENT.1990 Mar-Apr. 16(2). P 113-21.

Dreman-S. Orr-E. Aldor-R. Sense of competence, time perspective, and state-anxiety of separated versus divorced mothers.AMERICAN JOURNAL OF ORTHOPSYCHIATRY.1990 Jan. 60(1). P 77-85.

Duncan-Jones-P. Fergusson-D-M. Ormel-J. Horwood-L-J. A model of stability and change in minor psychiatric symptoms: results from three longitudinal studies.PSYCHOLOGICAL MEDICINE. MONOGRAPH SUPPLEMENT.1990. 18. P 1-28.

Elks-M-L. Pseudohypoglycemia in adult victims of adolescent incest.SOUTHERN MEDICAL JOURNAL.1990 Nov. 83(11). P 1338-40.

Ellis-E-M. Adult agoraphobia and childhood separation anxiety: using children's literature to understand the link.AMERICAN JOURNAL OF PSYCHOTHERAPY.1990 Jul. 44(3). P 433-44.

Emslie-G-J. Rush-A-J. Weinberg-W-A. Rintelmann-J-W. Roffwarg-H-P. Children with major depression show reduced rapid eye movement latencies.ARCHIVES OF GENERAL PSYCHIATRY.1990 Feb. 47(2). P 119-24.

Ernst-C. Are early childhood experiences overrated? A reassessment of maternal deprivation.EUROPEAN ARCHIVES OF PSYCHIATRY AND NEUROLOGICAL SCIENCES.1988. 237(2). P 80-90.

Famularo-R. Kinscherff-R. Fenton-T. Symptom differences in acute and chronic presentation of childhood post-traumatic stress disorder.CHILD ABUSE AND NEGLECT.1990. 14(3). P 439-44.

Feehan-M. McGee-R. Stanton-W. Silva-P-A. A 6 year follow-up of childhood enuresis: prevalence in adolescence and consequences for mental health.JOURNAL OF PAEDIATRICS AND CHILD HEALTH.1990 Apr. 26(2). P 75-9

Feinstein-C. Kaminer-Y. Barrett-R-P. Tylenda-B. The assessment of mood and affect in developmentally disabled children and adolescents: the Emotional Disorders Rating Scale.RESEARCH IN DEVELOPMENTAL DISABILITIES.1988. 9(2). P 109-21.

Fendrich-M. Weissman-M-M. Warner-V. Mufson-L. Two-year recall of lifetime diagnoses in offspring at high and low risk for major depression. The stability of offspring reports.ARCHIVES OF GENERAL PSYCHIATRY.1990 Dec. 47(12). P 1121-7.

Fisher-B-E. McGuire-K. Do diagnostic patterns exist in the sleep behaviors of normal children? J-Abnorm-Child-Psychol. 1990 Apr. 18(2). P 179-86.

Flament-M-F. Koby-E. Rapoport-J-L. Berg-C-J. Zahn-T. Cox-C. Denckla-M. Lenane-M. Childhood obsessive-compulsive disorder: a prospective follow-up study.JOURNAL OF CHILD PSYCHOLOGY AND PSYCHIATRY AND ALLIED DISCIPLINES.1990 Mar. 31(3). P 363-80.

Frets-Van-Buuren-J-J. Letuma-E. Daynes-G. Observations on early school failure in Zulu children.SOUTH AFRICAN MEDICAL JOURNAL.1990 Feb 3. 77(3). P 144-6.

Garber-J. Zeman-J. Walker-L-S. Recurrent abdominal pain in children: psychiatric diagnoses and parental psychopathology.JOURNAL OF THE AMERICAN ACADEMY OF CHILD AND ADOLESCENT PSYCHIATRY. 1990 Jul. 29(4). P 648-56.

Garland-E-J. Smith-D-H. Panic disorder on a child psychiatric consultation service.JOURNAL OF THE AMERICAN ACADEMY OF CHILD AND ADOLESCENT PSYCHIATRY. 1990 Sep. 29(5). P 785-8.

Gavshon-A. The analysis of a latency boy. The developmental impact of separation, divorce, and remarriage.PSYCHOANALYTIC STUDY OF THE CHILD. 1990. 45. P 217-33.

Gillman-R-D. The oedipal organization of shame. The analysis of a phobia.PSYCHOANALYTIC STUDY OF THE CHILD. 1990. 45. P 357-75.

Goodwin FK, Jamison KR (1990), Manic Depressive Illness. New York: Oxford University Press

Goodyer-I-M. Mitchell-C. Somatic emotional disorders in childhood and adolescence.JOURNAL OF PSYCHOSOMATIC RESEARCH.1989. 33(6). P 681-8.

Goodyer-I-M. Wright-C. Altham-P-M. Recent

friendships in anxious and depressed school age children.PSYCHOLOGICAL MEDICINE.1989 Feb. 19(1). P 165-74.

Goodyer-I-M. Wright-C. Altham-P-M. Maternal adversity and recent stressful life events in anxious and depressedchildren.JOURNAL OF CHILD PSYCHOLOGY AND PSYCHIATRY AND ALLIED1988 Sep. 29(5). P 651-67. DISCIPLINES.

Gortmaker-S-L. Walker-D-K. Weitzman-M. Sobol-A-M. Chronic conditions, socioeconomic risks, and behavioral problems in children and adolescents.PEDIATRICS.1990 Mar. 85(3). P 267-76

Graae-F. High anxiety in children.JOURNAL OF CLINICAL PSYCHIATRY.1990 May. 51 Suppl. P 18-9; discussion 50-3.

Graham-P. Stevenson-J. Temperament and psychiatric disorder: the genetic contribution to behaviour in childhood.AUSTRALIAN AND NEW ZEALAND JOURNAL OF PSYCHIATRY.1987 Sep. 21(3). P 267-74.

Guenther-R-K. Frey-C. Recollecting events associated with victimization.PSYCHOLOGICAL REPORTS.1990 Aug. 67(1). P 207-17.

Hammen-C. Burge-D. Burney-E. Adrian-C. Longitudinal study of diagnoses in children of women with unipolar and bipolar affective disorder.ARCHIVES OF GENERAL PSYCHIATRY.1990 Dec. 47(12). P 1112-7.

Harris JC, King SL, Reifler JP, Rosenberg L (1984). Emotional and learning disorders in 6-12 year old boys attending special school. J m Acad Child Psychiatry 2S:431-437

Hassanyeh F, Davidson K (1980). Bipolar affective psychosis with onset before age 16: report of 10 case. Br J Psychiatry 137:530-539

Hibbard-R-A. Hartman-G-L. Emotional indicators in human figure drawings of sexually victimized and nonabused children.JOURNAL OF CLINICAL PSYCHOLOGY.1990 Mar. 46(2). P 211-9.

Higgs-J-F. Goodyer-I-M. Birch-J. Anorexia nervosa and food avoidance emotional disorder. Journal Source: ARCHIVES OF DISEASE IN CHILDHOOD.1989 Mar. 64(3). P 346-51.

Hodges-K. Gordon-Y. Lennon-M-P. Parent-child agreement on symptoms assessed via a clinical research interview for children: the Child Assessment Schedule (CAS).JOURNAL OF CHILD PSYCHOLOGY AND PSYCHIATRY AND ALLIED DISCIPLINES.1990 Mar. 31(3). P 427-36.

Hodges-K. Saunders-W-B. Kashani-J. Hamlett-K. Thompson-R-J Jr. Internal consistency of DSM-III diagnoses using the symptom scales of the Child Assessment Schedule.JOURNAL OF THE AMERICAN ACADEMY OF CHILD AND ADOLESCENT PSYCHIATRY. 1990 Jul. 29(4). P 635-41.

Hojat-M. Borenstein-B-D. Shapurian-R. Perception of childhood dissatisfaction with parents and selected personality traits in adulthood.JOURNAL OF GENERAL PSYCHOLOGY.1990 Jul. 117(3). P 241-53.

Hughes-C-W. Preskorn-S-H. Weller-E. Weller-R. Hassanein-R. Tucker-S. The effect of concomitant disorders in childhood depression on predicting treatment response.PSYCHOPHARMACOLOGY BULLETIN.1990. 26(2). P 235-8.

Iwashige-T. Inoue-K. Nakajima-T. Renal transplantation: psychiatric aspects and interventions.JAPANESE JOURNAL OF PSYCHIATRY AND NEUROLOGY.1990 Mar. 44(1). P 7-18.

Jackson-P-L. Ott-M-J. Perceived self-esteem among children diagnosed with precociouspuberty.JOURNAL OF PEDIATRIC NURSING.1990 Jun. 5(3). P 190-203.

Jones-R-T. McDonald-D-W. Fiore-M-F. Arrington-T. Randall-J. A primary preventive approach to children's drug refusal behavior: the impact of rehearsal-plus.JOURNAL OF PEDIATRIC PSYCHOLOGY.1990 Apr. 15(2). P 211-23.

Joyce PR (1984). Age onset in bipolar affective disorder and misdiagnosis as schizophrenia. Psychol Med 14:145-149

Kaminer-Y. Feinstein-C. Seifer-R. Stevens-L. Barrett-R-P. An observationally based rating scale for affective symptomatology in child psychiatry.JOURNAL OF NERVOUS AND MENTAL DISEASE.1990 Dec. 178(12). P 750-4.

Kashani-J-H. Vaidya-A-F. Soltys-S-M. Dandoy-A-C. Katz-L-M. Reid-J-C. Correlates of anxiety in psychiatrically hospitalized children and their parents.AMERICAN JOURNAL OF PSYCHIATRY.1990 Mar. 147(3). P 319-23.

Kashani-J-H. Orvaschel-H. A community study of anxiety in children and adolescents.AMERICAN JOURNAL OF PSYCHIATRY.1990 Mar. 147(3). P 313-8.

Kashani-J-H. Dandoy-A-C. Vaidya-A-F. Soltys-S-M. Reid-J-C. Risk factors and correlates of severe psychiatric disorders in a sample of inpatient children.AMERICAN JOURNAL OF PSYCHIATRY.1990 Jun. 147(6). P 780-4.

Kaufman-A-M. The role of fantasy in the treatment of a severely disturbed child. PSYCHOANALYTIC STUDY OF THE CHILD. 1990. 45. P 235-56.

Kaufman-A-S. Eller-B-F. Applegate-B. An investigation of somatic anxiety and intelligence in children using the Kaufman-ABC and an Apple IIe program measuring heart rate.PERCEPTUAL AND MOTOR SKILLS.1990 Apr. 70(2). P 387-94.

Kearney-C-A. Silverman-W-K. A preliminary analysis of a functional model of assessment and treatment for school refusal behavior.BEHAVIOR MODIFICATION.1990 Jul. 14(3). P 340-66.

King-N-J. Gullone-E. Acceptability of fear reduction procedures with children.JOURNAL OF BEHAVIOR THERAPY AND EXPERIMENTAL PSYCHIATRY.1990 Mar. 21(1). P 1-8.

Klein-D-F. Further discussion of article on prodromal symptoms in panic disorder [letter].AMERICAN JOURNAL OF

PSYCHIATRY.1990 Nov. 147(11). P 1581-2.

Klein-D-F. Klein-R-G. Does panic disorder exist in c h i l d h o o d ? [letter].JOURNAL OF THE AMERICAN ACADEMY OF CHILD AND ADOLESCENT PSYCHIATRY. 1990 Sep. 29(5). P 834-5.

Knight-M-M. Wigder-K-S. Fortsch-M-M. Polcari-A. Medication education for c h i l d r e n . Is it worthwhile?JOURNAL OF CHILD AND ADOLESCENT PSYCHIATRIC AND MENTAL HEALTH NURSING. 25-8.1990 Jan-Mar. 3(1). P

Kosky-R. Silburn-S. Zubrick-S-R. Are children and adolescents who have suicidal thoughts different from those who attempt suicide? 1990 JOURNAL OF NERVOUS AND MENTAL DISEASE Jan.178(1). P 38-43..

Kovacs-M. Iyengar-S. Goldston-D. Obrosky-D-S. Stewart-J. Marsh-J. Psychological functioning among mothers of children with insulin-dependent diabetes mellitus: a longitudinal study.JOURNAL OF CONSULTING AND C L I N I C A L

PSYCHOLOGY.1990 Apr. 58(2). P 189-95.

Kovasznay B, Bromet E, Schwartz J, Ram R, Lavelle J, Brandon L (1993). Substance abuse and onset psychotic illness. Hosp Community Psychiatry 44:567-575

Kowal-A. Pritchard-D. Psychological characteristics of children who suffer from headache: a research note.JOURNAL OF CHILD PSYCHOLOGY AND PSYCHIATRY AND ALLIED1990 May. 31(4). P 637-49. DISCIPLINES.

La-Greca-A-M. Stone-W-L. LD status and achievement: confounding variables in the study of children's social status, self-esteem, and b e h a v i o r a l functioning.JOURNAL OF L E A R N I N G DISABILITIES.1990 Oct. 23(8). P 483-90.

Ladd-G-W. Having friends, keeping friends, making friends, and being liked by peers in the classroom: predictors of children's early school adjustment?CHILD DEVELOPMENT. 1990 Aug. 61(4). P 1081-100.

Najman-J-M. Morrison-J. Keeping-J-D. Andersen-M-J.

Williams-G-M. Social factors associated with the decision to relinquish a baby for adoption.COMMUNITY HEALTH STUDIES.1990. 14(2). P 180-9.

Lane-J-W. Pollard-C-A. Cox-G-L. Validity study of the Anxiety Symptoms Interview.JOURNAL OF CLINICAL PSYCHOLOGY.1990 Jan. 46(1). P 52-7.

Last-C-G. Strauss-C-C. School refusal in anxiety-disordered children and adolescents.JOURNAL OF THE AMERICAN ACADEMY OF CHILD AND ADOLESCENT PSYCHIATRY. 1990 Jan. 29(1). P 31-5.

Leung-A-K. Robson-W-L. Children of divorce.JOURNAL OF THE ROYAL SOCIETY OF HEALTH.1990 Oct. 110(5). P 161-3.

Lewin-C. Williams-R-J. Fear of AIDS: the impact of public anxiety in young people.BRITISH JOURNAL OF PSYCHIATRY.1988 Dec. 153. P 823-4.

Lewine RRJ (1988). Gender and schizophrenia. in: Nosology, Epidemiology and Genetics of Schizophrenia, Tsuang MT, Simpson JC, eds. Amsterdam: Elsevier, pp 379-398

Parker G, O'Donnell M, Walter S (1985). Changes in the diagnoses of functional psychoses associated with the introduction of lithium. Br J Psychiatry 146:377-382

Links-P-S. Boyle-M-H. Offord-D-R. The prevalence of emotional disorder in children.JOURNAL OF NERVOUS AND MENTAL DISEASE.1989 Feb. 177(2). P 85-91.

Lollis-S-P. Effects of maternal behavior on toddler behavior during separation.CHILD DEVELOPMENT.1990 Feb. 61(1). P 99-103.

Mahaney-N-B. Restoration of play in a severely burned three-year-old child. JOURNAL OF BURN CARE AND REHABILITATION.1990 Jan-Feb. 11(1). P 57-63.

McAdam-E-K. Cognitive behaviour therapy and its application with adolescents.JOURNAL OF ADOLESCENCE.1986 Mar. 9(1). P 1-15.

McCarthy-J-B. Abusive families and character formation.AMERICAN JOURNAL OF PSYCHOANALYSIS.1990 Jun. 50(2). P 181-6.

McClellan-J-M. Rubert-M-P. Reichler-R-J. Sylvester-C-E. Attention deficit disorder in children at risk for anxiety and depression.JOURNAL OF THE AMERICAN ACADEMY OF CHILD AND ADOLESCENT PSYCHIATRY. 1990 Jul. 29(4). P 534-9.

McFarlane-A-C. The relationship between patterns of family interaction and psychiatric disorder in children.AUSTRALIAN AND NEW ZEALAND JOURNAL OF PSYCHIATRY.1987 Sep. 21(3). P 383-90.

McGee-R. Stanton-W. Parent reports of disability among 13-year olds with DSM-III disorders.JOURNAL OF CHILD PSYCHOLOGY AND PSYCHIATRY AND ALLIED DISCIPLINES.1990 Jul. 31(5). P 793-801.

McGee-R. Feehan-M. Williams-S. Partridge-F. Silva-P-A. Kelly-J. DSM-III disorders in a large sample of adolescents.JOURNAL OF THE AMERICAN ACADEMY OF CHILD AND ADOLESCENT PSYCHIATRY. 1990 Jul. 29(4). P 611-9.

Meadow-S-R. Day wetting.PEDIATRIC NEPHROLOGY.1990 Mar. 4(2). P 178-84.

Offord-D-R. Prevention of behavioral and emotional disorders in children.JOURNAL OF CHILD PSYCHOLOGY AND PSYCHIATRY AND ALLIED DISCIPLINES. 1987 Jan. 28(1). P 9-19.

Place-M. Rajah-S. Crake-T. Combining day patient treatment with family work in a child psychiatry clinic.EUROPEAN ARCHIVES OF PSYCHIATRY AND NEUROLOGICAL SCIENCES.1990. 239(6). P 373-8.

Punamaki-R-L. Suleiman-R. Predictors and effectiveness of coping with political violence among Palestinian children.BRITISH JOURNAL OF SOCIAL PSYCHOLOGY.1990 Mar. 29 (Pt 1). P 67-77.

Radke-Yarrow-M. Cummings-E-M. Kuczynski-L. Chapman-M.

Patterns of attachment in two- and three-year-olds in normal families and families with parental depression.CHILD DEVELOPMENT.1985 Aug. 56(4). P 884-93.

Rae-Grant-N. Thomas-B-H. Offord-D-R. Boyle-M-H. Risk, protective factors, and the prevalence of behavioral and emotional disorders in children and adolescents.JOURNAL OF THE AMERICAN ACADEMY OF CHILD AND ADOLESCENT PSYCHIATRY. 1989 Mar. 28(2). P 262-8.

Rancurello-M. Antidepressants in children: indications, benefits, and limitations.AMERICAN JOURNAL OF PSYCHOTHERAPY.1986Jul. 40(3). P 377-92.

Reid-W-J. Crisafulli-A. Marital discord and child behavior problems: a meta-analysis.JOURNAL OF ABNORMAL CHILD PSYCHOLOGY.1990 Feb. 18(1). P 105-17.

Riddle-M-A. Scahill-L. King-R. Hardin-M-T. Towbin-K-E. Ort-S-I. Leckman-J-F. Cohen-D-J. Obsessive compulsive disorder in children and adolescents: phenomenology and family history.JOURNAL OF THE AMERICAN ACADEMY OF CHILD AND ADOLESCENT PSYCHIATRY. 1990 Sep. 29(5). P 766-72.

Robinson-J-O. Alverez-J-H. Dodge-J-A. Life events and family history in children with recurrent abdominal pain.JOURNAL OF PSYCHOSOMATIC RESEARCH.1990. 34(2). P 171-81.

Rogeness-G-A. Cepeda-C. Macedo-C-A. Fischer-C. Harris-W-R. Differences in heart rate and blood pressure in children with conduct disorder, major depression, and separation anxiety. PSYCHIATRY RESEARCH.1990 Aug. 33(2). P 199-206.

Rogeness-G-A. Javors-M-A. Maas-J-W. Macedo-C-A. Catecholamines and diagnoses in children.JOURNAL OF THE AMERICAN ACADEMY OF CHILD AND ADOLESCENT PSYCHIATRY. 1990 Mar. 29(2). P 234-41.

Rosen LN, Rosenthal NE, Van Dusen PH, Dunner DL, Fieve PR (1983), Age at onset and number of psychotic symptoms in bipolar I and schizoaffective disorder. Am J Psychiatry 140:1523-1524

Rubin-K-H. Mills-R-S. Maternal beliefs about adaptive and maladaptive social behaviors in normal, aggressive, and withdrawn preschoolers.JOURNAL OF ABNORMAL CHILD PSYCHOLOGY.1990 Aug. 18(4). P 419-35.

Ryde-Brandt-B. Anxiety and depression in mothers of children with psychotic disorders and mental retardation.BRITISH JOURNAL OF PSYCHIATRY.1990 Jan. 156. P 118-21.

Ryde-Brandt-B. Anxiety and defence strategies in mothers of children with different disabilities.BRITISH JOURNAL OF MEDICAL PSYCHOLOGY.1990 Jun. 63 (Pt 2). P 183-92.

Schachar-R. Wachsmuth-R. Hyperactivity and parental psychopathology.JOURNAL OF CHILD PSYCHOLOGY AND PSYCHIATRY AND ALLIED DISCIPLINES.1990 Mar. 31(3). P 381-92.

Schachar-R. Logan-G. Wachsmuth-R. Chajczyk-D. Attaining and maintaining preparation: a comparison of attention in hyperactive, normal, and disturbed control children.JOURNAL OF ABNORMAL CHILD PSYCHOLOGY.1988 Aug. 16(4). P 361-78.

Slough-N-M. Greenberg-M-T. Five-year-olds'representations of separation from parents: responses from the perspective of self and other.NEW DIRECTIONS FOR CHILD DEVELOPMENT.1990 Summer. (48). P 67-84.

Smith-G-J. Carlsson-I-M. The creative process: a functional model based on empirical studies from early childhood to middle age.PSYCHOLOGICAL ISSUES.1990. (57). P 1-243.

Spreen-O. The relationship between learning disability, emotional disorders, and neuropsychology; some results and observations.JOURNAL OF CLINICAL AND EXPERIMENTAL NEUROPSYCHOLOGY.1989 Jan. 11(1). P 117-40.

Steingard-R. Biederman-J. Keenan-K. Moore-C. Comorbidity in the interpretation of dexamethasone suppression test results in children: a review and report.BIOLOGICAL

PSYCHIATRY.1990 Aug 1. 28(3). P 193-202.

Steinhausen-H-C. Gobel-D. Convergence of parent checklists and child psychiatric diagnoses.JOURNAL OF ABNORMAL CHILD PSYCHOLOGY.1987 Mar. 15(1). P 147-51.

Stutzer-C-A. Pain and anxiety management program for pediatric oncology patients.JOURNAL OF PEDIATRIC ONCOLOGY NURSING.1990 Apr. 7(2). P 76-7.

Sugar-M. Developmental anxieties in adolescence.ADOLESCENT PSYCHIATRY.1990. 17. P 385-403.

Sugar-M. The inpatient borderline adolescent in group therapy.CHILD PSYCHIATRY AND HUMAN DEVELOPMENT.1990 Summer. 20(4). P 235-41.

Surrey-J. Swett-C Jr. Michaels-A. Levin-S. Reported history of physical and sexual abuse and severity of symptomatology in women psychiatric outpatients.AMERICAN JOURNAL OF ORTHOPSYCHIATRY.1990 Jul. 60(3). P 412-7.

Tambs-K. Vaglum-P. Alcohol consumption in parents and offspring: a study of the family correlation structure in a general population.ACTA PSYCHIATRICA SCANDINAVICA.1990 Aug. 82(2). P 145-51.

Tauschke-E. Merskey-H. Helmes-E. Psychological defence mechanisms in patients with pain.PAIN.1990 Feb. 40(2). P 161-70.

Tauschke-E. Merskey-H. Helmes-E. A systematic inquiry into recollections of childhood experience and their relationship to adult defence mechanisms.BRITISH JOURNAL OF PSYCHIATRY.1990 Sep. 157. P 392-8.

Taylor-E. Everitt-B. Thorley-G. Schachar-R. Rutter-M. Wieselberg-M. Conduct disorder and hyperactivity: II. A cluster analytic approach to the identification of a behavioural syndrome.BRITISH JOURNAL OF PSYCHIATRY.1986 Dec. 149. P 768-77.

Taylor-E. Schachar-R. Thorley-G. Wieselberg-H-M.

Everitt-B. Rutter-M. Which boys respond to stimulant medication? A controlled trial of methylphenidate in boys with disruptive behaviour.PSYCHOLOGICAL MEDICINE.1987 Feb. 17(1). P 121-43.

Tiedeman-M-E. Clatworthy-S. Anxiety responses of 5- to 11-year-old children during and after hospitalization.JOURNAL OF PEDIATRIC NURSING.1990 Oct. 5(5). P 334-43.

Vandvik-I-H. Mental health and psychosocial functioning in children with recent onset of rheumatic disease.JOURNAL OF CHILD PSYCHOLOGY AND PSYCHIATRY AND ALLIED DISCIPLINES.1990 Sep. 31(6). P 961-71.

Vidor-K-K. Anxiety related to impending surgery.TODAYS OR NURSE.1990 Sep. 12(9). P 36.

Vitiello-B. Behar-D. Wolfson-S. Mcleer-S-V. Children with panic disorder [letter; comment].AMERICAN JOURNAL OF PSYCHIATRY.1990 Mar. 147(3). P 377.

Vitiello-B. Behar-D. Wolfson-S. McLeer-S-V. Diagnosis of panic disorder in prepubertal children.JOURNAL OF THE AMERICAN ACADEMY OF CHILD AND ADOLESCENT PSYCHIATRY. 1990 Sep. 29(5). P 782-4.

Walker-D-K. Stein-R-E. Perrin-E-C. Jessop-D-J. Assessing psychosocial adjustment of children with chronic illnesses: a review of the technical properties of PARS III.JOURNAL OF DEVELOPMENTAL AND BEHAVIORAL PEDIATRICS.1990 Jun.11(3). P 116-21.

Weinberger-D-A. Tublin-S-K. Ford-M-E. Feldman-S-S. Preadolescents' social-emotional adjustment and selective attrition in family research.CHILD DEVELOPMENT.1990 Oct. 61(5). P 1374-86.

Weingourt-R. Wife rape in a sample of psychiatric patients.IMAGE - THE JOURNAL OF NURSING SCHOLARSHIP.1990 Fall. 22(3). P 144-7.

Weinstein-S-R. Noam-G-G. Grimes-K. Stone-K. Schwab-Stone-M. Convergence of DSM-III diagnoses and self-reported symptoms in child and adolescent inpatients.JOURNAL OF THE AMERICAN ACADEMY OF CHILD AND ADOLESCENT PSYCHIATRY. 1990 Jul. 29(4). P 627-34.

Wells-K-B. Manning-W-G Jr. Valdez-R-B. The effects of a prepaid group practice on mental health outcomes.HEALTH SERVICESRESEARCH.1990 Oct. 25(4). P 615-25.

Wells-K-B. Manning-W-G Jr. Duan-N. Newhouse-J-P. Ware-J-E Jr. Cost-sharing and the use of general medical physicians for outpatient mental health care.HEALTH SERVICES RESEARCH.1987 Apr. 22(1). P 1-17.

Wenning-K. Borderline children: a closer look at diagnosis and treatment.AMERICAN JOURNAL OF ORTHOPSYCHIATRY.1990 Apr. 60(2). P 225-32.

Werry JS, McClellan JM, Chard L (1991). Childhood and adolescent schizophrenic, bipolar and schizoaffective disorders: a clinical and outcome study. J Am Acad Child Adolesc Psychiatry 30:457-465

Whitaker-A. Johnson-J. Shaffer-D. Rapoport-J-L. Kalikow-K. Walsh-B-T. Davies-M. Braiman-S. Dolinsky-A. Uncommon troubles in young people: prevalence estimates of selected psychiatric disorders in a nonreferred adolescent population.ARCHIVES OF GENERAL PSYCHIATRY.1990 May. 47(5). P 487-96.

Whitman-B-Y. Accardo-P. Emotional symptoms in Prader-Willi syndrome adolescents.AMERICAN JOURNAL OF MEDICAL GENETICS.1987 Dec. 28(4). P 897-905.

Williams-S. Anderson-J. McGee-R. Silva-P-A. Risk factors for behavioral and emotional disorder in preadolescent children.JOURNAL OF THE AMERICAN ACADEMY OF CHILD AND ADOLESCENT PSYCHIATRY. 1990 May. 29(3). P 413-9.

Willock-B. From acting out to interactive play.INTERNATIONAL JOURNAL OF PSYCHO-ANALYSIS.1990. 71 (Pt 2). P 321-34.

Winland-Brown-J-E. Maheady-D-C. Using intuition

to define homesickness at summer camp.JOURNAL OF PEDIATRIC HEALTH CARE.1990 May-Jun. 4(3). P 117-21.

Winokur G, Clayton P, Reich T (1969). Manic Depressive Illness. St. Louis: CV Mosby

Wright-F-A. Giebartowski-J. McMurray-N-E. Determinants of dentists' management of difficult child patients.JOURNAL OF BEHAVIORAL MEDICINE.1990 Apr. 13(2). P 175-82.

Developmental Disorders, Autism and Childhood Schizophrenia

Author: Van Bourgondien M.E., Schopler,E.
Title: Critical issues in the residential care of people with Autism.
Journal Source: Journal of Autism and Developmental Disorders. 1990 Sep. 20(3). P 391-9.

Author: Mesibov, G.B.
Title: Normalization and its relevance today.
Journal Source: Journal of Autism and Developmental Disorders. 1990 Sep. 20(3). P 379-90.

Author: Schroeder-C-S. Schroeder-S-R.
Title: The future of children is now.
Journal Source: Journal of Autism and Developmental Disorders. 1990 Sep. 20(3). P 367-78.

Author: Wall, A.J.
Title: Group homes in North Carolina for children and adults with Autism.
Journal Source: Journal of Autism and Developmental Disorders. 1990 Sep. 20(3). P 353-66.

Author: Holmes, D.L.
Title: Community-based services for children and adults with Autism: the Eden Family of Programs.
Journal Source: Journal of Autism and Developmental Disorders. 1990 Sep. 20(3). P 339-51.

Author: Simonson, L.R., Simonson, S.M., Volkmar, F.R.
Title: Benhaven's residential program.
Journal Source: Journal of Autism and Developmental Disorders. 1990 Sep. 20(3). P 323-37.

Author: Kay, B.R.
Title: Bittersweet farms.
Journal Source: Journal of Autism and Developmental

Disorders. 1990 Sep. 20(3). P 309-21.

Author: Schopler, E., Hennike, J.M.
Title: Past and present trends in residential treatment.
Journal Source: Journal of Autism and Developmental Disorders. 1990 Sep. 20(3). P 291-8.

Author: Goodman, R., Ashby, L.
Title: Delayed Visual Maturation and Autism.
Journal Source: Developmental Medicine and Child Neurology. 1990 Sep. 32(9). P 814-9.

Author: Barthelemy, C., Adrien, J.L., Tanguay, P. Garreau, B., Fermanian, J., Roux, S., Sauvage, D., Lelord, G.
Title: The Behavioral Summarized Evaluation: validity and reliability of a scale for the assessment of Autistic behaviors.
Journal Source: Journal of Autism and Developmental Disorders. 1990 Jun. 20(2). P 189-204.

Author: Coe, D., Matson, J., Fee, V., Manikam, R., Linarello, C.
Title: Training nonverbal and verbal play skills to mentally retarded and Autistic children.
Journal Source: Journal of Autism and Developmental Disorders. 1990 Jun. 20(2). P 177-87.

Author: Carr, E.G., Darcy, M.
Title: Setting generality of peer modeling in children with Autism.
Journal Source: Journal of Autism and Developmental Disorders. 1990 Mar. 20(1). P 45-59.

Author: Harris-S-L. Handleman-J-S. Kristoff-B. Bass-L. Gordon-R.
Title: Changes in language development among Autistic and peer children in segregated and integrated preschool settings.
Journal Source: Journal of Autism and Developmental Disorders. 1990 Mar. 20(1). P 23-31.

Author: Factor, D.C., Perry, A., Freeman, N.
Title: Stress, social support, and respite care use in families with Autistic children.
Journal Source: Journal of Autism and Developmental Disorders. 1990 Mar. 20(1). P 139-46.

Author: Gillberg, C.
Title: Autism and pervasive developmental disorders.

Journal Source: Journal of Child Psychology and Psychiatry and Allied Disciplines. 1990 Jan. 31(1). P 99-119.

Author: Levitas, A.
Title: Developmental and family effects of Autism.
Journal Source: Pediatric Annals. 1990 Jan. 19(1). P 52-8.

Author: Love, S.R., Matson, J.L., West, D.
Title: Mothers as effective therapists for Autistic children's phobias.
Journal Source: Journal of Applied Behavior Analysis. 1990 Fall. 23(3). P 379-85.

Author: Harris, S.L., Handleman, J.S., Alessandri, M.
Title: Teaching youths with Autism to offer assistance.
Journal Source: Journal of Applied Behavior Analysis. 1990 Fall. 23(3). P 297-305.

Author: Atlas, J.A.
Title: Play in assessment and intervention in the childhood psychoses.
Journal Source: Child Psychiatry and Human Development. 1990 Winter. 21(2). P 119-33.

Author: Dalton, R. Bolding, D. Forman, M.A.
Title: Psychiatric hospitalization of preschool children: a follow-up study.
Journal Source: Child Psychiatry and Human Development. 1990 Fall. 21(1). P 57-64.

Author: Sullivan, A., Kelso, J., Stewart-M.
Title: Mothers' views on the ages of onset for four childhood disorders.
Journal Source: Child Psychiatry and Human Development. 1990 Summer. 20(4). P 269-78.

Author: Stone, W.L., Lemanek,K.L., Fishel, P.T., Fernandez, M.C., Altemeier, W.A.
Title: Play and imitation skills in the diagnosis of Autism in young children.
Journal Source: Pediatrics. 1990 August, 86(2). P 267-72.

Author: Sainato, D.M., Strain, P.S., Lefebvre, D., Rapp, N.
Title: Effects of self-evaluation on the independent work skills of preschool children with disabilities.
Journal Source: Exceptional Child. 1990 Apr. 56(6). P 540-9.

Author: Gillberg, C.
Title: Autism and pervasive developmental disorders.

Journal Source: Journal of Child Psychology and Psychiatry and Allied Disciplines. 1990 Jan. 31(1). P 99-119.

Author: Varley, C.K., Holm, V.A.
Title: A two-year follow-up of Autistic children treated with fenfluramine.
Journal Source: Journal of the American Academy of Child and Adolescent Psychiatry. 1990 Jan. 29(1). P 137-40.

Articles related to Childhood Schizophrenia

Asarnow, J.R., Horton, A.A. Coping and stress in families of child psychiatric inpatients: parents of children with depressive and schizophrenia spectrum disorders. Child Psychiatry and Human Development. 1990 Winter. 21(2). P 145-57.

Caplan, R., Foy, J.G., Asarnow, R.F., Sherman,T. Information processing deficits of schizophrenic children with formal thought disorder. Psychiatry Research. 1990 Feb. 31(2). P 169-77.

Play Therapy

Atlas-J-A. Play in assessment and intervention in the childhood psychoses. CHILD PSYCHIATRY AND HUMAN DEVELOPMENT.1990 Winter. 21(2). P 119-33.

Robinson-R. Child's play. NURSING TIMES.1990 Oct 31-Nov 6. 86(44). P 20-1.

Celano-M-P. Activities and games for group psychotherapy with sexually abused children. INTERNATIONAL JOURNAL OF GROUP PSYCHOTHERAPY.1990 Oct. 40(4). P 419-29.

Author: Vessey-J-A. Mahon-M-M.
Title: Therapeutic play and the hospitalized child.
Journal Source: JOURNAL OF PEDIATRIC NURSING.1990 Oct. 5(5). P 328-33.

Author: Post-C-A.
Title: Play therapy with an abused child: a case study.
Journal Source: JOURNAL OF CHILD AND ADOLESCENT PSYCHIATRIC AND MENTAL HEALTH NURSING. 34-6.1990 Jan-Mar. 3(1).

Author: Willock-B.
Title: From acting out to interactive play.

Journal Source: INTERNATIONAL JOURNAL OF PSYCHO-ANALYSIS. 1990. 71 (Pt 2). P 321-34.

Rae-W-A. Worchel-F-F. Upchurch-J. Sanner-J-H. Daniel-C-A. The psychosocial impact of play on hospitalized children. JOURNAL OF PEDIATRIC PSYCHOLOGY.1989 Dec. 14(4). P 617-27.

Walker-C. Use of art and play therapy in pediatric oncology. JOURNAL OF PEDIATRIC ONCOLOGY NURSING.1989 Oct. 6(4). P 121-6.

Gray-E. The emotional and play needs of the dying child. ISSUES IN COMPREHENSIVE PEDIATRICNURSING.1989. 12(2-3). P 207-24.

Saucier-B-L. Play therapy: a nursing intervention.
Journal Source: ADVANCING CLINICAL CARE.1989 Sep-Oct. 4(5). P 22-3.

Conn-J-H. Play interview therapy: its history, theory and practice--a fifty year retrospective account.
CHILD PSYCHIATRY AND HUMAN DEVELOPMENT.1989 Fall. 20(1). P 3-13.

Goodwin-J-M. Talwar-N. Group psychotherapy for victims of incest. PSYCHIATRIC CLINICS OF NORTH AMERICA.1989Jun. 12(2). P 279-93.

Edwards-K-S. Send in the clowns. OHIO MEDICINE.1989 May. 85(5). P 343-5.

Schibuk-M. Treating the sibling subsystem: an adjunct of divorce therapy. AMERICAN JOURNAL OF ORTHOPSYCHIATRY.1989 Apr. 59(2). P 226-37.

Author: Saucier-B-L.
Title: The effects of play therapy on developmental achievement levels of abused children.
Journal Source: PEDIATRIC NURSING.1989 Jan-Feb. 15(1). P 27-30.

Author: Sugar-M.
Title: A preschooler in a disaster.
Journal Source: AMERICAN JOURNAL OF PSYCHOTHERAPY.1988 Oct. 42(4). P 619-29.

Author: Walker-C-L.
Title: Use of art and play therapy in pediatric oncology.

Journal Source: JOURNAL OF THE ASSOCIATION OF PEDIATRIC ONCOLOGY NURSES.1988. 5(1-2). P 34.

Author: Johnson-M-L.
Title: Use of play group therapy in promoting social skills.
Journal Source: ISSUES IN MENTAL HEALTH NURSING.1988. 9(1). P 105-12.

Author: Dubow-E-F. Huesmann-L-R. Eron-L-D.
Title: Mitigating aggression and promoting prosocial behavior in aggressive elementary schoolboys.
Journal Source: BEHAVIOUR RESEARCH AND THERAPY. 1987. 25(6). P 527-31.

Author: Jack-L-W.
Title: Using play in psychiatric rehabilitation.
Journal Source: JOURNAL OF PSYCHOSOCIAL NURSING AND MENTAL HEALTH SERVICES.1987 Jul. 25(7). P 17-20.

Author: Gilman-C-M. Frauman-A-C.
Title: Use of play with the child with chronic illness.
Journal Source: ANNA JOURNAL.1987 Aug. 14(4). P 259-61.

Author: Tregloan-L. Oberklaid-F.
Title: The hospitalized child.
Journal Source: AUSTRALIAN PAEDIATRIC JOURNAL.1987 Apr. 23(2). P 85-7.

Author: Bates-T-A. Broome-M.
Title: Preparation of children for hospitalization and surgery: a review of the literature.
Journal Source: JOURNAL OF PEDIATRIC NURSING.1986 Aug. 1(4). P 230-9.

Author: Steward-M-S. Farquhar-L-C. Dicharry-D-C. Glick-D-R. Martin-P-W.
Title: Group therapy: a treatment of choice for young victims of child abuse.
Journal Source: INTERNATIONAL JOURNAL OF GROUP PSYCHOTHERAPY.1986 Apr. 36(2). P 261-77.

Author: Garot-P-A.
Title: Therapeutic play: work of both child and nurse.
Journal Source: JOURNAL OF PEDIATRIC NURSING.1986 Apr. 1(2). P 111-6.

Author: Deering-C-G.
Title: The inhibited child.

Journal Source: JOURNAL OF PSYCHOSOCIAL NURSING AND MENTAL HEALTH SERVICES.1986 Feb. 24(2). P 16-21.

Author: Linn-S. Beardslee-W. Patenaude-A-F.
Title: Puppet therapy with pediatric bone marrow transplant patients.
Journal Source: JOURNAL OF PEDIATRIC PSYCHOLOGY.1986 Mar. 11(1). P 37-46.

Author: Edington-G.
Title: Hand puppets and dolls in psychotherapy with children.
Journal Source: PERCEPTUAL AND MOTOR SKILLS.1985 Dec. 61(3 Pt 1). P 691-6.

Author: Meer-P-A.
Title: Using play therapy in outpatient settings.
Journal Source: MCN; AMERICAN JOURNAL OF MATERNAL CHILD NURSING.1985 Nov-Dec. 10(6). P 378-80.

Author: Irwin-E-C.
Title: Puppets in therapy: an assessment procedure.
Journal Source: AMERICAN JOURNAL OF PSYCHOTHERAPY.1985Jul. 39(3). P 389-400.

Art Therapy and Drama Techniques

Author: Rollins-J-H.
Title: The arts: helping children cope with hospitalization.
Journal Source: IMPRINT.1990 Nov. 37(4). P 79-83.

Author: McIntyre-B-B.
Title: Art therapy with bereaved youth.
Journal Source: JOURNAL OF PALLIATIVE CARE.1990 Spring. 6(1). P 16-25.

Author: Walker-C.
Title: Use of art and play therapy in pediatric oncology.
Journal Source: JOURNAL OF PEDIATRIC ONCOLOGY NURSING.1989 Oct. 6(4). P 121-6.

Author: Davis-C-B.
Title: The use of art therapy and group process with grieving children.
Journal Source: ISSUES IN COMPREHENSIVE PEDIATRIC NURSING.1989. 12(4). P 269-80.

Author: Stern-R-S.
Title: Many ways to grow: creative art therapies.
Journal Source: PEDIATRIC ANNALS.1989 Oct. 18(10). P 645, 649-52.

Author: ONeill-E-W.
Title: Art therapy with children with cancer.
Journal Source: JOURNAL OF THE ASSOCIATION OF PEDIATRIC ONCOLOGY NURSES.1989. 6(2). P 36-7.

Author: Walker-C-L.
Title: Use of art and play therapy in pediatric oncology.
Journal Source: JOURNAL OF THE ASSOCIATION OF PEDIATRIC ONCOLOGY NURSES.1988. 5(1-2). P 34.

Author: Rollins-J-A.
Title: Art supplies and high risk children.
Journal Source: PEDIATRIC NURSING. 1988 May-Jun. 14(3). P 251-2.

Author: Zimmerman-M-I. Wolbert-W-A. Burgess-A-W. Hartman-C-R.
Title: Art and group work: interventions for multiple victims of child molestation (Part II).
Journal Source: ARCHIVES OF PSYCHIATRIC NURSING.1987 Feb. 1(1). P 40-6.

Author: Hughes-J-N. Boodoo-G. Alcala-J. Maggio-M-C. Moore-L. Villapando-R.
Title: Validation of a role-play measure of children's social skills.
Journal Source: JOURNAL OF ABNORMAL CHILD PSYCHOLOGY.1989 Dec. 17(6). P 633-46.

Author: Renaud-L. Suissa-S.
Title: Evaluation of the efficacy of simulation games in traffic safety education of kindergarten children.
Journal Source: AMERICAN JOURNAL OF PUBLIC HEALTH.1989 Mar. 79(3). P 307-9.

Author: Fryer-G-E Jr. Kraizer-S-K. Miyoshi-T.
Title: Measuring children's retention of skills to resist stranger abduction: use of the simulation technique.
Journal Source: CHILD ABUSE AND NEGLECT.1987. 11(2). P 181-5.

Author: Irwin-E-C.
Title: Drama therapy in diagnosis and treatment.
Journal Source: CHILD WELFARE.1986 Jul-Aug. 65(4). P 347-57.

Additional Bibliographic References

Achenbach TM (1991), Manual for the Child Behavior Checklist/4-18 and 1991 Profile. Burlington, VT: University of Vermont Department of Psychiatry

American Psychiatric Association (1994), Diagnostic and Statistical Manual of Mental Disorders, 4th edition (DSM-IV). Washington, DC: American Psychiatric Association

Anderson JC, Williams S, McGee R, Silva PA (1987), DSM-III disorders in proadolescent children: prevalence in a large sample from the general population. Arch Gen Psychiatry 44:69-76

Arnsten AFT, Contant TA (1992), Alpha-2 adrenergic agonists decrease distractibility in aged monkeys performing a delayed response task. Psychopharmacology 108:159-169

Arnsten AFT, Cai JX, Goldman-Rakic PS (1988), The alpha-2 adrenergic agonist, guanfacine improves memory in aged monkeys without sedative or hypotensive side effects: evidence for alpha-2 receptor subtypes. J Neurosci 8:4287-4298

Arnsten AFT, Goldman-Rakic PS (1985), Alpha-2 adrenergic mechanisms in prefrontal cortex associated with cognitive decline in aged nonhuman primates. Science 230:1273-1276

Arnsten AFT (1993), Catecholamine mechanisms in age-related cognitive decline. Neurobiol Aging 14:639-641

Arnsten AFT, Leslie FM (1991), Behavioral and receptor binding analysis of the alpha-2 adrenergic agonist UK-14304 (5-bromo-6 2-imidazoline-2-yl amino quinoxaline): evidence for cognitive enhancement at an alpha-2 adrenoceptor subtype. Neuropharmacology 30:1279-1289

Benoit D, Zeanah CH, Barton ML (1989), Maternal attachment disturbances in failure to thrive. Infant Ment Health J 10:185-202

Berwick DM (1980) Nonorganic failure to thrive. Pediatr Rev 1:265-270

Biederman J, Rosenbaum JF, Hirshfeld DR, et al. (1990), Psychiatric correlates of behavioral inhibition in young children of parents with and without psychiatric disorders. Arch Gen Psychiatry 47:21-26

Biederman J, Faraone SV, Keenan K, et al. (1992a), Further evidence for family-genetic risk factors in attention deficit hyperactivity disorder (ADHD): patterns of comorbidity in probands and relatives in psychiatrically and pediatrically referred samples. Arch Gen Psychiatry 49:728-738

Biederman J, Faraone SV, Lapey K (1992b), Comorbidity of diagnosis in attention deficit hyperactivity disorder (ADHD). Child and Adolescent Psychiatric Clinics of North America 1:335-360

Biederman J, Faraone SV, Spencer T et al. (1993), Patterns of psychiatric comorbidity, cognition, and psychosocial functioning in adults with attention deficit hyperactivity disorder. Am J Psychiatry 150:1792-1798

Biederman J, Newcorn J, Sprich S (1991), Comorbidity of attention deficit hyperactivity disorder with conduct, depressive, anxiety, and other disorders. Am J Psychiatry 148:564-577

Bithoney WG, Dubowitz H, Egan H (1992), Failure to thrive/growth deficiency. Pediatr Rev 13:453-460

Brown CM, MacKinnon AC, McGrath JC, Spedding M, Kilpatrick AT (1990), Alpha-2-adrenoceptor subtype and imidazoline-like binding sites in the rat brain. Br J Pharmacol 99:803-809

Clarren, S.K.; Astley, S.J.; and Bowden D.M. Physical anomalies and developmental delays in non-human primates exposed to weekly doses of ethanol during gestation. Teratology 37(6):561-569, 1988.

Coles, C.D.; Brown, R.T.; Smith, I.E., Platzman, K.A.; Erickson, S.; and Falek. A. Effects of prenatal alcohol exposure at school age: 1. Physical and cognitive development. Neurotoxicology and Teratology, 13(4):1-11, 1991.

Coles, C.D.; Smith, I.E., Fernhoff, P.M.; and Falek, A. Neonatal neurobehavioral characteristics as correlates of maternal alcohol use during gestation. Alcoholism: Clinical and Experimental Research 9(5):1-7,1985.

Conners CK (1973), Rating scales for use in drug studies with children. Am J Psychiatry 126:884-888

Conners CK (1973), Rating scales for use in drug studies in children.Psychopharmacol Bull (special edition) 9:24-84

Creer TL, Gustafson KE (1989), Psychological problems associated with drug therapy in childhood asthma. American Journal of Pediatrics 115:850-855

Day, N.L.; Robles, N.: Richardson, G.; Geva, D., Taylor, P.; Scher, M.; Staffer, D.; Cornelius, M.; and Goldschmidt, L. The effects of prenatal alcohol use on the growth of children at three years of age. Alcoholism: Clinical and Experimental Research 15(1):67-71, 1991.

Day, N.L.: Jasperse, D.: Richardson, G., Robles, N.: Sambamoorthi, U.; Scher, M.; Staffer, D.: and M. Prenatal exposure to alcohol: Effect on infant growth and morphological characteristics. Pediatrics 84(3):536-541, 1989.

Dobbing, J. The later development of the brain and its vulnerability. In: Davis, J.A., and Dobbing, J., eds. Scientific Foundations of Paediatrics. 2nd ed. Baltimore: University Park Press, 1981. pp. 744-758.

Drotar D, ed. (1985), New Directions in Failure to Thrive: Implications for Research and Practice. New York: Plenum Press

Drotar D, Eckerle D, Satola J, Pallotta J, Wyatt B (1990), Maternal interactional behavior with nonorganic failure-to-thrive: a case comparison study. Child Abuse Negl 14:41-51

Ernhart, C.B.; Sokol, R.J.; Martier, S.: Moron, P.; Nadler, D.; Ager, J.W.; and Wolf, A. Alcohol teratogenicity in the human: A detailed assessment of specificity, critical period, and threshold. American Journal of Obstetrics and Gynecology 156(l):33-39, 1987.

Fabro, S.; McLachilan, J.A.; and Dames, N.M. Chemical exposure of embryos during the preimplantation stages of pregnancy: Mortality rate and intrauterine development. Amerinscan Journal of Obstetrics and Gynecology 148:929, 1984.

Faraone SV, Biederman J, Keenan K, Tsuang MT (1991), Separation of DSM-III attention deficit disorder and conduct disorder: evidence from a family-genetic study of American child psychiatric patients. Psychol Med 21:109-121

Firestone P (1982), Factors associated with children's adherence to stimulant medication. Am J Orthopsychiatry 52:447-457

Fowler MG, Davenport MG, Garg R (1992), School functioning of US children with asthma. Pediatrics 90:939-944

Frank DA, Zeisel SH (1988), Failure to thrive. Pediatr Clin North Am 35:1187-1206

Gorman J, Leifer M, Grossman G (1993), Nonorganic failure to thrive: maternal history and current maternal functioning. J Clin Child Psychol 22:327-336

Goyette CH, Conners CK, Ulrich RF (1978), Normative data on Revised Conners Parent and Teacher Rating Scales. J Abnorm Child Psychol 6:221-236

Graham, J.M.; Hanson, J.W.; Darby, B.L.; Barr, H.M. and Streissguth, A.P. Independent dysmorphology evaluations at birth and 4 years of age for children exposed to varying amounts of alcohol nsin utero. Pediatrics 81(6):772-778, 1988.

Gutstadt LB, Gillette JW, Mrazek DA, Fukuhara JT, LaBrecque JF, Strunk RC (1989), Determinants of school performance in children with chronic asthma. Am J Dis Child 143:471-475

Hollingshead AB (1975), Four Factor Index of Social Status. New Haven, CT: Yale University Department of Sociology

Hunt RD (1987), Treatment effects of oral and transdermal clonidine in relation to methylphenidate: an open pilot study in ADDH. Psychopharmacol Bull 23:111-114

Hunt RD, Minderaa RB, Cohen DJ (1985), Clonidine benefits children with attention deficit disorder and hyperactivity: report of a double-blind placebo-controlled crossover study. J Am Acad Child Psychiatry 24:617-629

Hunt RD, Capper L, O'Connell P (1990), Clonidine in child and adolescent psychiatry. J Child Adolesc Psychopharmacol 1:87-101

Hunt RD, Lau S, Ryu J (1991), Alternative therapies for ADHD. In: Ritalin: Theory and Practice, Greenhill L, ed. New York: Mary Ann Liebert, Inc, pp 75-95

Hunt RD (1988), Attention deficit disorder: diagnosis, assessment and treatment. In: Handbook of Clinical Assessment of Children and Adolescents: A Biopsychosocial Approach, Vol II, Kestenbaum C, Williams D, eds. New York: New York University Press

Jackson WJ, Buccafusco JJ (1991), Clonidine enhances delayed matching-to-sample performance by young and aged monkeys. Pharmacol Biochem Behav 39:79-84

Jones, K.L., and Smith, D.W. Recognition of fetal alcohol syndrome in early infancy. Lancet 2(783b): 999-1001,1973.

Kagan J, Snidman N, Julia-Sellers M, Johnson MO (1991), Temperament and allergic systems. Psychosom Med 53:332-340

Klein D (1993), False suffocation alarms, spontaneous panics, and related conditions: an integrative hypothesis. Arch Gen Psychiatry 50:306-318

Kugler J, Seus R, Krauskopf R, Brecht HM, Raschig A (1990), Differences in psychic performance with guanfacine and clonidine in normotensive subjects. Br J Clin Pharmacol 99:803-809

Lambert MN, Sandoval J, Sasone DM (1981), Prevalence of hyperactivity and related treatments among elementary school children. In: Psychosocial Aspects of Drug Treatment for Hyperactivity, Gadow KD, Loney J, eds. Washington, DC: American Association for the Advancement of Science, pp 241-291

Larsson, G.; Bohlin A.-B.; and Tunell, R. Prospective study of children exposed to variable amounts of alcohol in utero. Archives of the Diseases of Children 60:315-321, 1985.

Lindgren S, Lokshin B, Stromquist A, et al. (1992), Does asthma or treatment with theophylline limit children's academic performance? N Engl J Med 327:926-930

McGee R, Stanton W, Sears M (1993), Allergic disorders and attention deficit disorder in children. J Abnorm Child Psychol 21:79-88

Milich R, Loney J, Landau S (1982), The independent dimensions of hyperactivity and aggression: a validation with playroom observation data. J Abnorm Psychol 91:183-198

Orvaschel H (1985), Psychiatric interviews suitable for use in research with children and adolescents. Psychopharmacol Bull 21:737-745

Pauls DL, Towbin KE, Leckman JF, Zahner GE, Cohen DJ (1986), Gilles de la Tourette's syndrome and obsessive-compulsive disorder. Evidence supporting a genetic relationship. Arch Gen Psychiatry 43:1180-1182

Rosett, H.L.; Weiner, L., Zuckerman, B.; McKinlay, S.; and Edelin, K.C. Reduction of alcohol consumption during pregnancy with benefits to the newborn. Alcoholism: Clinical and Experimental Research 4:178-184, 1980.

Roth N, Beyreiss J, Schlenzka K, Beyer H (1991), Coincidence of attention deficit disorder and atopic disorders in children: empirical findings and hypothetical backround. J Abnorm Child Psychol 19:1-13

Schlieper A, Alcock D, Beaudry P, Feldman W, Leikin L (1991), Effect of therapeutic plasma concentrations of theophylline on behavior, cognitive processing, and affect in children with asthma. J Pediatr 118:449-455

Scialli, A.R. A Clinical Guide to Reproductive and Developmental Toxicology. Boca Raton, FL: CRC Press, 1992.

Smith, I.E.; Lancaster, J.S., Moss-Wells, S., Coles, C.D. and Falek, A. Identifying high risk pregnant drinkers: Biological and behavioral correlates of continuous heavy drinking during pregnancy. Journal of Studies on Alcohol 48(4):304-309, 1986.

Sly MR (1992), Asthma. In: Nelson Textbook of Pediatrics, Behrman RE, ed. Philadelphia: WB Saunders Company, pp 587-596

Sorkin EM, Heel RC (1986), Guanfacine: a review of its pharmacodynamic and pharmacokinetic properties, and therapeutic efficacy in the treatment of hypertension. Drugs 31:301-336

Streissguth, A.P.; Bookstein, F.L.; Sampson, P.D.; and Barr, H.M. Neurobehavioral effects of prenatal alcohol: Part III. PLS analyses of neuropsychologic tests. Neurotoxicology and Teratology 11 (5):493-507, 1989.

Sulik, K.K., and Johnston, M.C. Sequence of developmental alterations following acute ethanol exposure in mice: Craniofacial features of the fetal alcohol syndrome. American Journal of Anatomy 166:257-269, 1983. West, J.R. and Goodlett, C.R. Teratogenic effects of alcohol on brain development. Annals of Medicine 22:319-325, 1990.

Teiramaa E (1979), Asthma, psychic disturbances and family history of atopic disorders. J Psychosom Res 23:209-217

US Department of Health and Human Services (1991), Guidelines for the Diagnosis and Management of Asthma. (National Asthma Education Program Expert Panel Report No. 91-3042). Bethesda, MD: National Institutes of Health

U.S. Department of Health and Human Services. Down Syndrome prevalence at birth - United States, 1983-1990. Morbidity and Mortality Weekly Report August 26 1994, v43, n33, p617(6)

Ward MF, Wender PH, Reimherr FW (1993), The Wender Utah Rating Scale: an aid in the retrospective diagnosis of childhood attention deficit hyperactivity disorder. Am J Psychiatry 150:885-890

Weinberger M, Lindgren S, Bender B, Lerner JA, Szefler S (1987), Effects of theophylline on learning and behavior: reason for concern or concern without reason? J Pediatr 111:471-474

Weiss G, Hechtman L, Milroy T, Perlman T (1985), Psychiatric status of hyperactives as adults: a controlled prospective 15-year follow-up of 63 hyperactive children. J Am Acad Child Psychiatry 24:211-220

Wender PH, Wood DR, Reimherr FW (1985), Pharmacological treatment of attention deficit disorder residual type in adults. Psychopharmacol Bull 21:222-227

Wender PH, Reimherr FW, Wood DR (1981), Attention deficit disorder ("minimal brain dysfunction") in adults. Arch Gen Psychiatry 38:449-456

Smart Parenting

Appendix A

Biopsychosocial History

Name of Child:_____ Informant:_____ Date:_____
Age:____ DOB:_____ Phone No :_____
School:_____ Grade:____ Contact:_____
Child's Physician: _____ Last Visit:_____
Primary Concern about Child:_____

Parents with Whom the Child Resides: (A=adoptive, B=biological, F=foster, S=Step-parent or O=other)

Father:_____ Relationship: A B F S O   WK Phone:_____
Mother:_____ Relationship: A B F S O   WK Phone:_____

Other Parents:

Father:_____ Relationship: A B F S O   WK Phone:_____
Mother:_____ Relationship: A B F S O   WK Phone:_____

If your Child has a biological parent who does not reside in the same home please indicate the circumstances:

Death   Month:____   Year:_____   Cause of Death:_____
Divorce   Month:____   Year:_____   Legal Custodian:_____
Separation Month:____   Year:_____   Legal Custodian:_____
Foster
Placement   Month:____   Year:_____   Legal Custodian:_____

If divorce or separation has occurred, does your child have visitations with his or her other biological parent? _____ Are Visitations Regular?_____   Frequency of Visitations:_____

Names and Ages of Siblings
Residing with the Child   Not Residing with the Child

_____   _____
_____   _____
_____   _____
_____   _____

Were there any complications with the pregnancy or delivery of this child?
_____

How would you describe your child as an infant? toddler? Pre-schooler?
_____
_____

Did your child attend a pre-school? Kindergarten? What was his or her attitude toward it?
_____
_____

Please make any descriptive comment regarding school adjustments attitude or performance.

1st grade_____   4th grade_____   7th grade_____   10th grade_____
2nd grade_____   5th grade_____   8th grade_____   11th grade_____
3rd grade_____   6th grade_____   9th grade_____   12th grade_____

Child's Name_____   Biopsychosocial History page 2

Current Difficulties: (please circle Y=Yes, N=No S=Sometimes).

Learning Y N S	School Behavioral Y N S	Home Behavioral Y N S
Destructive Y N S	Shyness Y N S	Allergies Y N S
Hyperactivity Y N S	Bedwetting Y N S	Withdrawn Y N S
Few Friends Y N S	Bossiness Y N S	Picky Eater Y N S
No Friends Y N S	Over Eating Y N S	Aggressive Y N S
Headaches Y N S	Irritable Y N S	Defiant Y N S
Moody Y N S	Immature Y N S	Light Sleeper Y N S
Stomach aches Y N S	Inattention Y N S	Soiling Pants Y N S
Dizziness Y N S	Impulsive Y N S	Cries easily Y N S
Poor Appetite Y N S	Poor Concentration Y N S	Sound Sleeper Y N S
Sleep prob. Y N S	Fearful Y N S	Legal Y N S

Has your child had previous psychiatric or psychological care or evaluation? Describe with whom, when and where.

_____

Is or has your child been on any medication other than that prescribed for general childhood illnesses? If so please indicate type, dose, date prescribed and by whom.
Past:

_____

Current:

_____

Has your child ever had seizures that you are aware of?_____ Is your child allergic to any medicines that you are aware of?_____ Does your child have any current or chronic medical illnesses? _____

Has your child suffered any recent of past trauma? (if so please explain)

_____

Please Circle if any biological relatives of your child have any of the following conditions: (Y=Yes N=No P=Possibly)

Depression Y N P	Alcoholism Y N P	Epilepsy Y N P
Diabetes Y N P	Autism Y N P	Developmental Disability Y N P
Schizophrenia Y N P	Bipolar Illness Y N P	Suicide Y N P
Anxiety Y N P	Other illness Y N P	Obsessive Compulsive Disorder Y N P

Has your child's behavior or personality changed recently or dramatically in the last year? Have these difficulties been developing for some time? How long? Please describe.

_____

Are you and your spouse and/or the other biological parent in agreement as to the nature of your child's difficulties?

_____

Additional Comments:_____

_____

Appendix B

The Systematic Observation Scale (SOS)
©1988. Duke Children's Clinic

General Description and Instructions for using the Systematic Observation Scale

The SOS offers a method of observation and documentation that facilitates the physician-parent partnership in the treatment and on-going evaluation of a child. It is particularly valuable in observing, recording, tracking and evaluating children's responses to psychopharmacological and/or psychotherapeutic interventions. Observations by parents and teachers in the form of the Systematic Observation Scale (SOS) record, provides a direct communication link between the educational or child care setting, parents and the clinician. The SOS was developed to provide a method to make specific multiple observations over time, quantify the observations and graphically represent these observations over individually determined time intervals. The SOS is comprised of five specific observational scales and an observation summary graph. The PH scale observes physiological symptoms. The AD scale tracks symptoms that are associated with attention deficit and hyperactivity. The AG scale tracks physical, verbal and self aggression. The AF scale tracks affective or emotional states. The fifth scale is the specific problem tracking scale. The SPT scale tracks any specified problem the parent and clinician wish to observe. The uses of the SOS include it's utility in documenting and graphically demonstrating relative changes over a treatment course. Parental and educational settings observations aid in assessing treatment results and variations of treatment. The SOS is easy to use and step by step instructions and tips are provided for observers and evaluators.

An example of the flexibility of the SOS is it's ability to observe on a daily, weekly or monthly schedule. Observations will most commonly be characterizations of the day, week or month, but can also be made more rigorous by planning direct observations at randomly assigned times. Systematic observations usually begin with one or more observations representing pre-treatment conditions. In order to avoid the effects of inter-rater differences in a series of observations, the individual observing should ideally remain consistent. Multiple observers, should have his or her individual SOS records of dated observations to be made available as needed. If an observer must be changed during an observational series, it can be indicated and taken into consideration when evaluating the observations. The SOS establishes a data base from which treatment responses can be evaluated, monitored and documented.

The SOS consists of these descriptive and instructional remarks, item definitions, an observation sheet and an observational summary graph. Instructions are provided for accommodating single or multiple observers. Each observation summary graph allows for thirty observations on each of the five dimensions. The instructional remarks, item definitions, an observation sheet and an observational summary graph can be found in the appendix. The purchaser of this book is permitted to make unlimited photocopies of the SOS and other forms in the appendix for personal and non-commercial use.

SOS Item Definitions

Sleep- This item relates to daytime sleeping and nighttime sleep disturbances. Daytime sleep disturbances refer to falling asleep during the other than that usually occuring during a nap time or excessive sleep. Nighttime sleep diffculties refer to difficulty falling asleep, awakening during the night or early morning awakening. The frequency of the sleep difficulty is indicated as daily, two or more times a week, weekly or monthly. Circle the appropriate score related to the frequency of the observed difficulty.

Fatigue-Circle if complaints of fatigue seem excessive and not related to boredom.

Tremors, Twiches, Mannerisms or Tics-Tremors, trembling, twiches, muscle spasms, mannerisms, habitual perculiarity of manner, lip smacking, eye blinking or other tics.

Appetite or Eating Patterns- Score if there has been a change from normal eating patterns; overeating or lack of appetite.

Hypoactivity- Lack of energy, little enthusiasm or interest.

Physical complaints-Score if headaches, stomachaches or physical complaints seem excessive.

Hyperactive-Overactive. More active than most same age children. Always in action.

Short Attention Span-Unable to sustain focus of attention more than a few minutes at a time.

Impulsive-Acts without thinking. Acts without regard for social norms or expectations.

Highly Distractible-Easily taken off task. Focus of attention is easily interrupted.

Constantly Seeking Attention-Clowns around, disruptive, silly or attention demanding behavior.

Squirms, Fidgets-Wiggling, constant finger or foot tapping or manipulation of objects.

Physical Aggression-Hitting, biting, kicking, spitting or throwing objects at others.

Verbal Aggression-Verbal attacks, name calling and strong argumentativeness.

Self Aggression-Self abuse, negative or self demeaning statements.

Moody-Easily changes from cheerful and animated to serious or sad. Mood swings.

Explosive-Loss of control that results in verbal or physical assault or destruction of property.

Withdrawal-Stays to him or her self. Doesn't initiate activity with others.

Easily Frustrated-Easily upset when faced with difficult tasks or situations.

Seeks Immediate Gratification-Difficulty delaying gratification-impulsive eating, spending-difficulty waiting.

Appears Sad-Looks unhappy. Cries or appears tearful. Minimal verbal interaction.

Worried-Frequently anxious or tense

Irritable-Anger easily aroused. Grumpy, easily irritated. Low tolerance of others.

Smart Parenting

Child's Name: _____   Observer: _____
                              Date: _____

                                           Circle the affirmative observations

PH SCALE
Sleep- daytime sleeping and nighttime sleep disturbances.
Frequency: daily =4; two or more times a week=3; weekly=2;   Yes=4,3,2
Fatigue-   Yes=1
Tremors, Twiches, Mannerisms or Tics   Yes=1
Appetite or Eating Patterns   Yes=1
Hypoactivity- Lack of energy   Yes=1
Physical complaints   Yes=1

                            PH Total= _____

AD SCALE
Hyperactive   Yes=2
Short Attention Span   Yes=2
Impulsive   Yes=1
Highly Distractible   Yes=2
Constantly Seeking Attention   Yes=1
Squirms, Fidgets   Yes=2

                            AD Total= _____

PH SCALE
Aggression
    a) Physical
    Frequency-Hourly=4; Daily=3; Weekly=2   Yes=4,3,2
    a) Verbal
    Frequency-Hourly=3; Daily=2; Weekly=1   Yes=3,2,1

Aggression generally directed toward:
    Peers   Yes=1
    Adults   Yes=1
    Self   Yes=1

                            AG Total= _____

AF SCALE
Moody   Yes=2
Explosive   Yes=1
Withdrawn   Yes=1
Easily Frustrated   Yes=1
Seeks Immediate Gratification   Yes=1
Appears Sad   Yes=2
Worried-Frequently anxious or tense   Yes=1
Irritable   Yes=1

                            AF Total= _____

SPT SCALE

_____
(Specific Problem)
Frequency: Hourly=5; 2 or more x Daily=4;   Yes=5,4,3,2,1
Daily=3; 2 or more Weekly=2; Weekly=1.   SPT Total= _____

Observation Summary Graph

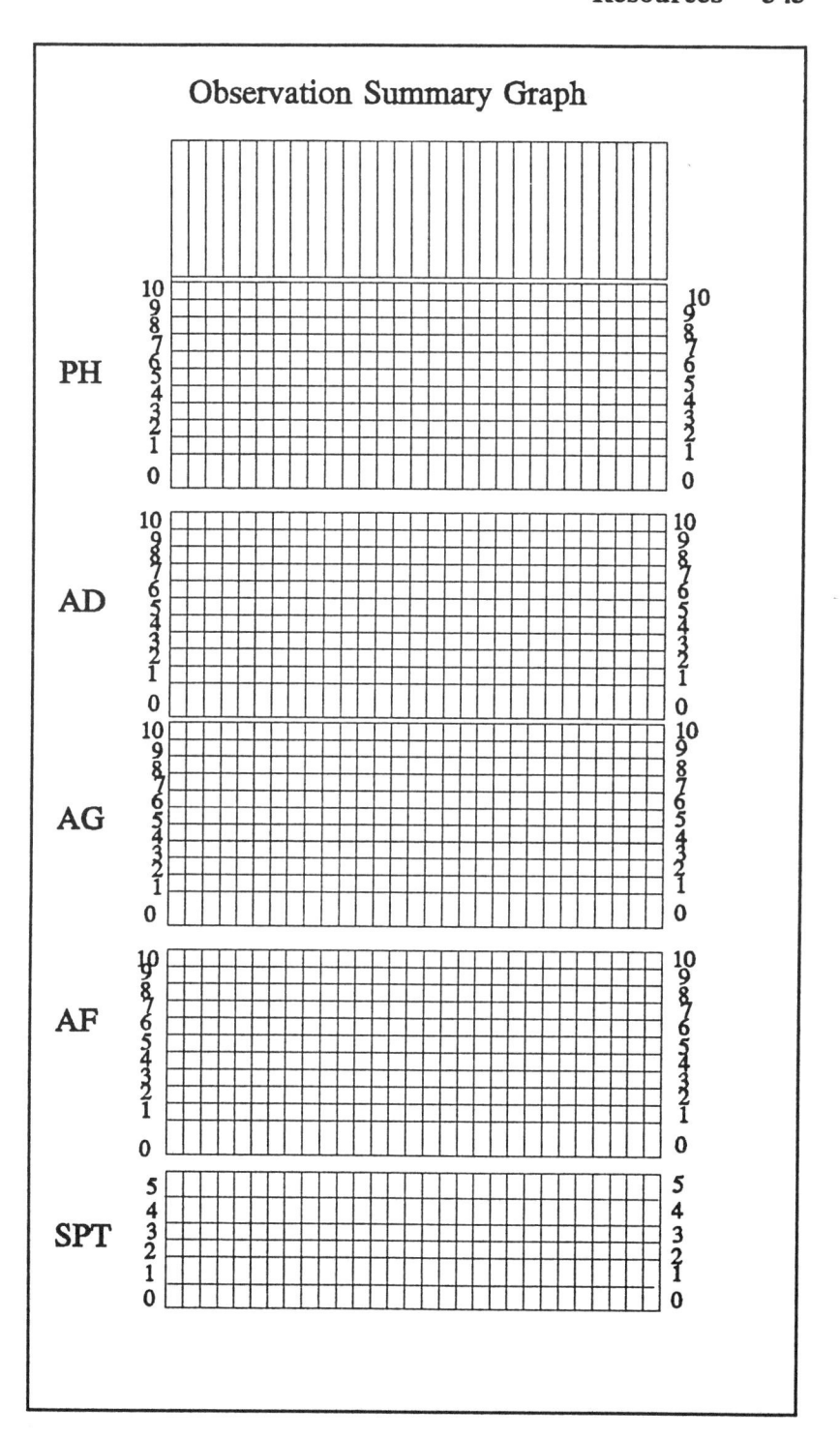

PH 10 9 8 7 6 5 4 3 2 1 0

AD 10 9 8 7 6 5 4 3 2 1 0

AG 10 9 8 7 6 5 4 3 2 1 0

AF 10 9 8 7 6 5 4 3 2 1 0

SPT 5 4 3 2 1 0

344 Smart Parenting

Appendix C

Time-out Log

Name: _____

Date:

Behavior:

Length of Time-out:

Other Consequences:

Circumstances:

Comments:

Parents Initials: _____

Name:

Date:

Behavior:

Length of Time-out:

Other Consequences:

Circumstances:

Comments:

Parents Initials:

Appendix D

Play Session Log

Date:

Session #____

Was session ontime?
Was session interrupted?

Toys selected:

Emotional State:

Themes:
ie. Mommy and sister doll are going shopping without the baby.

Behaviors:

Parent Reflections:

Comments:

Index

Abdominal pain	313
Accidents	95
Adaptivity	22
ADHD	149
Adjustment Disorders	135
Adjustment during preadolescence	309
Aggression	24, 161, 172
in attention deficit disorder	152
in conduct disorders	163
in play sessions	266
Antidepressant	172
Antidepressant Medications	243
Antihistaminic Medications	250
Antihypertensive Medications	242
Anxiety	24, 37, 171
adolescent	306
contagious	52
disorders	175
hospitalization	323
hyperactivity	151
in adjustment disorders	136
in child cancer patients	322
in children	307
in normal children	307
in play sessions	265
in serious sibling illness	308
parental	77
school refusal	318
separation anxiety	96, 191
surgical	323
trauma	78
with phobic disorders	302
Appetite	171
Arguements	
Refusing	118
Argumentativeness	156
Arson	174
Art therapy	331

Assaultive 26
Assessment 57
    Parent Assessment 57
Attention
    deficit 149
Attention Deficit Hyperactivity Disorder 149
Attention seeking 24
Autism 211
Axon 46
Behavior Modification 254
Behavioral Disorders 136
Behavioral interventions 126
Biological interventions 234
Borderline children: 324
Child Anger 129
Childhood enuresis:
    urinary incontinence 312
Circadian rhythms 174
Cognitive Behavioral Interventions 256
Cognitive behavioral treatment 309
Compulsions 199
Compulsive 172
Conduct Disorders 161
Creative process: 321
Cruelty 174
Death 77
Defiance 155
Dendrites 46
Depression 172
    childhood depression 171
    defining 171
    effect of coexisting disorders 315
    in adjustment disorders 136
    in mothers 321
    major depression 171
    maltreated children 70
    neurological aspects 304
    seasonal 311
    treatment 172

348 Smart Parenting

with anxiety	191
with attention deficit	35
with parental depression	320
Developmental Disorders	147
Discipline	101
Disobedience	155
Disorganization	151
Disruptive behavior	172
Divorce	81
Drama therapy	332
Effective communication	130
Emotional Disorders	145
Evaluation of Medication Response	
Medication	250
Example of a Female with Conduct Disorder	
Conduct Disorder	165
Example of a Male with Conduct Disorder	
Conduct Disorder	163
Explosiveness	151
Family	
environment	69
Fidgeting	152
Foster placements	69
Group homes	325
Head injury.	307
Hostility	156
Impulse control	173
Impulsivity	152
in attention deficit disorder	152
Irritability	151, 171
Limits	273
Love	101
Marital difficulties	73
Maternal behavior	318
Medication	235
Mental retardation	216
Mood	173
Mood Stabilizers and Anticonvulsant Medications	
Mood Stabilizers	248

Moodiness	171
Mothers' views	
age of difficulty onset	327
Negativism	155
Neuroleptic Medications	249
Neurotransmitters	47
Non-professional therapists	263
Observations	55
Systematic	60
Obsessions	199
Obsessive	172
Oppositional	155
Oppositional Defiant Disorder	155
Panic attacks	309
Panic disorder	308
Parental Observations	
Parental Observations	56
Parents anger	128
Parents as therapists	306
Pharmacotherapy	234
Pharmacotherapy for school refusal.	308
Phototherapy	234
Play materials	267
Play therapy environment	264
Poor school performance.	
behavior problems	305
Psychoactive medications	238
Reflection	265
Reinforcement	108
Residential care	325
Residential treatment	26, 169
Schizophrenia	47, 211, 213
School	52
School refusal	318
Self esteem	
risk for damage	152
Serotonin	172
Severely ill child	92
Sleep	171

Sleep behaviors 313
Social exclusion 24
SSRI's 172
Stimulant Medications 239
Substance abuse 151
Suicidal thoughts 317
Suicidality 174
The Mental Health Association 291
Tics 151
Time Out Guidelines 120
Time out logs
    interpreting 127
Time Outs
    parent behavior 124
Treatment of Conduct Disordered Children
    Conduct Disorder 168

Order Form

Smart Parenting ISBN 0-9648838-3-X
A Guide to Child Assessment and
Therapeutic Interventions   Unit Price $19.95 x quantity=_____

(Purchase four or more)   Unit Price $16.95 x quantity=_____

Systematic Observation Scale   Unit Price $9.95 x quantity=_____
Tablet with 25 complete scales

Biopsychosocial History   Unit Price $9.95 x quantity=_____
Tablet with 25 History Forms

Sub-Total   =_____

Sales Tax (where applicable)   =_____

Shipping and Handling 10% of sub-total   =_____

Total Enclosed   =_____

Please attach order and make cheque or money order payable to:

        DCC Publishing
        Post Office Box 10458
        Fargo, ND 58103-0458 U.S.A.

Order Form

Smart Parenting   ISBN 0-9648838-3-X
A Guide to Child Assessment and
Therapeutic Interventions   Unit Price $19.95 x quantity=_____

(Purchase four or more)   Unit Price $16.95 x quantity=_____

Systematic Observation Scale   Unit Price $9.95 x quantity=_____
Tablet with 25 complete scales

Biopsychosocial History   Unit Price $9.95 x quantity=_____
Tablet with 25 History Forms

Sub-Total   =_____

Sales Tax (where applicable)   =_____

Shipping and Handling 10% of sub-total   =_____

Total Enclosed   =_____

Please attach order and make cheque or money order payable to:

        DCC Publishing
        Post Office Box 10458
        Fargo, ND 58103-0458 U.S.A.